HOUSE-MUSEUM GALA DALÍ CASTLE
PÚBOL

ANTONI PITXOT
MONTSE AGUER
JORDI PUIG

TRIANGLE ▼ POSTALS

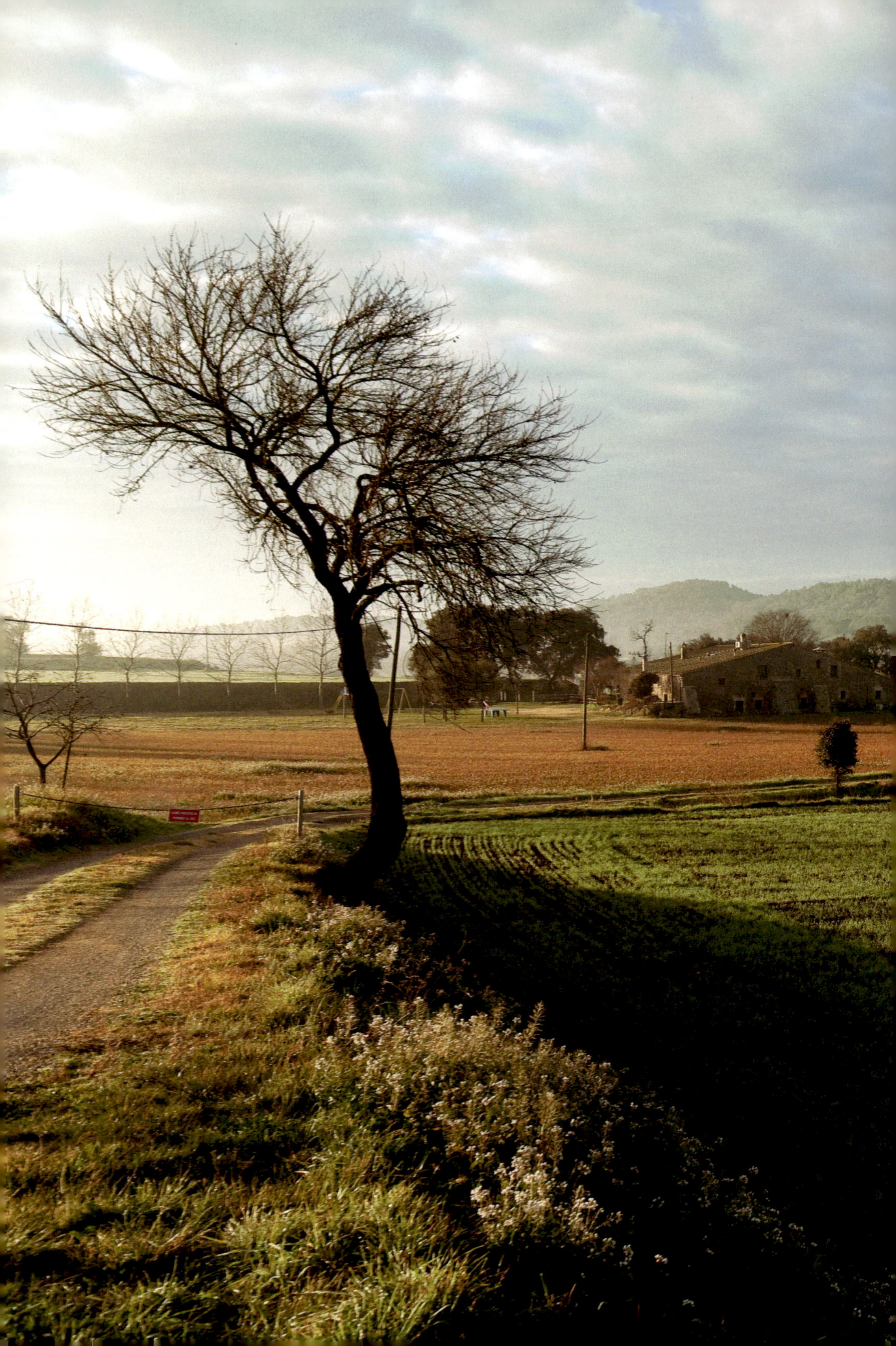

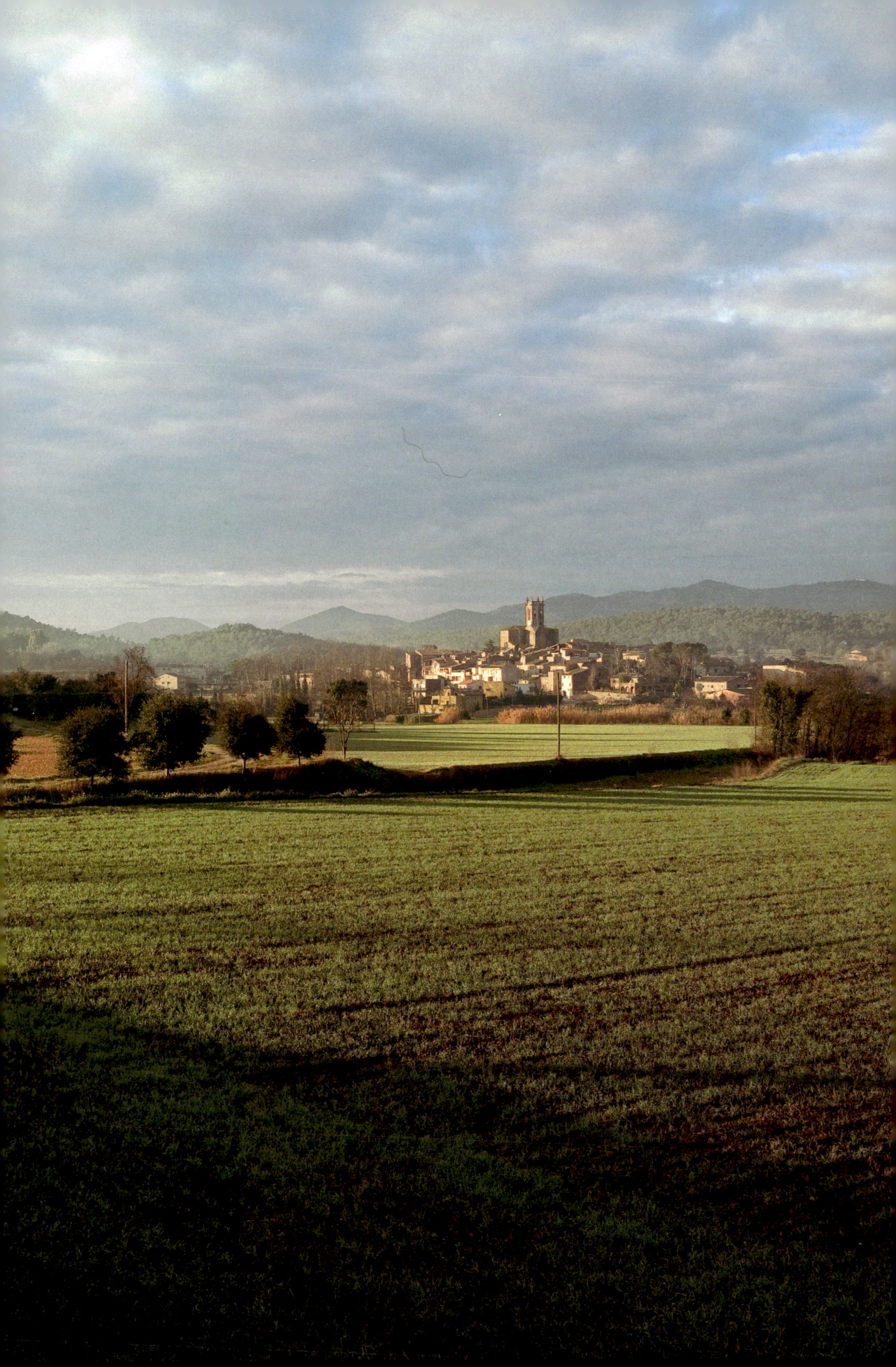

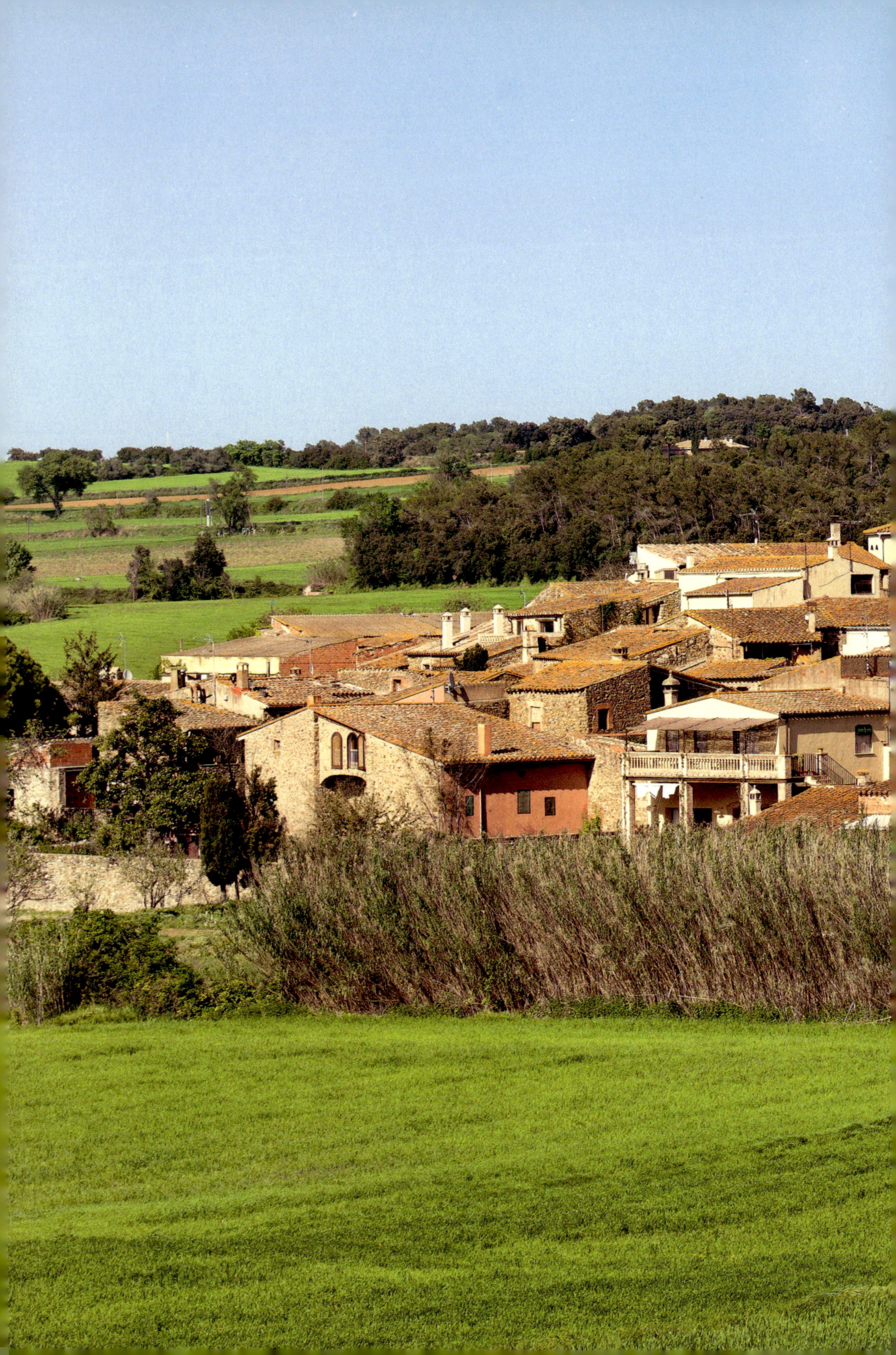

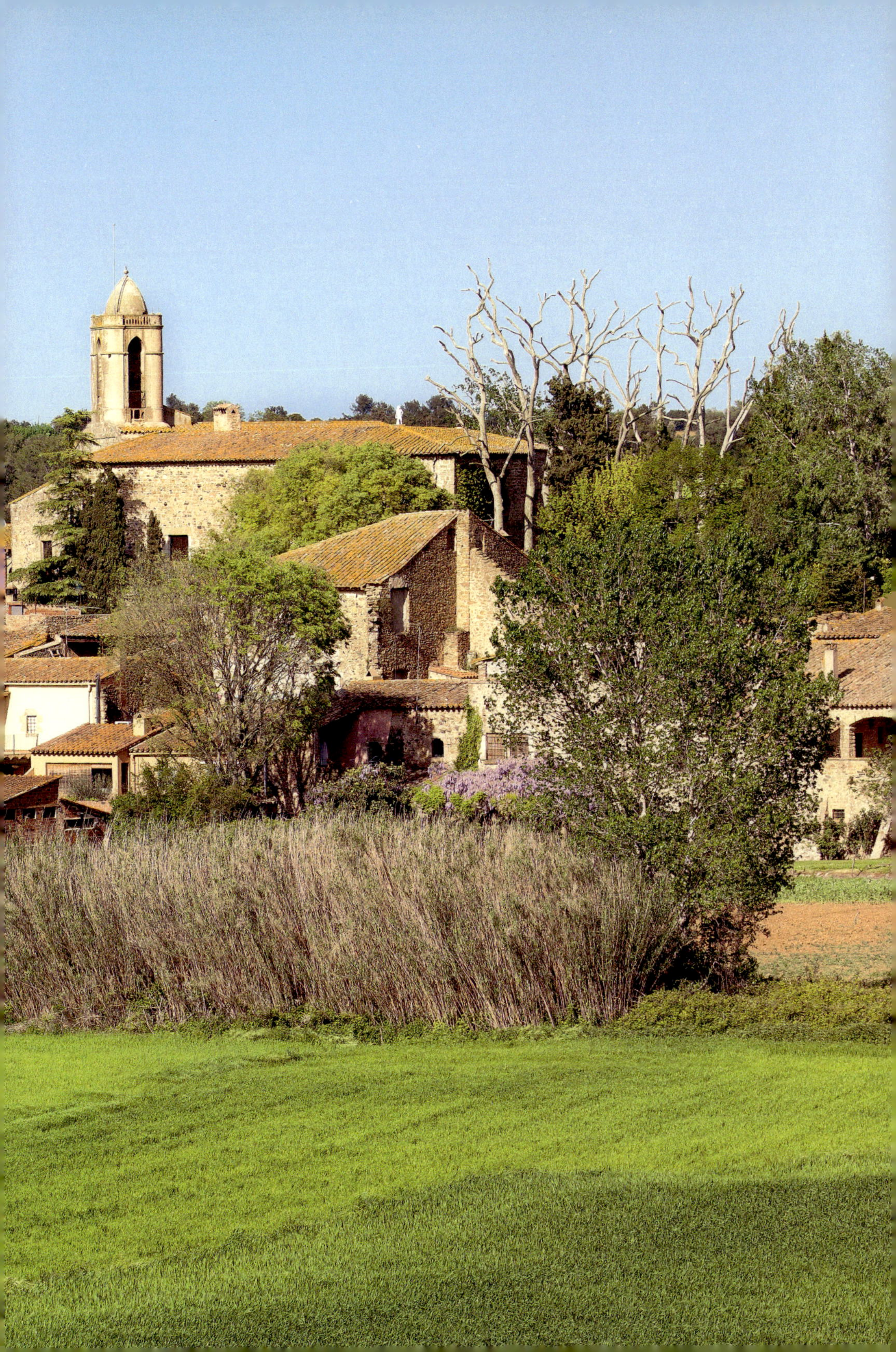

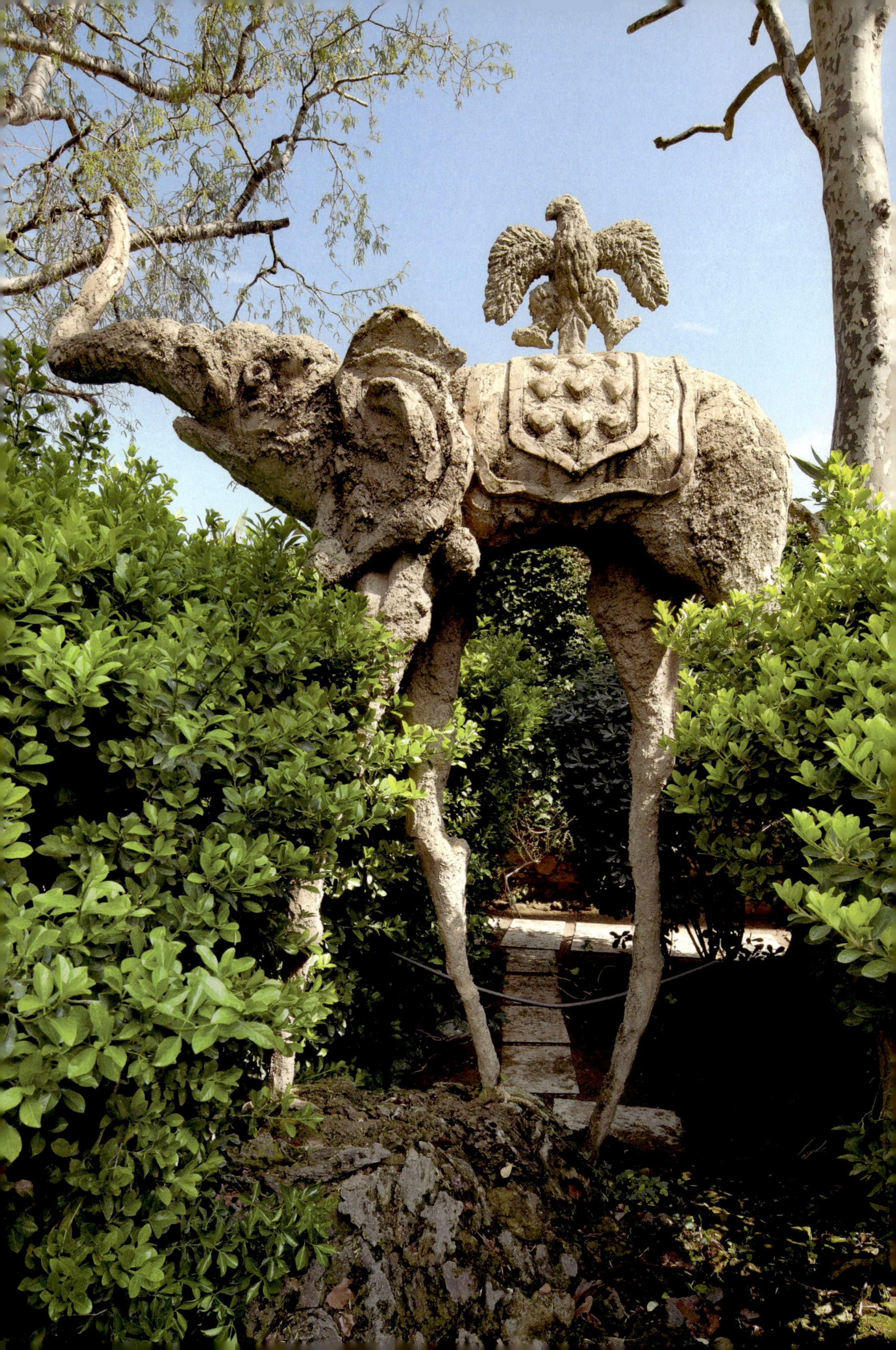

HOUSE-MUSEUM GALA DALÍ CASTLE
PÚBOL

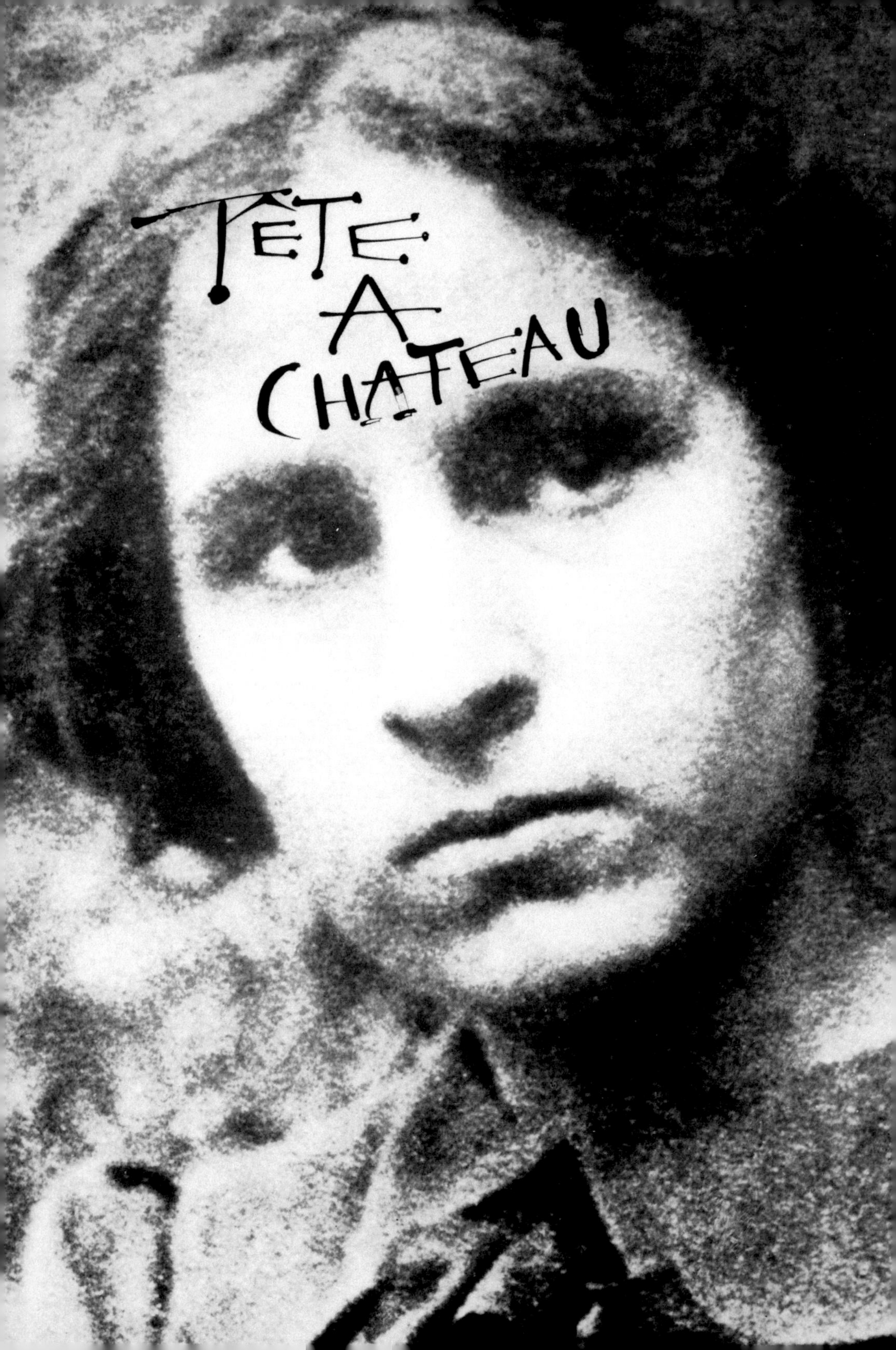
TÊTE
A
CHATEAU

THE REFUGE OF THE VISIBLE WOMAN

The castle of Púbol is the second side of what is called the Dalinian Triangle. In chronological order, this triangle is made up of, firstly, the painter's house in Portlligat; secondly, the castle of Púbol, for Gala, and where, on her death, the painter moved into until 1984; and third, the Dalí Theatre-Museum in Figueres, which was opened on the 28 of September 1974.

The castle of Púbol —a medieval building acquired in 1969, where Dalí undertook an overwhelming creative effort thinking of one person, Gala, and of one function, an appropriate place for the rest and refuge of his wife— delighted Gala, who especially loved the garden and the flowers, above all the roses, which reminded her of a garden in Crimea, where she had spent her summer holidays as a child. Gala frequented the castle, her space and refuge, between 1970 and 1980, usually in short stays during the summer, where she received some of her lovers.

Dalí's creative versatility, on the other hand, gave the architectural aspect of Púbol another reading and it is in this sense that we can highlight the condensed narrative that exists in this creation: it is not simply another place to live, it is not only an accumulation of objects —despite the fact that in very specific spaces there are—, the castle is a construction, reconstruction, where he wanted to give meaning to a space, and Gala, in this case, was an active part in finally providing a multiplicity of meanings to the castle, of intervening in the work, in a way that that this architecture interweaves in the biography of Dalí and Gala, and forms an inseparable part of the final stages of both figures.

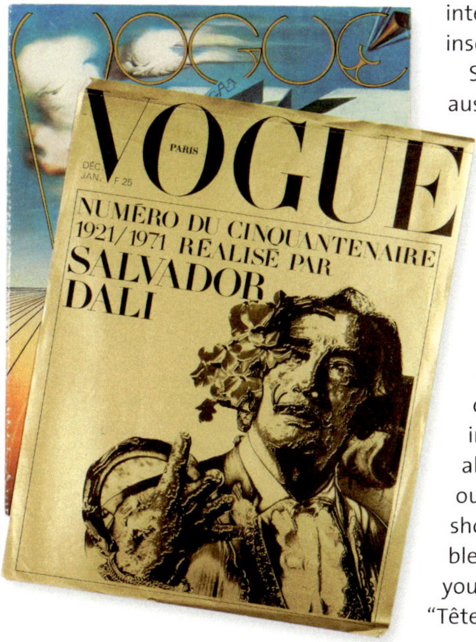

Some of the other keys for understanding this universe, austere yet beautiful, are provided by Dalí himself —in the special issue of *Vogue*— published in 1971 to celebrate the fiftieth anniversary of the French edition of the magazine— when he recounts how he took Gala to Púbol with her eyes blindfolded, offered the castle to her as a gift and immediately explains: "Gala took me by the hand and soon she said to me, 'Thank you once again. I accept the castle of Púbol but on one condition, that you do not come to visit me at the castle unless by written invitation'. This condition gratified, above all, my masochistic sentiments and thrilled me; Gala became the impregnable castle that she had always been. Intimacy and, above all, familiarities, decrease passions. Sentimental rigour and distances, as the neurotic ceremony of courtly love shows, increases passion"[1]. The image of Gala as impregnable castle was emblematised by Dalí in a photograph of a young Gala, on show in the castle library, over which he wrote "Tête a chateau".

[1] Dalí, Salvador, "Le point de vue de Dalí", *Vogue*. A: Dalí, Salvador, *Obra completa*, vol. 4, Destino, Fundació Gala-Salvador Dalí, Barcelona, Figueres, 2005, p. 821.

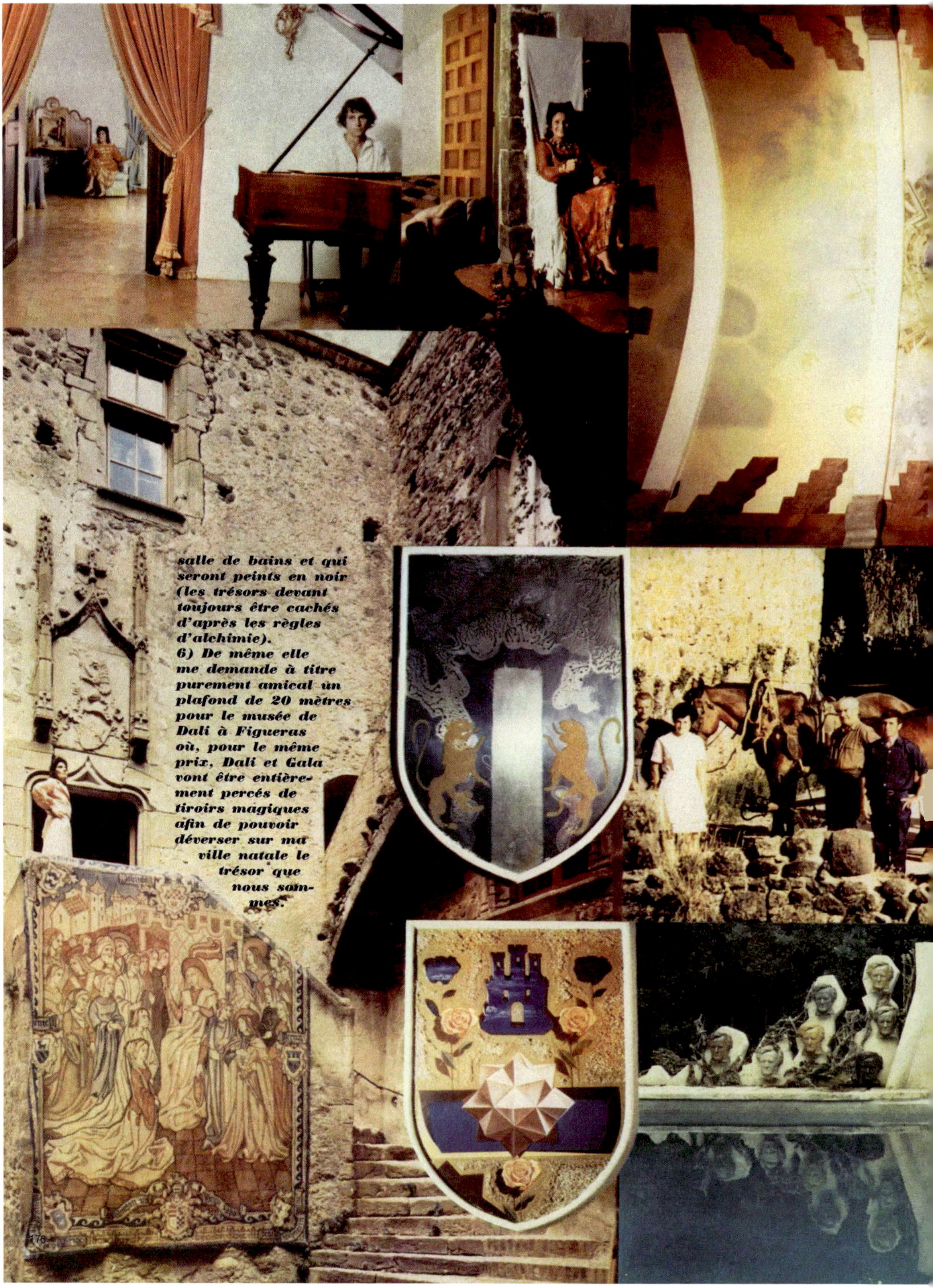
salle de bains et qui seront peints en noir (les trésors devant toujours être cachés d'après les règles d'alchimie).
6) De même elle me demande à titre purement amical un plafond de 20 mètres pour le musée de Dali à Figueras où, pour le même prix, Dali et Gala vont être entièrement percés de tiroirs magiques afin de pouvoir déverser sur ma ville natale le trésor que nous sommes.

Vogue magazine, "Numero du cinquantenaire 1921-1971, realisé par Salvador Dalí"

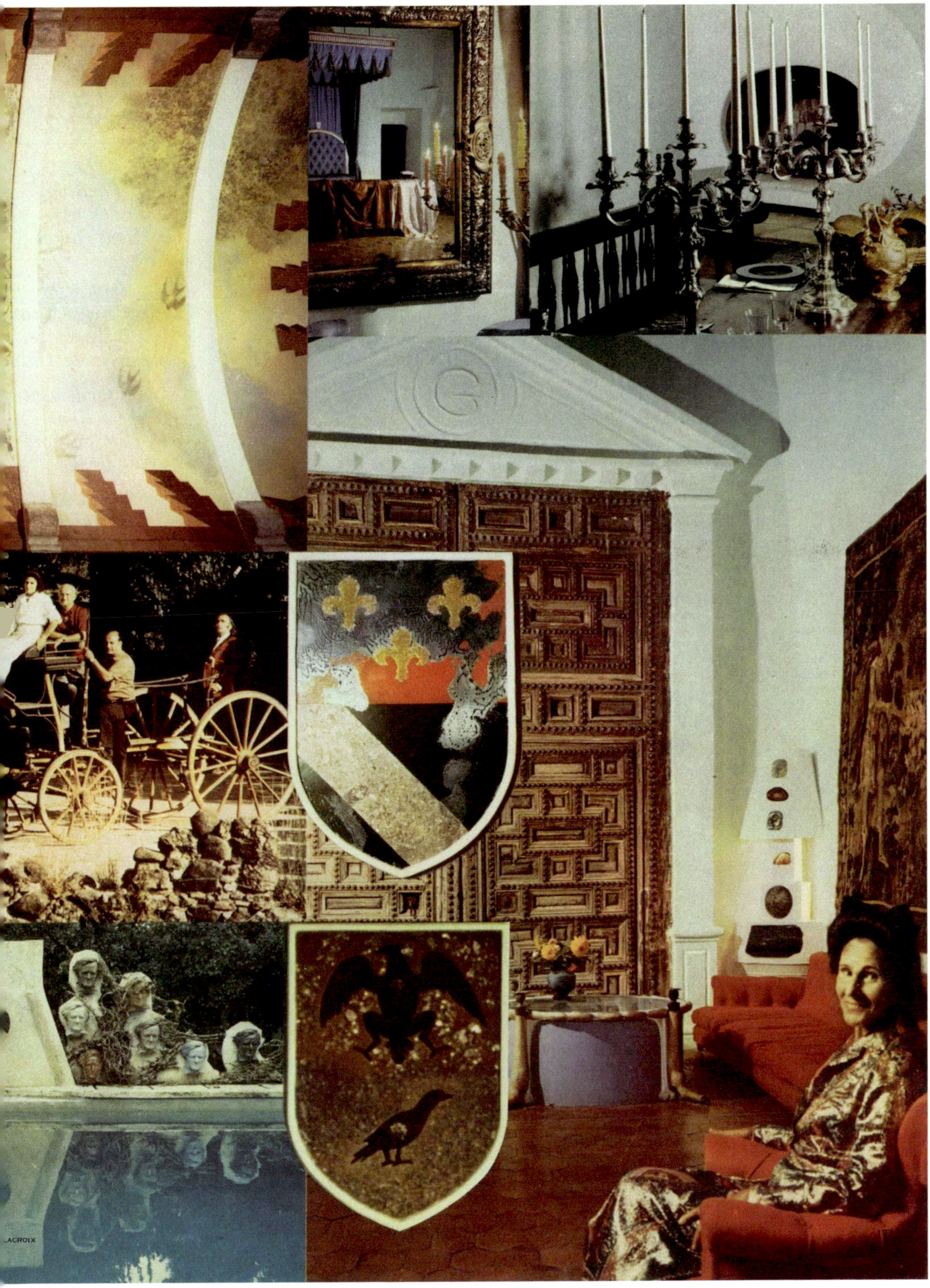

LACROIX

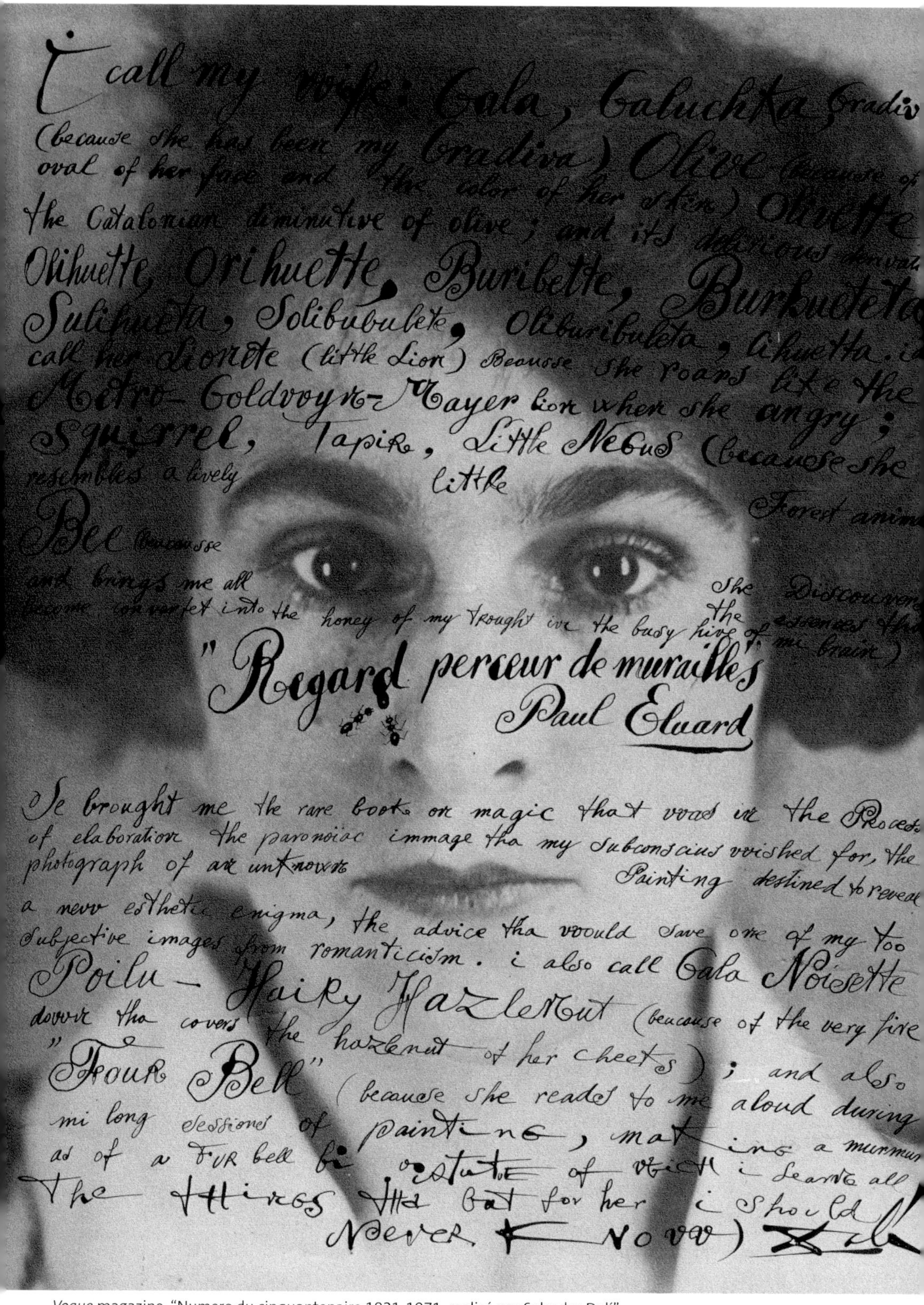

Vogue magazine, "Numero du cinquantenaire 1921-1971, realisé par Salvador Dalí"

GALA, THE LADY OF THE CASTLE [2]

Of Gala, born Helena Ivanova Diakonova, we know very little, the documents and data about her being practically inexistent. She was born in Kazan on the 26 August 1894, had two elder brothers, Vadim and Nicolai, and a younger sister, Lidia. Her father died when she was 11 and her mother remarried a Moscow lawyer, a liberal bourgeois with whom Gala had a very good relationship. She was a model student, who completed her studies in Moscow with a very high average mark and, by decree of the Tsar, was authorised to work as a primary school teacher and give classes in her home. Two of her friends from this period were the Tsvetaeva sisters, Marina, poetess, and Anastasia. A victim of tuberculosis, in 1912 her family decided to admit her to the sanatorium of Clavadel, in Davos, Switzerland, where she met the young poet Eugène Grindel, who would be known by the name of Paul Éluard [3]. Their age and the passion for reading brought them together. In 1914 both of them were given a clean bill of health, Gala returning to Russia and Éluard joining up with the front, but they had become engaged. The outbreak of the First World War did not help them. The families were also not particularly in favour. Nevertheless, and despite all the difficulties (Europe was at war and Gala moved from Russia to Paris) they married in 1917 and in 1918 their only daughter, Cécile, was born. They mixed with the standard-bearers of the surrealist movement and Gala was not merely a fellow traveller but attended many of its meetings. Paul Éluard loved her greatly, as the correspondence between them [4] shows and Dalí also mythologised her. In 1922 she began a relationship with Max Ernst which ended in 1924. Testimony to this relationship and Gala's activities is the picture by Ernst, *Le rendez-vous des amis* from 1922.

[2] This question was extensively analysed in the catalogue: Aguer, Montse; de Diego, Estrella, *Gala. Àlbum*. Distribucions d'Art Surrealista, Figueres, 2007.

[3] Pseudonym with which the writer and poet Eugène Grindel was known. After taking part in the First World War, he came into contact with other writers such as André Breton, Tristan Tzara or Louis Aragon, with whom he became an active member of several avant-garde movements, especially surrealism. Paul Éluard, one of the most important names in surrealist literature, had also formed part of the Dadaist movement. Among his main writings we can highlight: *Le Devoir et l'Inquiétude* (1917), *Capitale de la douleur* (1926), *L'Immaculée Conception*, with André Breton (1930), *Cours naturel* (1938), *Poésie et Véritiene* (1942) or *Les Sentiers et les Routes de la poésie* (1954).

[4] Published in Éluard, Paul, *Lettres á Gala: 1924-1948*, Gallimard, Paris, 1984.

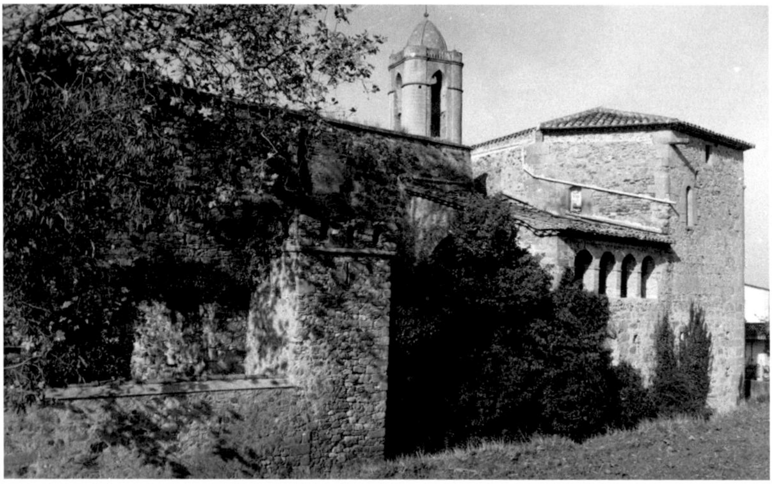

Púbol

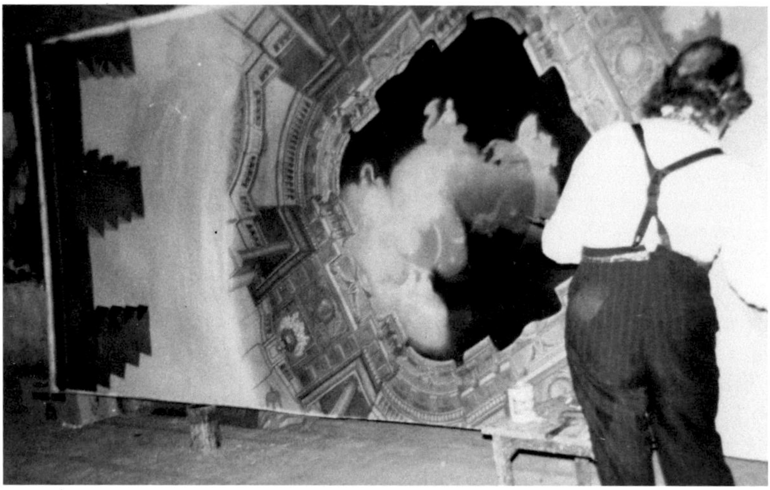

Salvador Dalí painting the canvas for the ceiling of the Coat of Arms Room

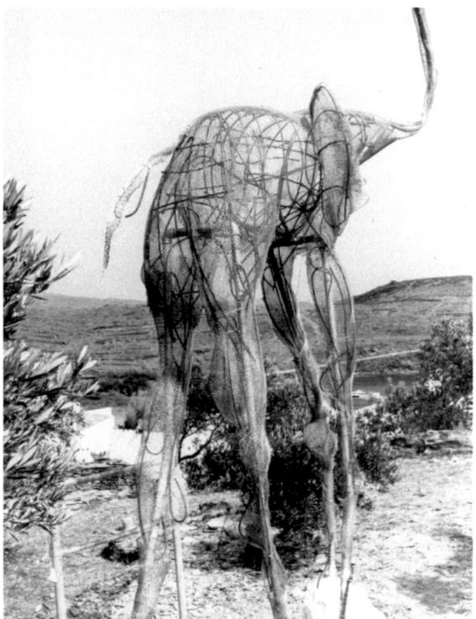

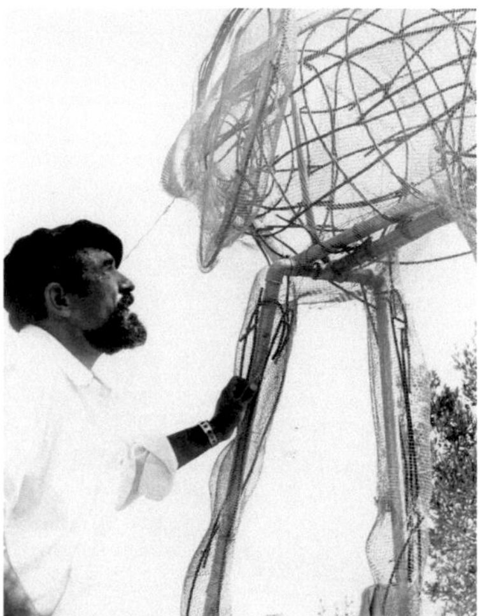

Construction of the elephants of the garden of Púbol, in Portlligat

It was not until 1929 that she met Salvador Dalí. In April, the painter went to Paris to present the film that he had made with Luis Buñuel, *Un chien andalou*, and there the Belgian gallery owner and poet Camille Goemans introduced him to Paul Éluard. Dalí invited them to spend the summer in Cadaqués. Goemans and his companion, René Magritte and his wife, Luis Buñuel, Paul Éluard and Gala, and their daughter, Cécile, spent some time there. When the painter met Gala, he was totally taken aback and fell in love. He wrote in his autobiography *The Secret Life of Salvador Dalí*: "She was destined to be my Gradiva, 'she who advances', my victory, my wife" [5] (this name comes from the title of the novel of the same name by W. Jensen, in which Gradiva, the heroine, makes possible the psychological cure of the main character). Gala would be at the painter's side for always. From then on her biography is connected to that of Dalí and his establishment as a painter in both France and, later in the 1940s, the United States. In 1948 they returned from America. In 1958 they were married in the Sanctuary dels Àngels, very close to both Púbol and Girona. In 1969 the painter bought the castle of Púbol for Gala. Between 1970 and 1980, Gala spent some periods of time there, usually in summer. In 1982 Gala died and is buried in the castle.

Gala has always been considered as Salvador Dalí's muse, an inspiring muse and a mysterious woman, a clichéd adjective, but one that clearly defines the little we actually know about her. Loved by some, hated by others, she left no-one indifferent. She was a woman of great intuition that knew how to recognise the artistic and creative genius of artists and intellectuals such as Paul Éluard, Max Ernst, René Char, René Crevel and Salvador Dalí, to mention just a few. Paul Éluard describes her look as "the eyes that pass through walls" and Salvador Dalí speaks to us of "her intuition of a medium" [6].

Throughout his autobiography, Dalí provides us with diverse visions of Gala. Firstly, she appears as an example of the "serene perfections of the Renaissance" [7]. In the second part, Gala is presented to us in different ways which, like a puzzle, end up forming a determined personality. Dalí speaks to us of Gala in relation to desire and discovery of the sexual act:

"I kissed her on the mouth, inside her mouth. It was the first time I did this. I had not suspected until then that one could kiss in this way. With a single leap all the Parsifals of my long bridled and tyrannised erotic desires rose, awakened by the shocks of the flesh[8]." (...) "Gala had begun to explain to me minutely the reasons for her wish, and it suddenly occurred to me that she, too, had an inner world of desires and frustrations, and moved with a rhythm of her own between the poles of lucidity and madness" [9].

Later, also in his autobiography, the more surrealist Dalí, and with an ironic tone, associates food with his loved one, who must be devoured in order to achieve total love, the fusion of loved ones. However, Dalí also presents a different Gala to us, much closer to that which he calls the principle of reality:

"Since Málaga I had become Gala's pupil. She had revealed to me the principle of pleasure. She taught me also the meaning of the principle of reality in all things (...) She also taught me the 'principle of proportion' which slumbered in my intelligence. She was the Angel of Equilibrium. The precursor of my classicism" [10].

[5] Dalí, Salvador, *The Secret Life of Salvador Dalí*. A: Dalí, Salvador, in *Complete Works*, vol. 1, Destino, Fundació Gala-Salvador Dalí, Barcelona, Figueres, 2003, p. 622 (English version published by Dover, New York, 1993. P. 233).

[6] *Ibid.* [7] *Op. cit.*, p. 233 [8] *Op. cit.*, p. 640 (English version p. 243) [9] *Op. cit.*, p. 642 (English version p. 245) [10] *Op. cit.*, p. 759-760 (English version p. 316-317)

There also had to be Gala the model and muse, "destined to be my Gradiva, 'she who advances', my victory, my wife. But for this, she had to cure me, and she did cure me!"[11]. An inspiring muse who, always according to Dalí, "discovers and brings me all the essences that that become converted into the honey of my thought in the busy hive of my brain"[12]; she also brought him "the rare book on magic that was to nourish my magic"[13] and "she reads to me aloud during my long sessions of painting, making a murmur as of a fur bell by virtue of which I learn all the things that but for her I should never know"[14]. A vision that provides us with a not-much highlighted aspect of Gala: a cultured Gala, related to the circles of intellectuals and artists, above all to the surrealist group around André Breton. An encouraging, tenacious, collaborative Gala, inseparable from and diligent of: "(...) Gala and I went to the Bonwit-Teller's, where my two displays were being set up. I thought up on the spot a whole series of new lyric inventions, and we stayed to put the finishing touches to the two displays till six o'clock in the morning. Gala had completely torn her dress in the ardour of nailing and hanging false jewels everywhere. Dead tired, we went to bed"[15].

At the same time a great driving force, a driving force for Dalí, who was convinced of spending the rest of her life with the painter and helping him in establishing himself internationally:

"Gala alone was a witness to my furies, my despairs, my fugitive ecstasies, and my relapses into the bitterest pessimism. She alone knows to what point painting became for me at this period a ferocious reason for living, while at the same time it became an even more ferocious and unsatisfied reason for loving her, Gala, for she and she alone was reality; and all that my eyes were capable of seeing was 'she', and it was the portrait of her that would be my work, my idea, my reality"[16].

There is also a merchant Gala, the economic administrator of the couple. As well as a creative Gala, with a clear vocation as a writer, we can also sense from her brief but irreplaceable autobiography, *Gala Dalí, La vida secreta. Diari inèdit* (Gala Dalí, The Secret Life. Unpublished diary), that had remained unknown until very recently, that she was an editor: she ordered Dalí's texts, corrected them, looked after them, he gave her instructions and the authority of the task of publishing, such as with the book *La femme visible* (The Visible Woman) in 1930.

We can add that Gala was also a person interested in the world of clairvoyance, tarot and gambling; a person often classified as standoffish, hard and unfriendly; who was separated from her only daughter, Cécile; that there was a vulnerable Gala, who sought eternal youth; an independent Gala who also fought all her life to choose what and who she loved; a woman who related to her partners beyond the limits established by conventional morals; a woman who, according to Dalí, "has built all the success of my life".

[11] *Op. cit.*, p. 622 (English version p. 233) [12] *Op. cit.*, p. 647 (English version p. 248) [13] *Ibid.* [14] *Ibid.*
[15] *Op. cit.*, p. 857 (English version p. 372) [16] *Op. cit.*, p. 874 (English version p. 383)

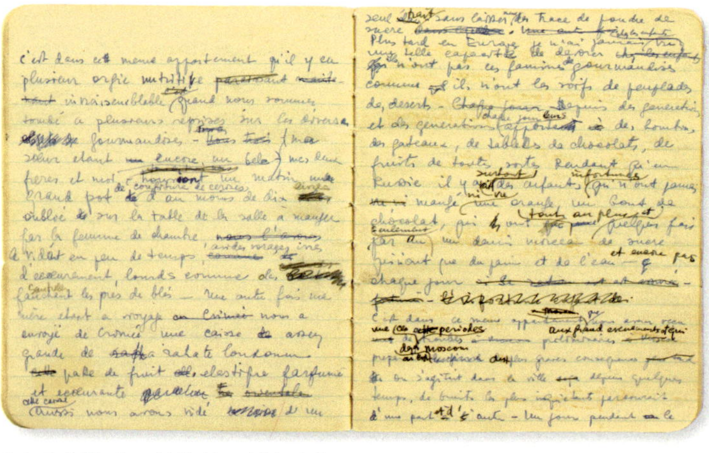

Gala Dalí, The Secret Life. Unpublished diary

Salvador Dalí and Gala before de *Corpus Hypercubus* (detail), 1954

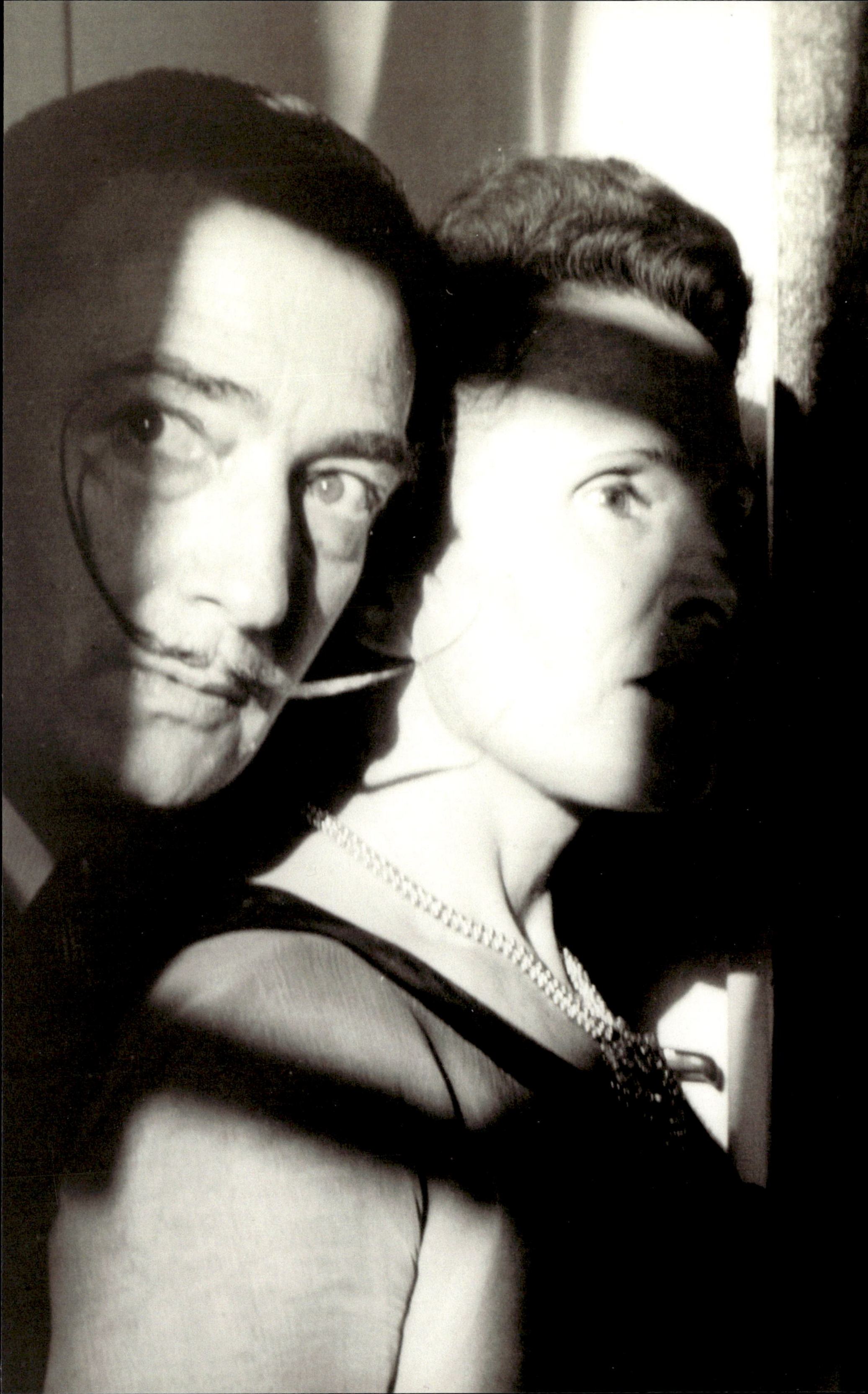

—I give you a Gothic castle Gala.
—I accept on one condition, that you only come to visit me in the castle by invitation.
—I accept, since I accept in principle all on condition there are conditions. It is the same principle of courtly love.

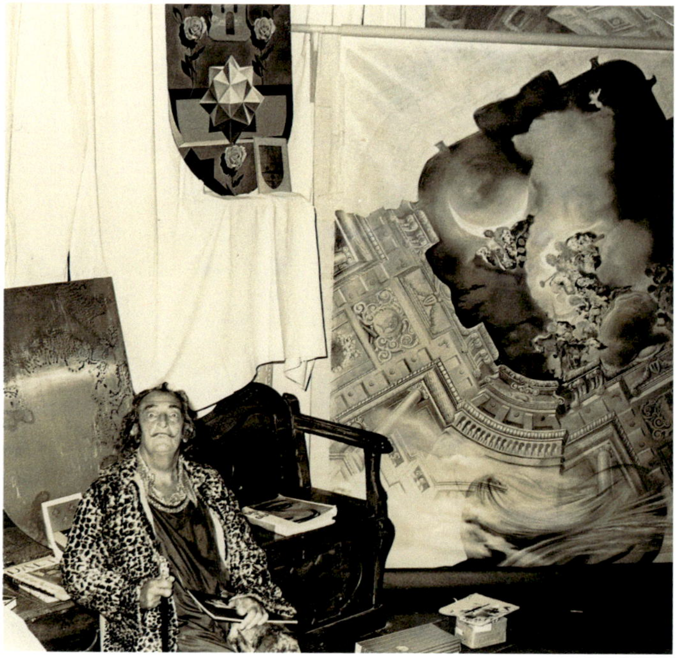

Dalí in his studio in Portlligat, 1971

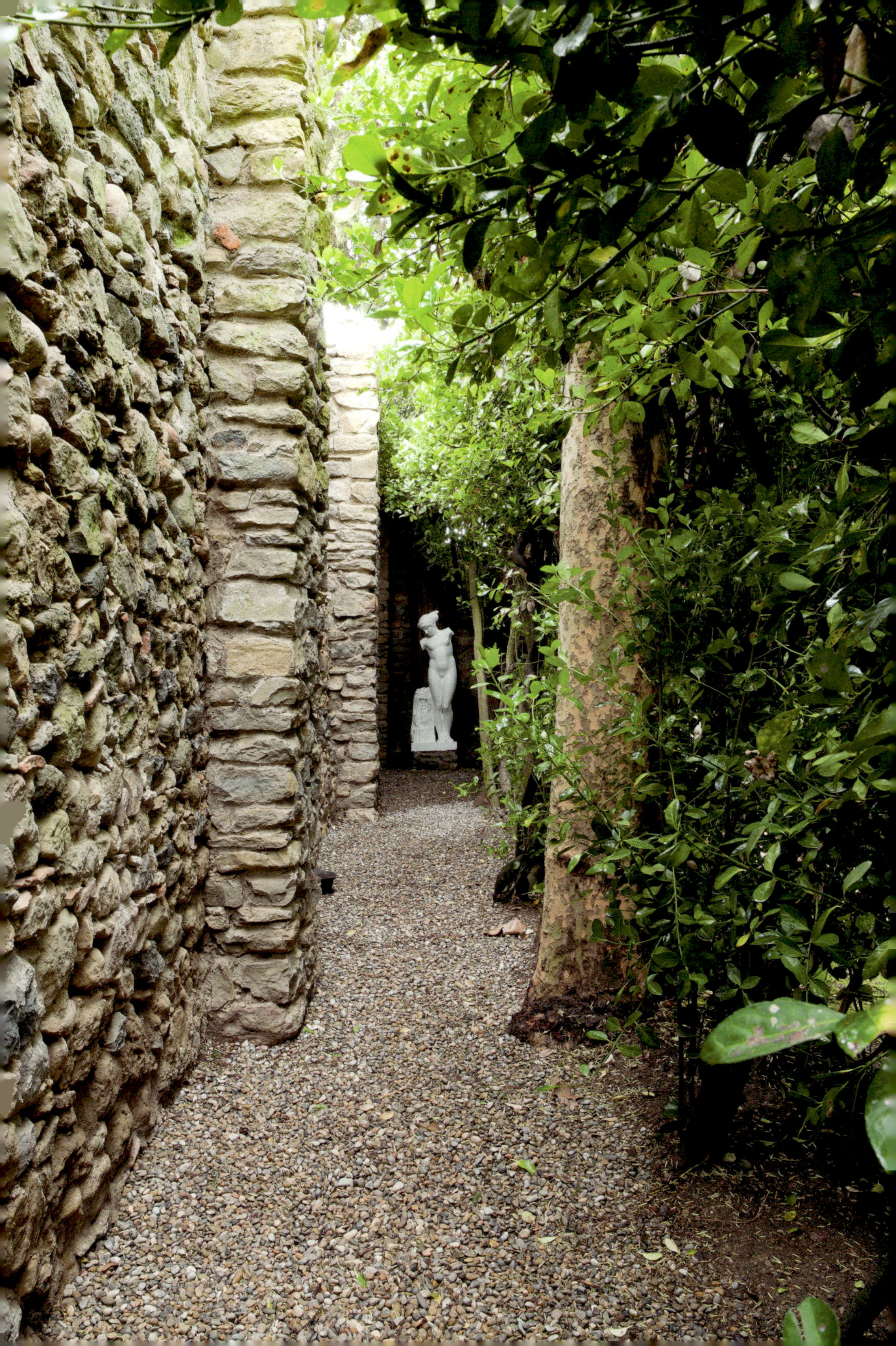

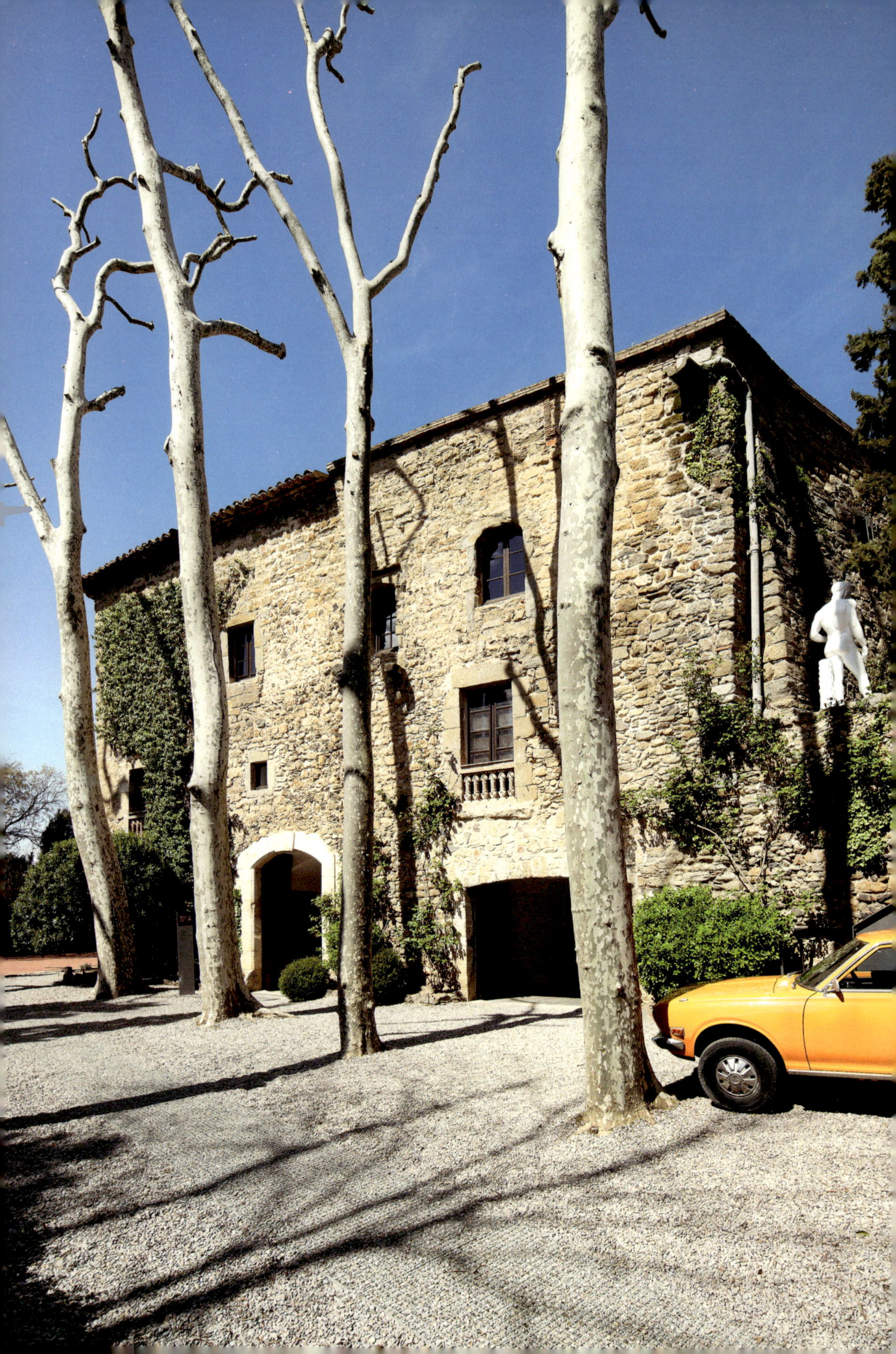

THE CASTLE

Of what is known as the Dalinian Triangle, the castle of Púbol is the most austere place associated with Gala and related above all with the final creative stage of the artist. It is the place that Dalí offered to his lady, where he pays homage, a place of isolation, melancholy, of Proust-like airs, of the search for a lost world, of subjective projection.

Dalí refers to the castle in his written work. It is interesting to see how in *The Unspeakable Confessions* of Salvador Dalí (1973) he presents it as a continuation of Portlligat —precisely through the round or oval room, Gala's place—, understood as a place destined for his lady and to an amorous ideal. This association is made very clear in the following paragraph:

"Everything there celebrates the cult of Gala, even to the round bedroom, with its perfect echo, that crowns the complex of buildings and is like the dome of this Gala-ctic cathedral; and when I go through this house, I am looking at myself, living my own concentricity. I love its Mauresque severity. I had to give Gala a setting more solemnly worthy of our love. That is why I gave her the twelfth-century castle in which she reigns, and which I shall not speak of, for I have meant her to be its absolute sovereign, to the point that I go there only when invited by her own hand. It was enough that I decorated the ceilings so that whenever she looks up she finds me in her heaven" [17].

And in the abovementioned article for the special issue of *Vogue* he adds:

"Since my surrealist period, I have signed my best paintings: Gala Salvador Dalí. You do not have to be Sartre to state that the name is the person, but you do have to be Dalí to state that the super-person, the superman of Nietzche and the Dalinian superwoman are his castle" [18].

The castle of Púbol is, therefore, a very significant spot in Dalinian creation: a continuation of Portlligat with its own personality. It is Dalí's gift to Gala, his lady, to whom he renders vassalage, and to which he cannot enter without her written permission. In this sense the manuscript text by Dalí, "Le chateau de Gala, la Gala du chateau" (sic), in the book by Jean-Charles Pichon, *L'Homme et les dieux*, is illustrative [19]. Dalí, in a written autograph refers to Gala and the castle:

"I give you a Gothic castle Gala.
I accept on one condition, that you
only come to visit me in the castle
by invitation. I accept, since I accept
in principle all on condition there
are conditions It is the same
principle of courtly love".

[17] Dalí, Salvador, Parinaud, André, *Unspeakable Confessions of Salvador Dalí*. A: Dalí, Salvador, *Complete Works*, vol. 2, Destino, Fundació Gala-Salvador Dalí, Barcelona, Figueres, 2003, p. 689 (English version. Quartet Books. 1977).

[18] Dalí, "Le point de vue de Dalí", op. cit., p. 821.

[19] Pichon, Jean-Charles, *L'Homme et les dieux*, Robert Laffont, Paris, 1969.

The architectural whole of the castle of Púbol is made up of the current parish church, the fortified farmhouse-palace surrounded by a walled garden and the adjoining building known as the tithe, a basement. Around it are crowded together the houses protected by the remains of the medieval wall, and, framing the whole complex, the stream, with its characteristic plant life, where the leading figures are the poplars (which the village's name, Púbol, comes from) and other trees suited to a humid ecosystem. All this completes this icon of Empurdà medieval village, where we can still find remains of the early walled precinct or numerous architectural vestiges from the time of maximum splendour of the barony, at the end of the 14th and early 15th centuries. On several occasions Dalí presents this complex in both his pictorial and written work.

We get our first perception of the castle on climbing the current Carrer Gala Dalí, from where we see the west wall of the farmhouse, protected by the battlements of the basement area and the remains of

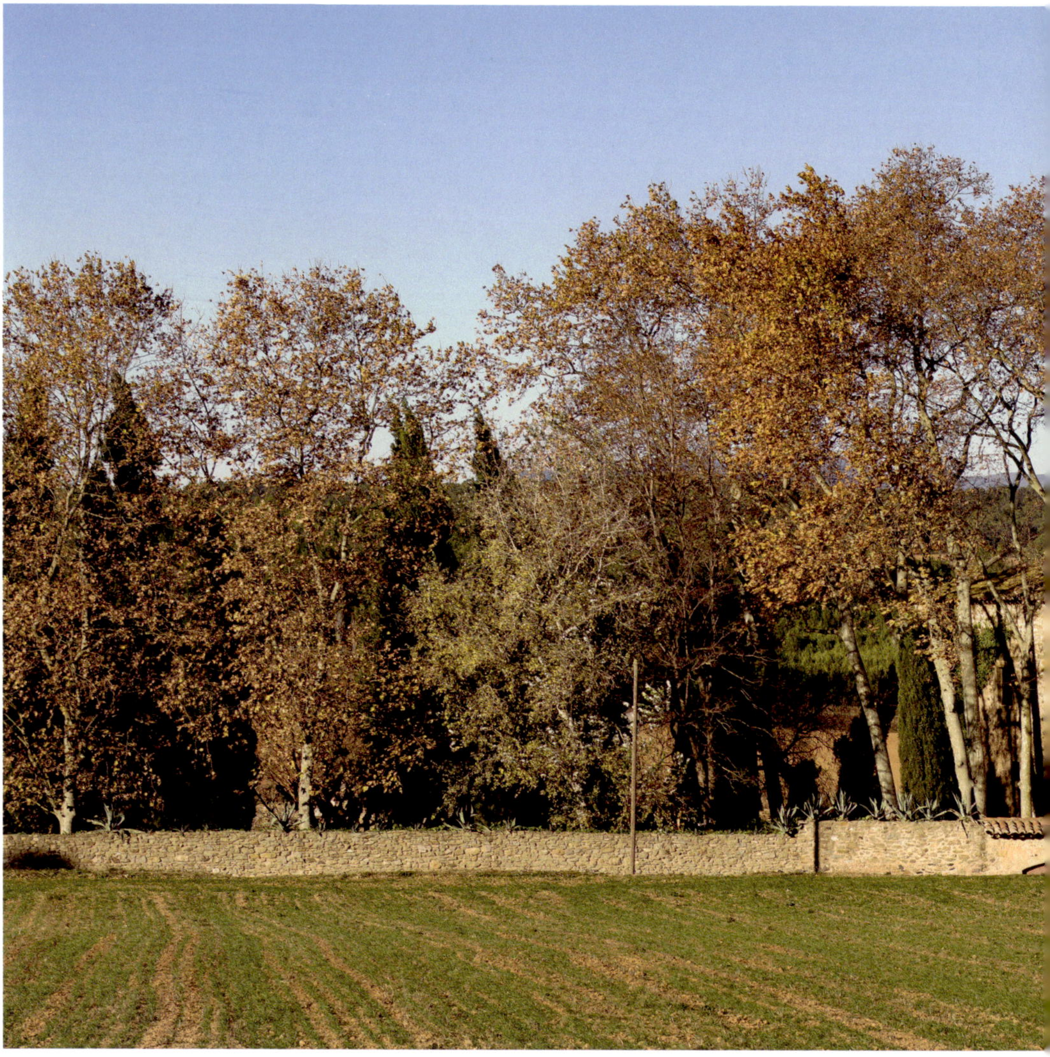

Púbol

the machicolation that must have protected the main entrance of the house. The cobbled street leads us to the main entrance, where we discover a small square, formerly a cemetery, presided over by the Gothic church, and bordered to the north by the remains of the town walls —a section that was broken up by the residents themselves— and to the south, by the walls of Gala's private rooms. Precisely on one of these walls of the castle we can still discover a cavity with the remains, as popular legend goes, of three skulls of some bandits put to death and exposed to public ridicule.

Now before the main façade, the words of Emili Puignau, constructor and friend of Dalí, make the painter's desire clearer to us: "(...) I have seen something sublime on the façade: not only is it cracked, but a burr forms in the crack that gives the impression that a cataclysm had occurred here, an earthquake; that a part held firm and the other part separated and tumbled. Therefore, this must not be touched, it must be left just as it is" [20].

[20] Puignau, Emili. *Vivències amb Salvador Dalí*, Juventud, Barcelona, 1995, p. 107-108.

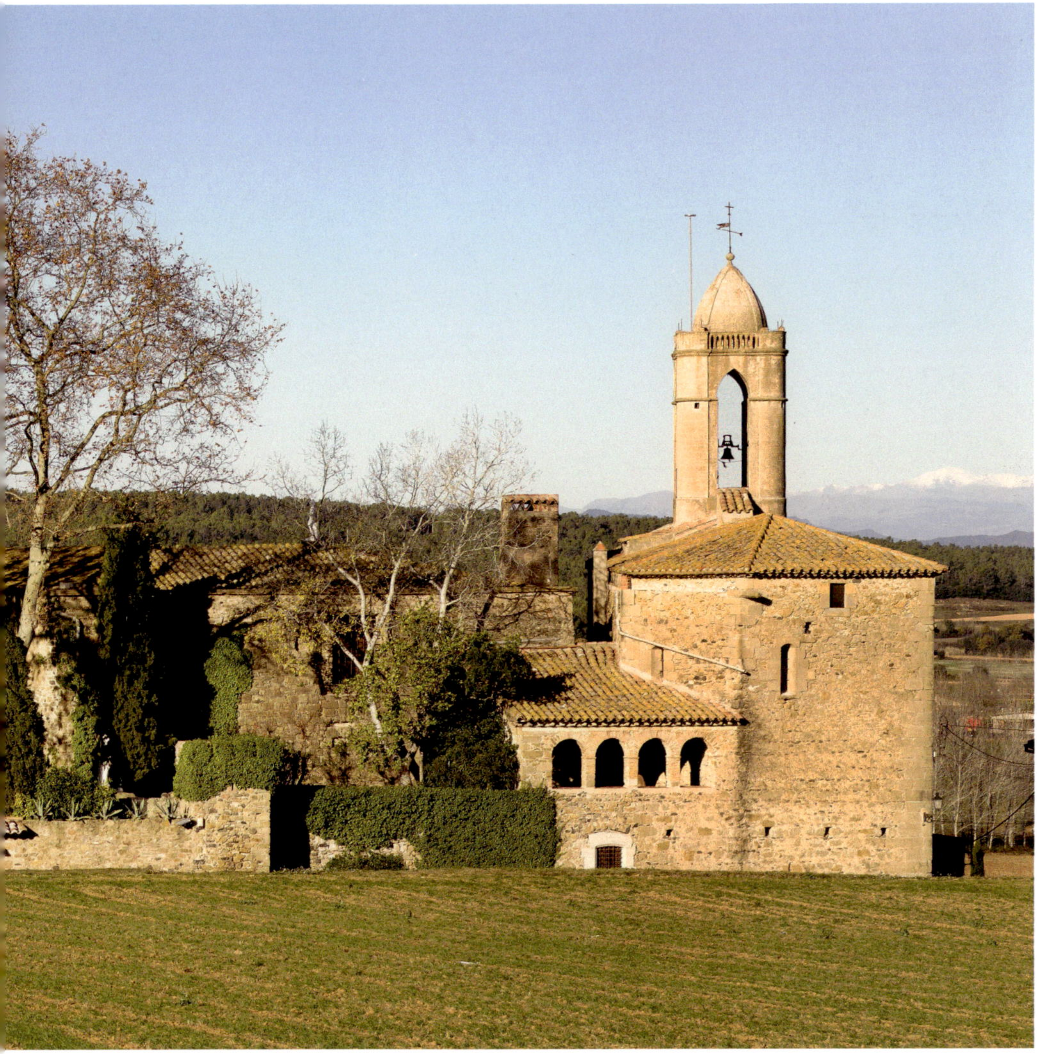

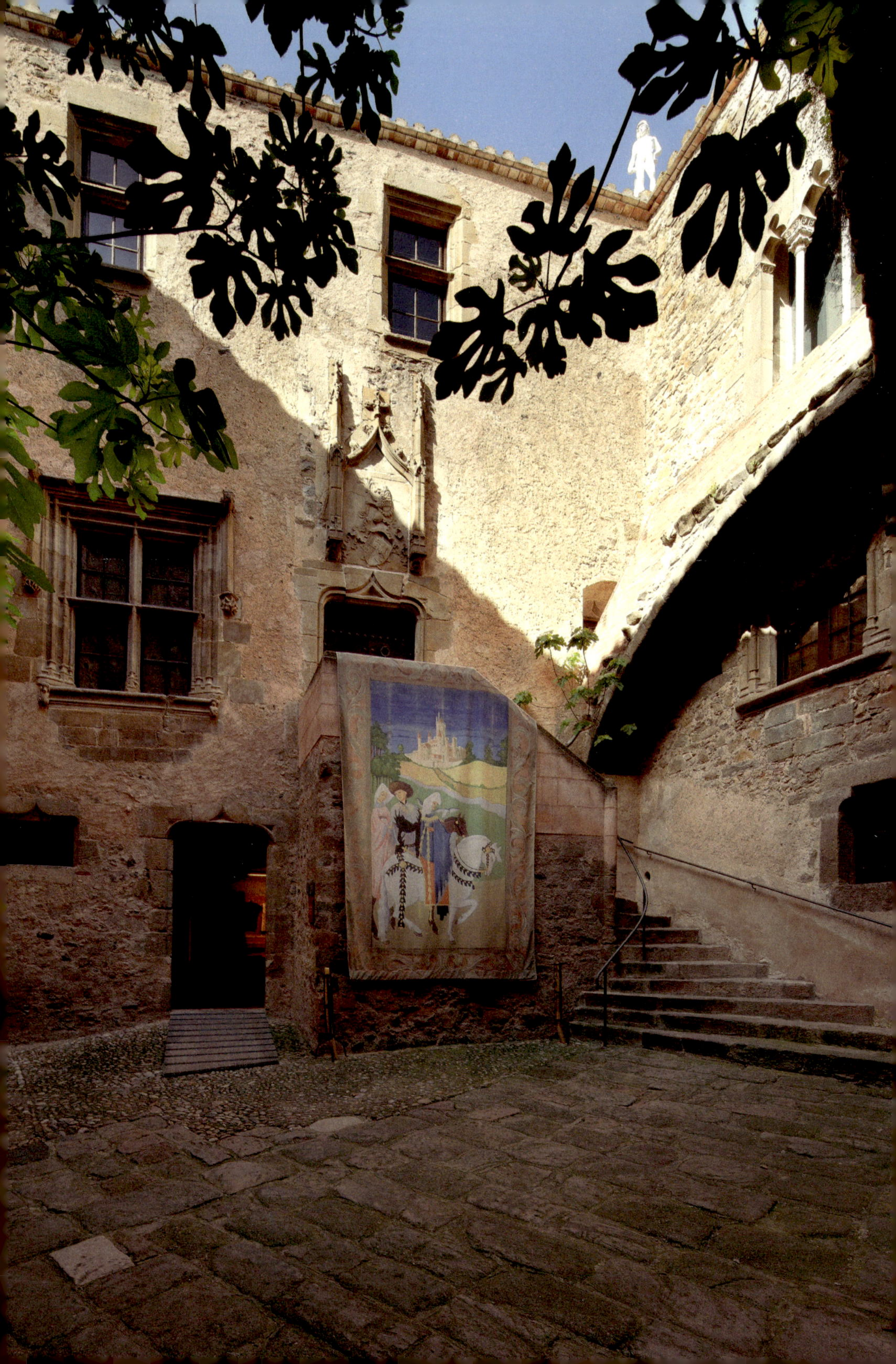

THE ENTRANCE AND THE COURTYARD

On entering the premises, we come to a crenelated terrace overlooked by the multicolour rose trees and the aromatic lavender that adorn the main façade of the castle at the express desire of Gala; colours and aroma that recalled for her the holidays as a child on the shores of the Black Sea. From here we can begin to sense the romantic approach that Salvador Dalí wanted to give the whole complex and the determinant role of Gala in its execution. From the point of view of architectural finish, the Empordà artist laid great emphasis on the idea of ruin –as in the Dalí Theatre-Museum there is the conception of rehabilitating a more or less ruined building, scrupulously respecting the appearance deteriorated by the passing of time, which he called the signs and stigmas of time.

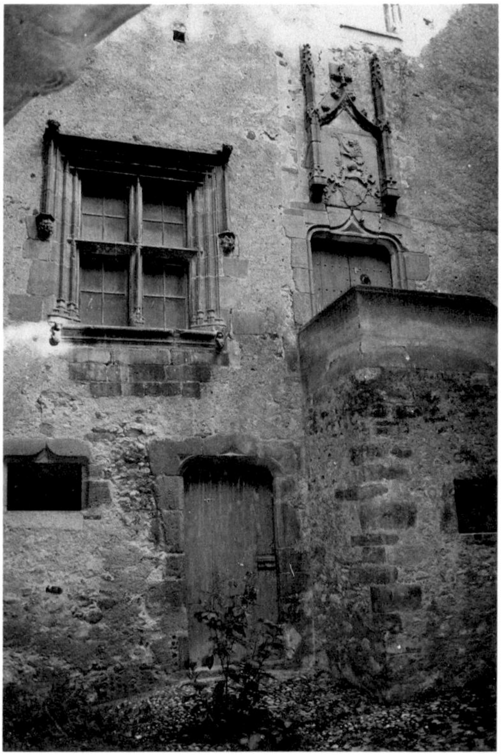

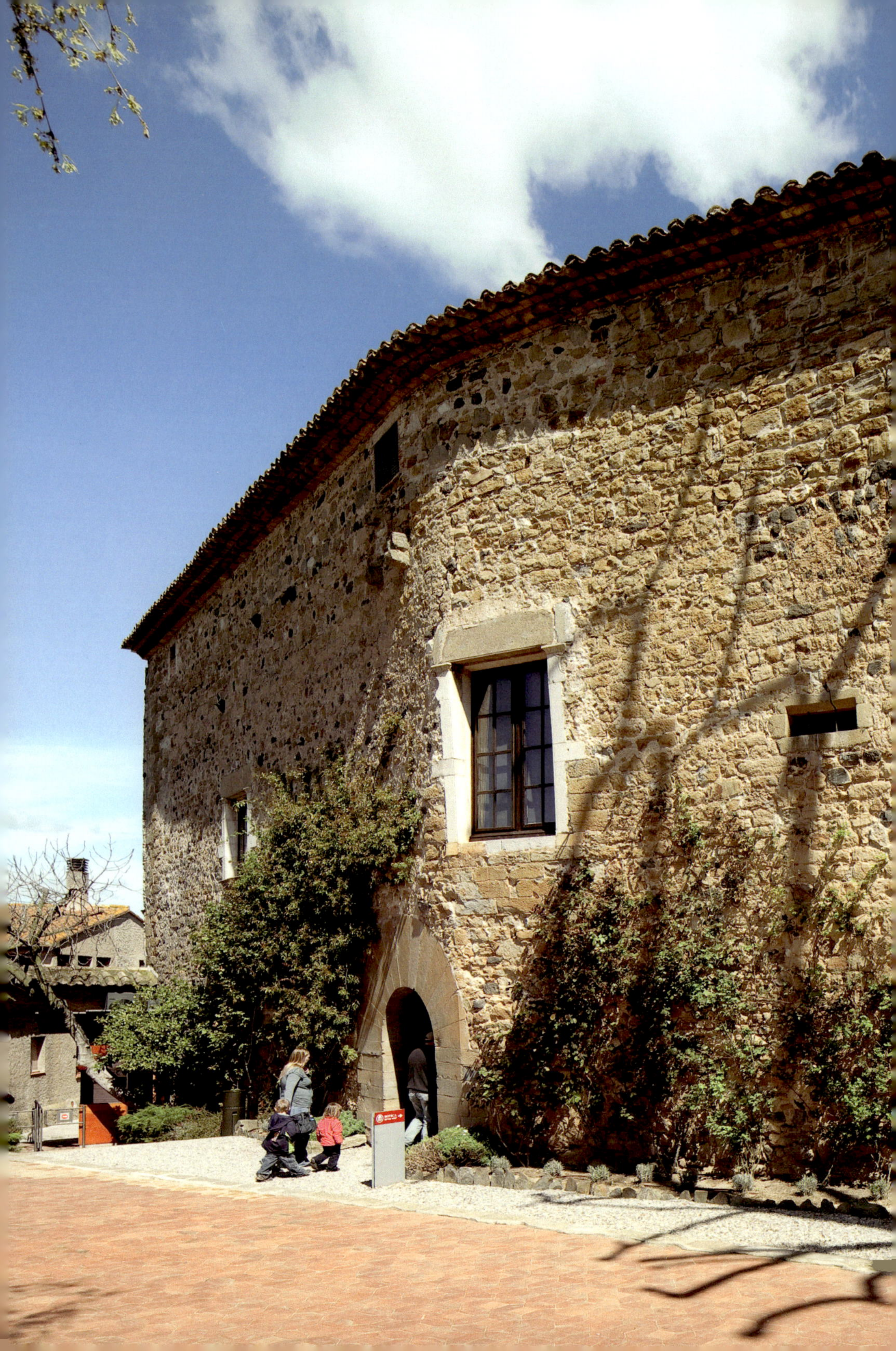

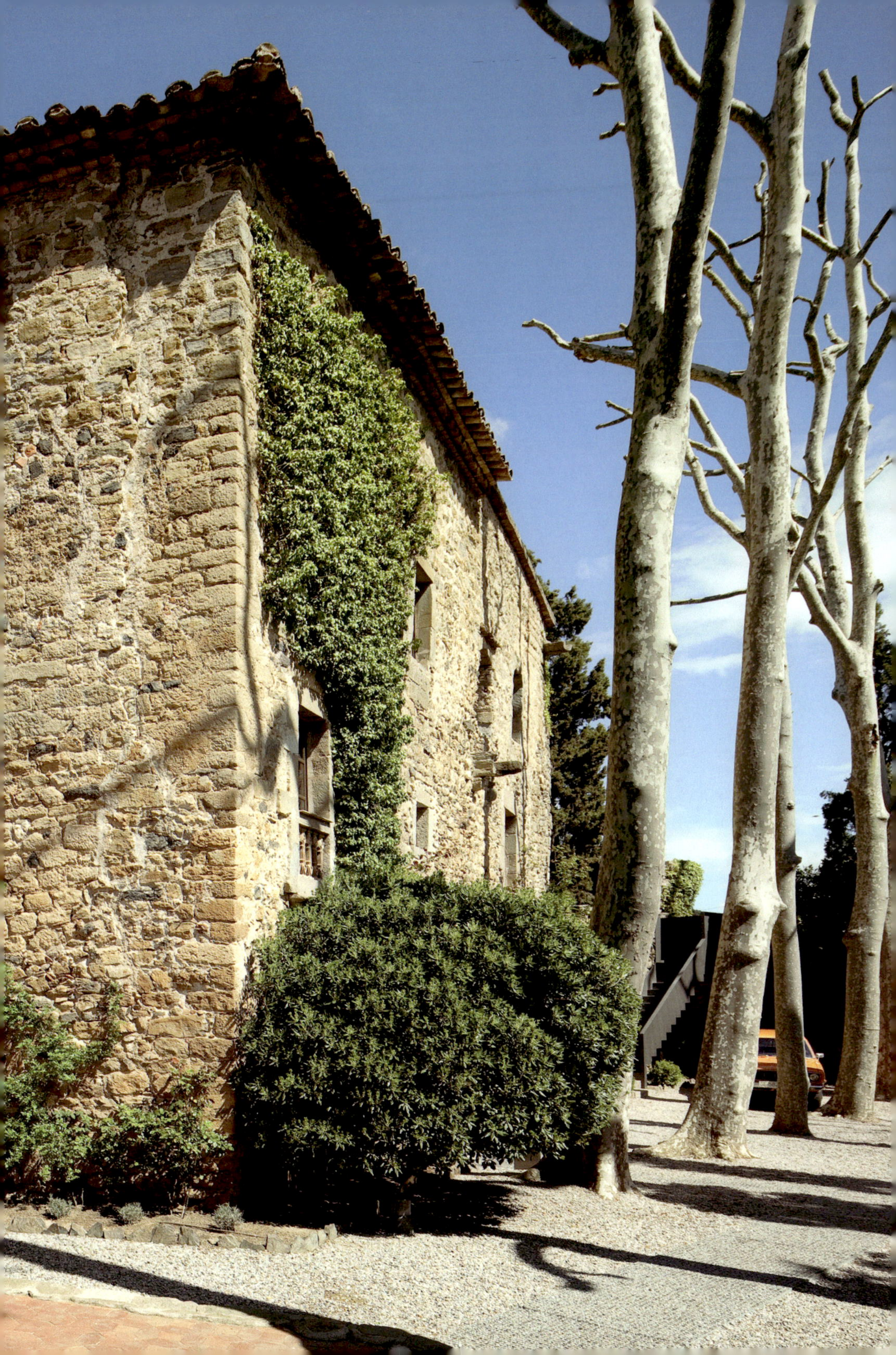

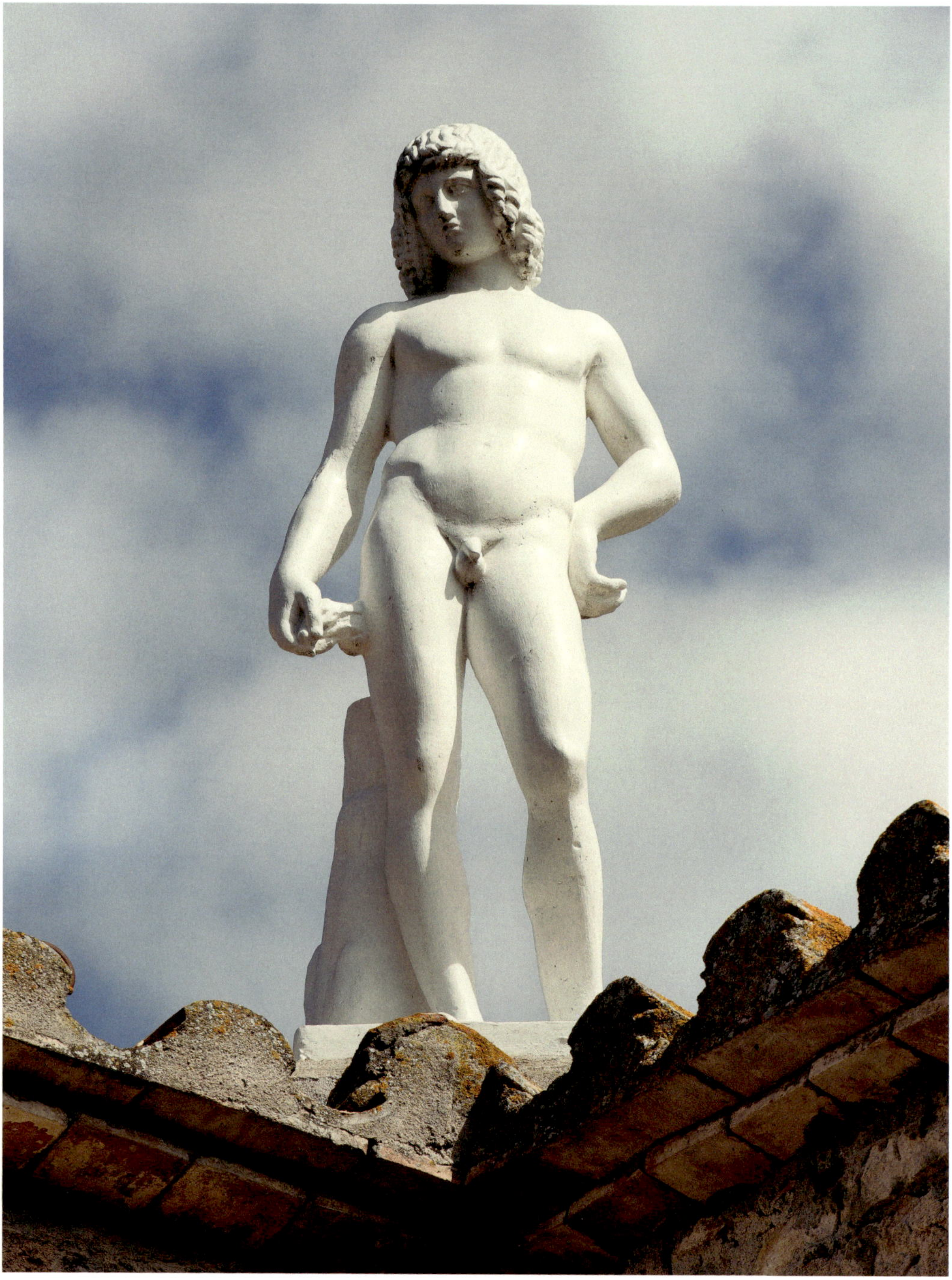

Plaster statue that overlooks the courtyard | Carriage of the barons of Púbol

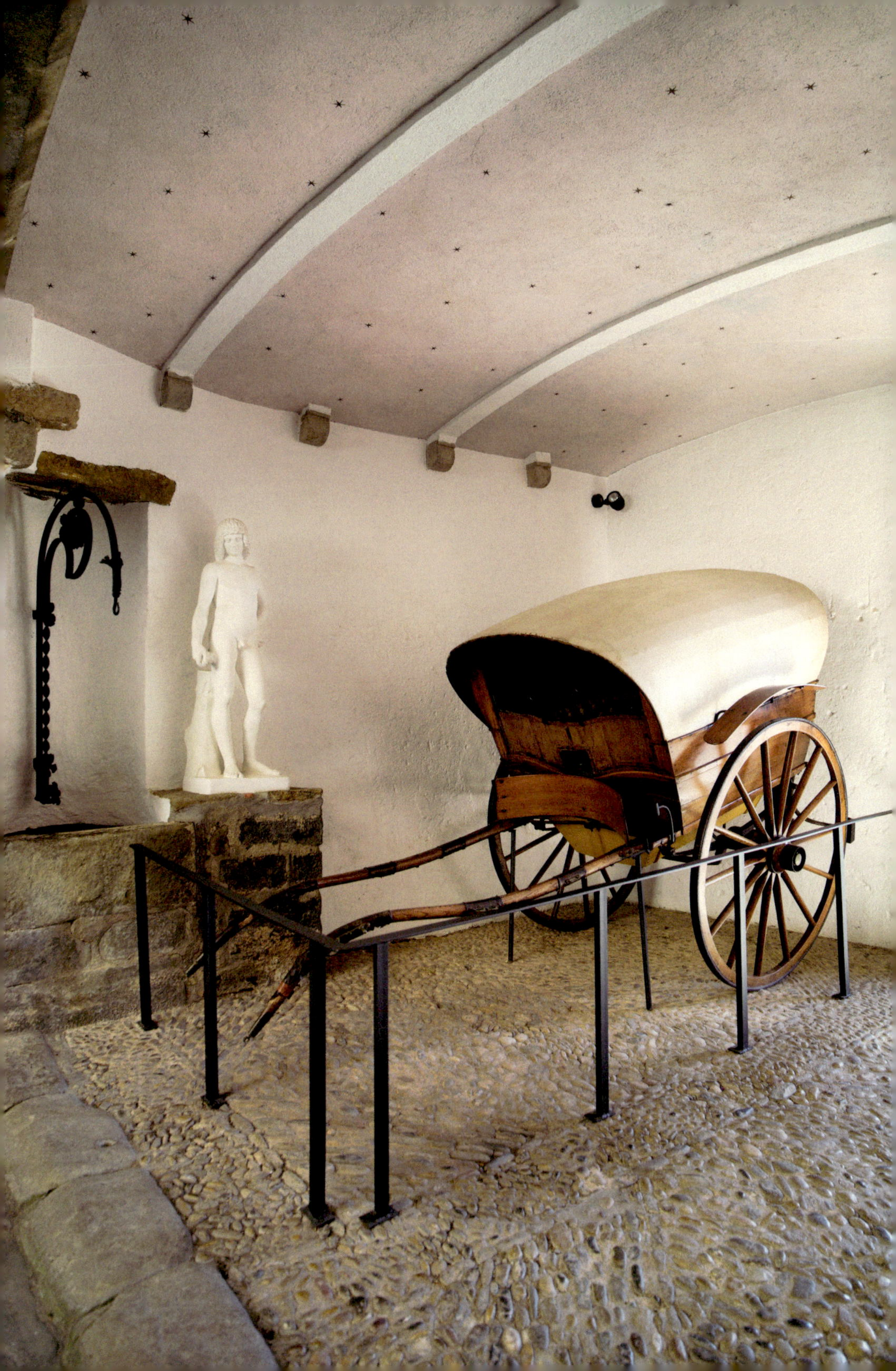

Here we see reflected Gala's pragmatism, who wanted an austere building and which went unnoticed, a building that protected her privacy; she wanted to avoid the Dalinian external evidence of the house in Cadaqués. As regards the garden, Dalí went beyond the structure in French style of the original garden of the barons of Púbol, to transform it into a garden inspired by the aesthetic experience and the senses that remained etched in his mind after his visit to the gardens of Bomarzo, Rome, and also inspired by all the tradition of bestiary, so popular in the Middle Ages. A decadent air, recalling Wagner and King Ludwig, as well as Luchino Visconti [21], impregnates the whole atmosphere, both in the garden specifically and the castle as a whole.

The voussoired door of the rose tree façade is flanked by two types of old corbels finished in the form of human head with moustache, that seem to be caricatures of Dalí and, through a porch, the entrance to the cobbled central courtyard opens to us, of trapezoidal ground plan, which is the axis from which the building is structured and distributed: a ground floor and two floors with which Dalí would play to create the spaces appropriate for the residency of Gala on the first floor, reducing the second floor to the minimum surface with a function more like a loft. The courtyard conserves the medieval air that defines the whole village.

The most characteristic element of the courtyard is the Gothic-Renaissance main façade, with the coat of arms of the barony from the late 14th century, and the carriage of the barons of Púbol that Dalí conserved in its place (the carriage, a symbol that appears in different oil paintings by the artist). Here is the entrance door to the old stables of the castle and a well.

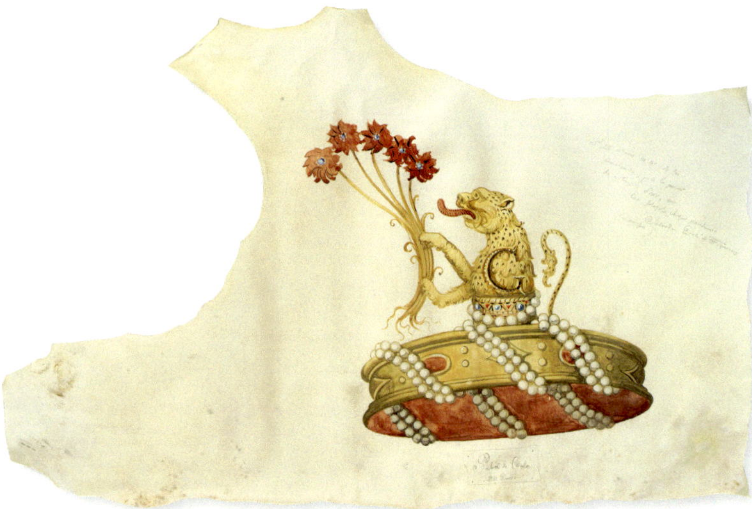

Púbol of Gala, watercolour by Dalí inspired by the coat of arms of the barony

[21] Dalí worked with Visconti in 1948 producing the costumes and the set for the work by William Shakespeare, *As you like* it, directed by the Italian director.

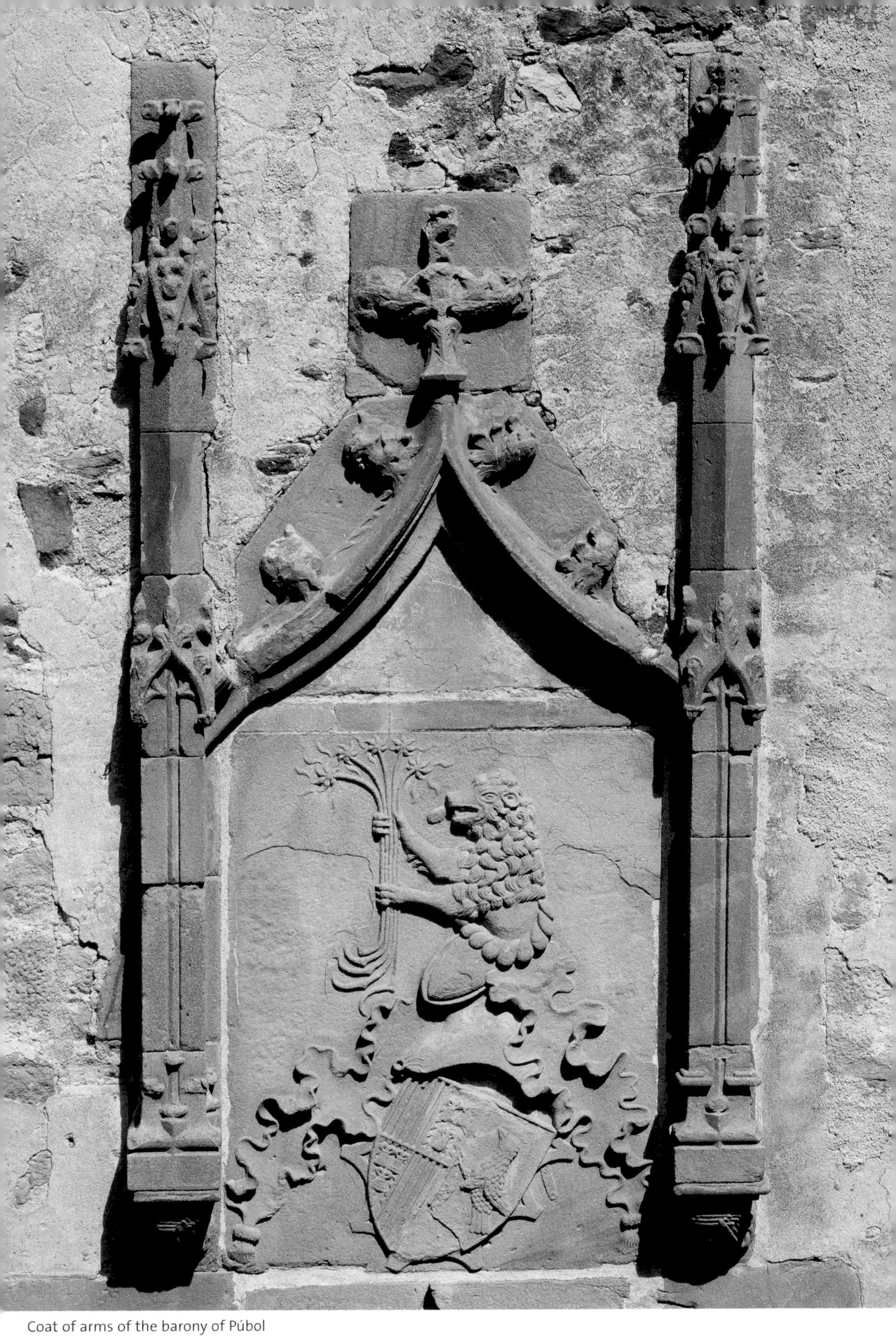

Coat of arms of the barony of Púbol

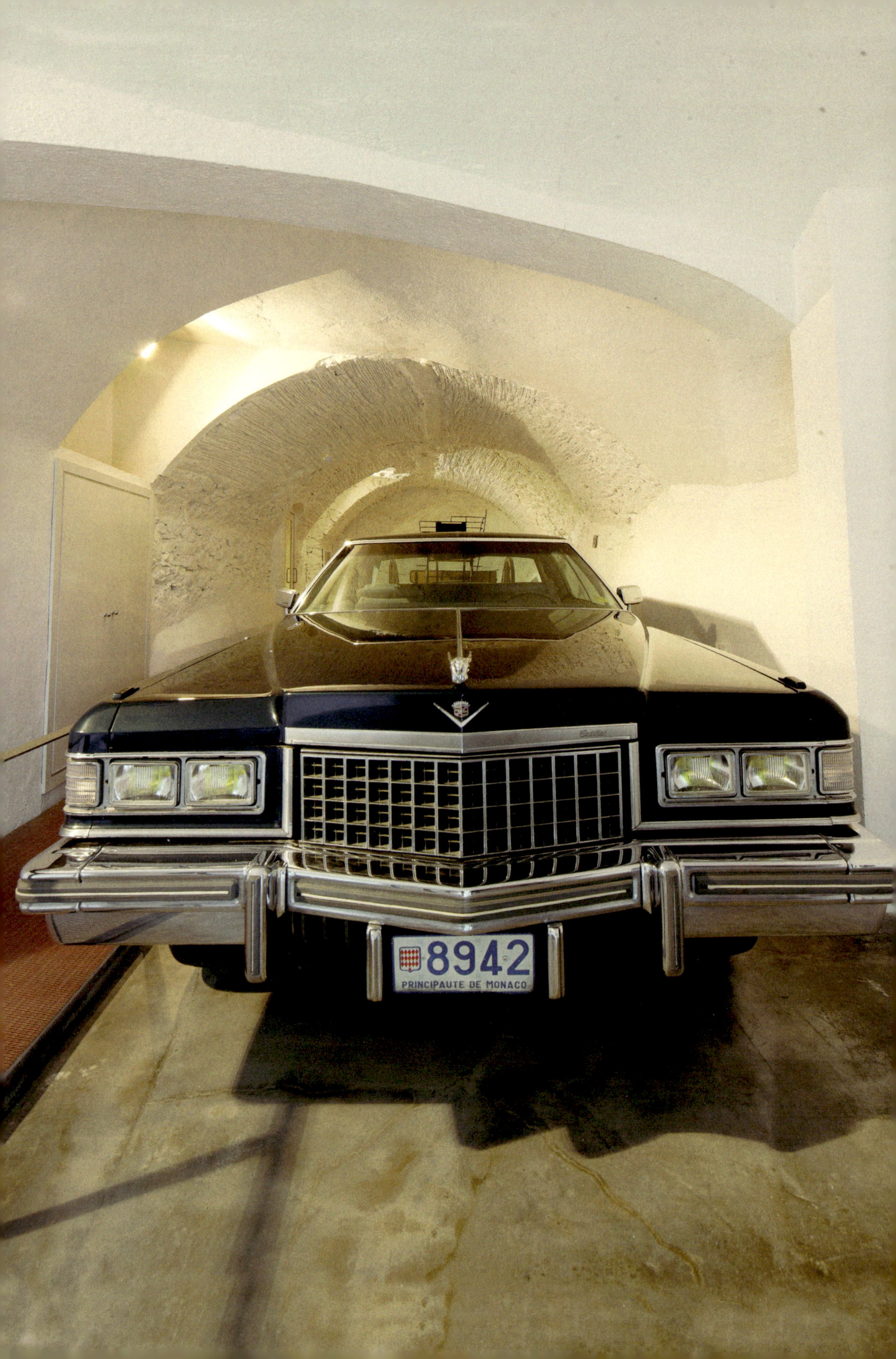
8942
PRINCIPAUTE DE MONACO

THE GARAGE

In Gala's time, the garage could be reached from both the garden and from a room called "the Persian room", currently the shop of the House-Museum. It was given this name due to the old decoration such as a glass lantern, with a crown on top, designed by Dalí.

In this lengthened space, with a vaulting that conserves the form of reeds, is an old calash, named by the painter as "the calash of the forgotten", left by the old owners of the castle. The calash only came out once from the time Dalí and Gala stayed in the castle, for the photographic session for the previously mentioned special issue of *Vogue* magazine. It was taken round the garden, pulled by two horses of a farmer. As well as Gala and the painter, Emili Puignau and Artur Caminada also rode in it. Marc Lacroix took the photo that Dalí described and enriched with these words: "I am behind, as servant of Gala, while she leads everyone, whip in hand".

In the garage we can also see other more modern means of transport, such as the cars used by the Dalí couple, for short trips or for running errands. In fact, Gala was the one who drove, or later on, Artur Caminada, chauffeur, butler and right-hand man. We can therefore see a small orange Datsun for which Dalí produced an advertisement for American television in 1972.

The other car is a blue Cadillac, with registration number 8942 from the Principality of Monaco, a Sedan Deville model bought for 10,000 dollars in 1976 in the United States. It was registered on the 16 March of that year with the registration number 568 YUL-USA in the name of Mrs. Helen Dalí, resident at the Hotel Saint Regis. But in 1977, when the Dalí couple established their home in Monte Carlo (in 36 de la Rue des Remparts), they took the car to Europe and changed the registration number for the current one.

The presence of the Cadillac is highly significant, since it appears as motif in some of the painter's outstanding works. We find it in early works, such as the oil painting titled *Bather* (1924), a portrait of his friend Joan Xirau, or in *Girl of Figueres*, from 1926. Dalí enriched the many meanings attributed to the car and applied his paranoiac-critical method and his special conception of the world. Thus, he used the fossilised car that appears in *Imperial monument to the child-woman* (1929) to extend in time the mineral and timeless presence of the rocks of Cap de Creus. The presence of dynamic machines in his work such as cars or planes creates a disassociation of ideas. He joins fossil material, immemorial time, with the most recent element in the history of mankind: the machine that provides mobility. The contrast of ideas and images serves to awaken the imagination of the spectator, to provoke them.

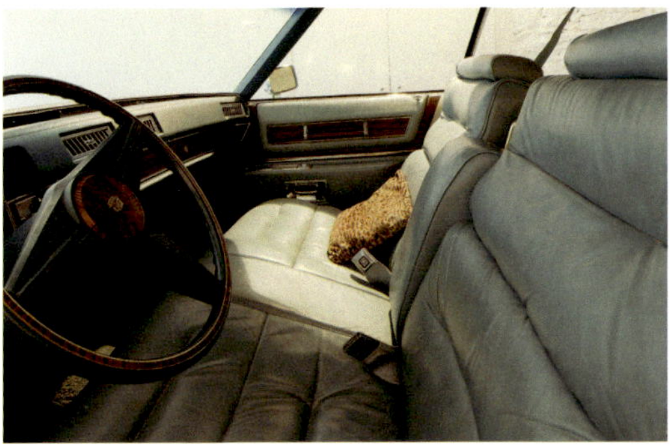

The Cadillac Sedan Deville, in the garage

A Cadillac, a 1941 Sedan model, is also the car that Dalí used to reproduce the action that the painter presented in 1938 in the International Exhibition of Surrealism in Paris and which, currently, is the central element of the courtyard of the stalls of the municipal theatre of Figueres, today the Dalí Theatre-Museum.

According to Jaume Miravitlles, childhood friend of the painter, in an article for *Revista de Girona*: "General Motors had launched a *Deluxe Cadillac* onto the market that had been a big commercial success, and wanted to repeat the test with a more expensive and sophisticated model. Dalí received an official notification to launch a new model. He immediately had an idea: the car would be called *Gala Cadillac*: a bombshell of a name and within the artist's obsession. He accompanied the name with a brief sketch he drew with a ballpoint pen, on headed writing paper of the Hotel Saint Regis. It was very interesting, although I do not know if it could be 'mass' produced. It was a regular Cadillac covered with a sumptuous metallic layer in cardinal red, which covered the roof of the car and came down the sides and back, leaving only the windows uncovered. He did it in less than five minutes, but the result was really quite amazing: a real car, a gala car!

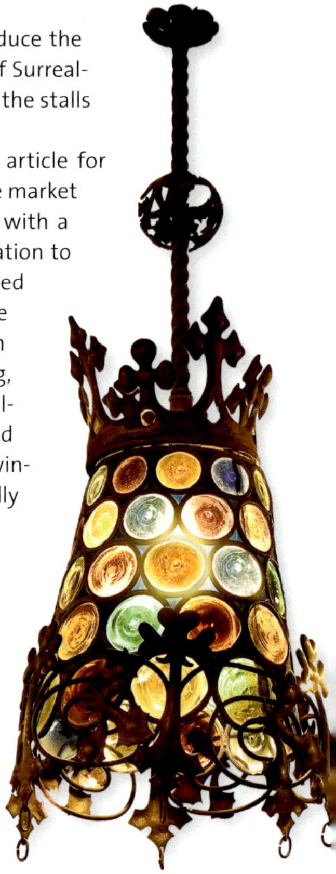

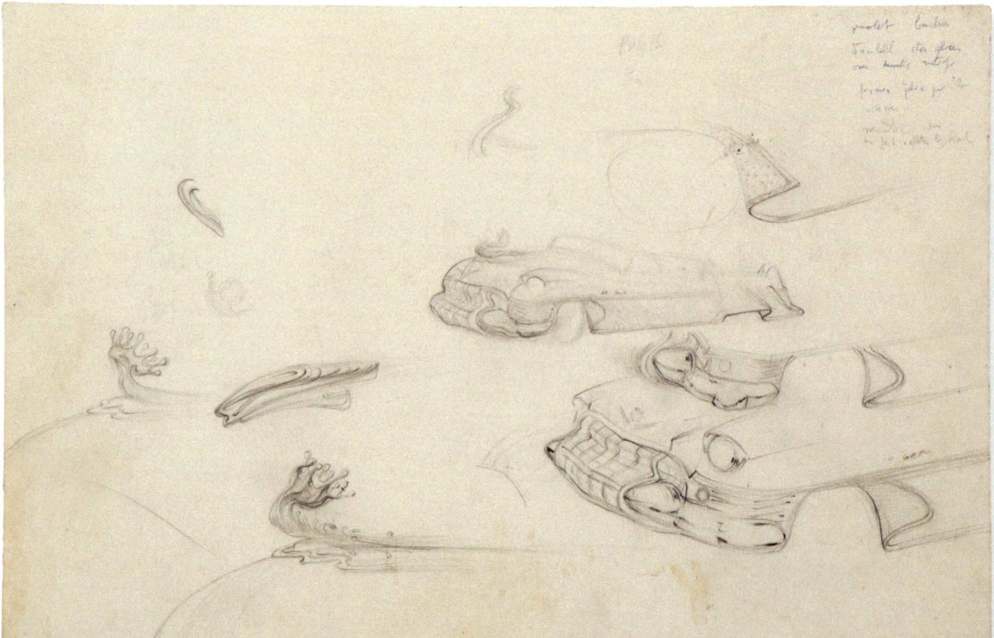

Sketch by Dalí for Gala's Cadillac | Glass lamp inspired by Puig i Cadafalch

I do not know what happened. There was no reply, neither positive nor negative, from General Motors. But a year or two later the company announced the appearance of a new model: the *Gala Cadillac*! The name only, without any of the innovations that Dalí had suggested"[22].

In 1976, in the first issue of his *Setmanari artístic empordanès*, Dalí wrote these words about the *Rainy Taxi*, exhibited in the Theatre-Museum:

"... the famous Cadillac that Dalí gave to Gala and of which there are six examples. One of them belonged to President Roosevelt, another to Clark Gable, etc. This is the fourth reproduction of the *Rainy Taxi*, today all destroyed.

The first was exhibited with great success in the surrealist exhibition of Paris; the second, in the International Exhibition of Nueva York, and the third in the surrealist retrospective of the Museum of Modern Art of New York. And the fourth is this one, which is on permanent show in the Dalí Museum".

This car was the one that Gala had driven on long trips from California to New York and which, finally, Artur Caminada used. It was also involved in two trips of a more tragic note: one for the movement of Gala, once dead, from Portlligat to Púbol; and the second, on the 31 of August 1984, when Dalí was moved from the castle to the Pilar clinic in Barcelona, after the fire in his bedroom.

The window that joins this room with the garage is the proof that at some time there had been a prison in the basement of the stately home, since it is certain that a small gap in the window allowed the prisoner's food to be passed through without the jailor having to enter.

[22] Miravitlles, Jaume. "Dalí i l'aritmètica". *Revista de Girona*, July 1974, Girona, p. 34.

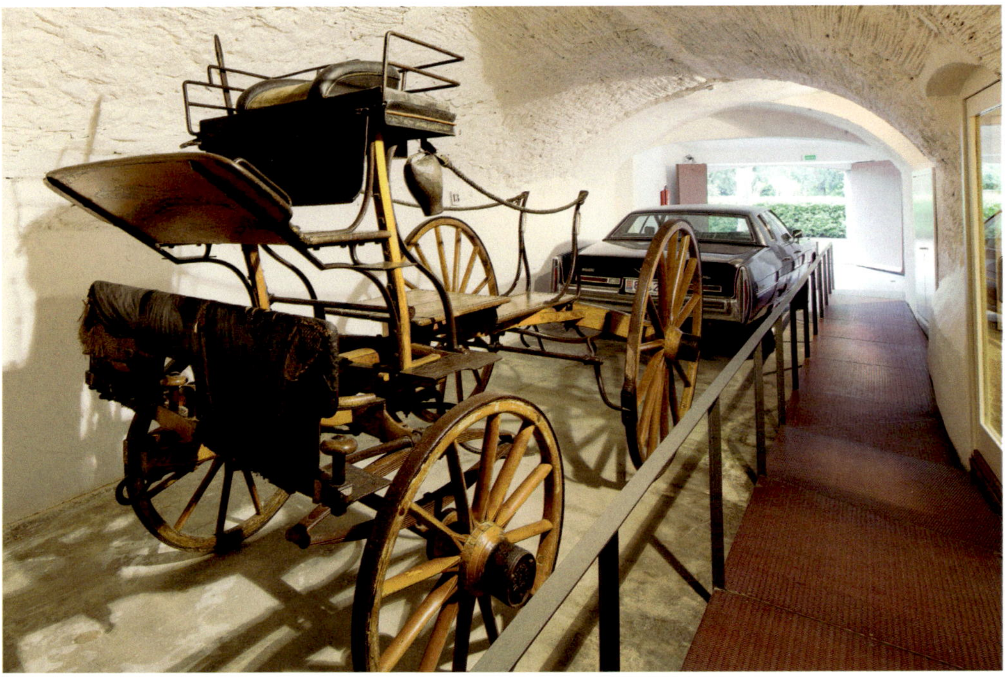

The "calash of the forgotten"

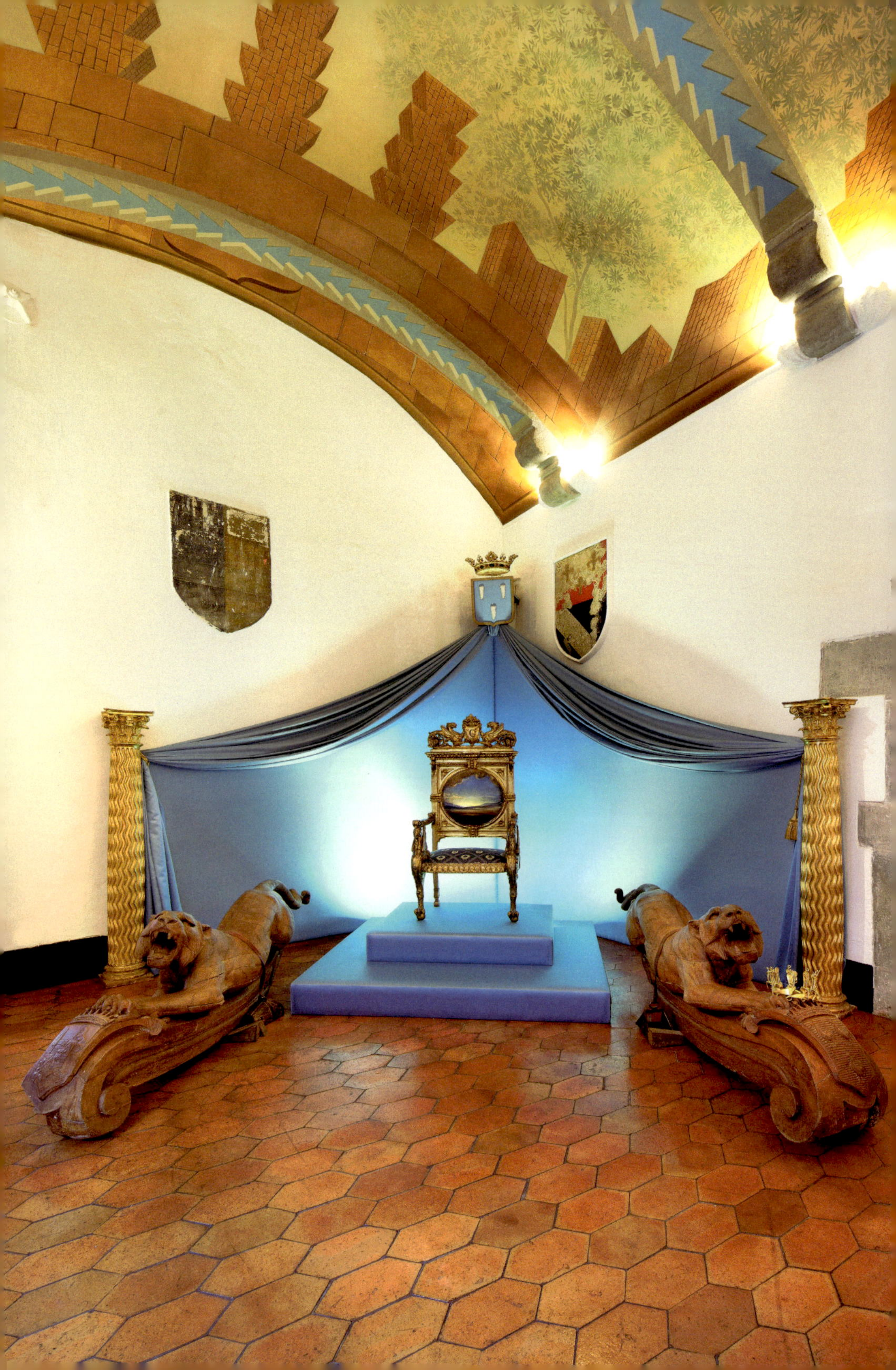

THE COAT OF ARMS ROOM

The first floor of the castle was the area of residence, and both the entrance door, at the end of the stone stairway, and a large window, on the same side, now reveal a sumptuousness that is not perceived on the outside walls. The historian Badia i Homs wrote a detailed description of these two openings that explain part of the genealogical history of the castle. Of the "Renaissance window divided into four" [23] he says that "the base of the mullions and columns have motifs in relief; in the upper angles each of the corbels represent lions and the lower ones, dragons" [24]. The door features a large emblem in bas-relief added in the 16th century: "It is framed by two false columns crowned by pinnacles with floral motifs, among them an arcade of arris enhanced by a cross. In the lower part of each column there are two curious reliefs: they aim to represent ribbons with tassels. The coat of arms, in the centre, is inclined towards the left and belongs to the Requesens-Corbera [25] (matched: the crow on one side and four consoles on the other). Above there is a warrior's helmet from which four ribbons hang, and above everything a rampant lion that grips a bunch, perhaps, of spears "[26].

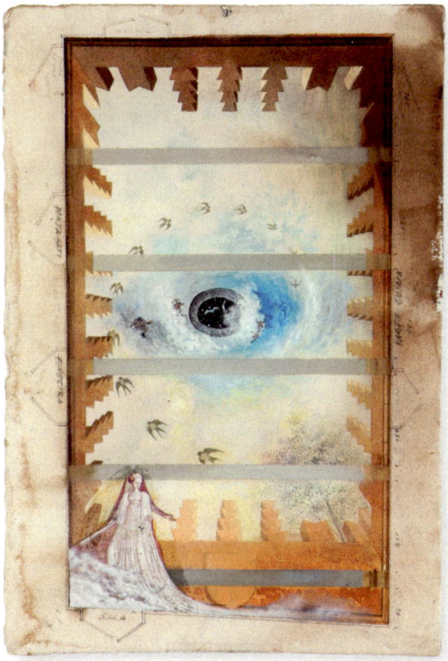

Preparatory watercolour of the painting of the ceiling

[23] Badia i Homs, *L'arquitectura medieval de l'Empordà*, Vol. I, Diputació de Girona, Girona, 1977, p. 307.

[24] *Ibid.*

[25] The coat of arms mentioned is a combination of two noble families who owned the castle. On the right appears the crow, symbol of the Corbera, which is also found over the door of the church, and on the left, the heraldry of the Requesens represented in the 1st and 4th quadrants by four *pals de gules* (equivalent to red) over a golden field, and in the 2nd and 3rd quadrants, by three golden towers over a field of azure (dark blue). Josep M. Marquès identifies the ribbon with tassels with Sança, who was the widow of Gispert de Campllong in 1400. (Pitxot, Antoni; Playà, Josep, *Gala Dalí's Castle: The Road to Púbol*, Fundació Gala-Salvador Dalí, Escudo de Oro, Figueres, Barcelona, 1997, p. 20)

[26] *Op. cit.*, p. 307.

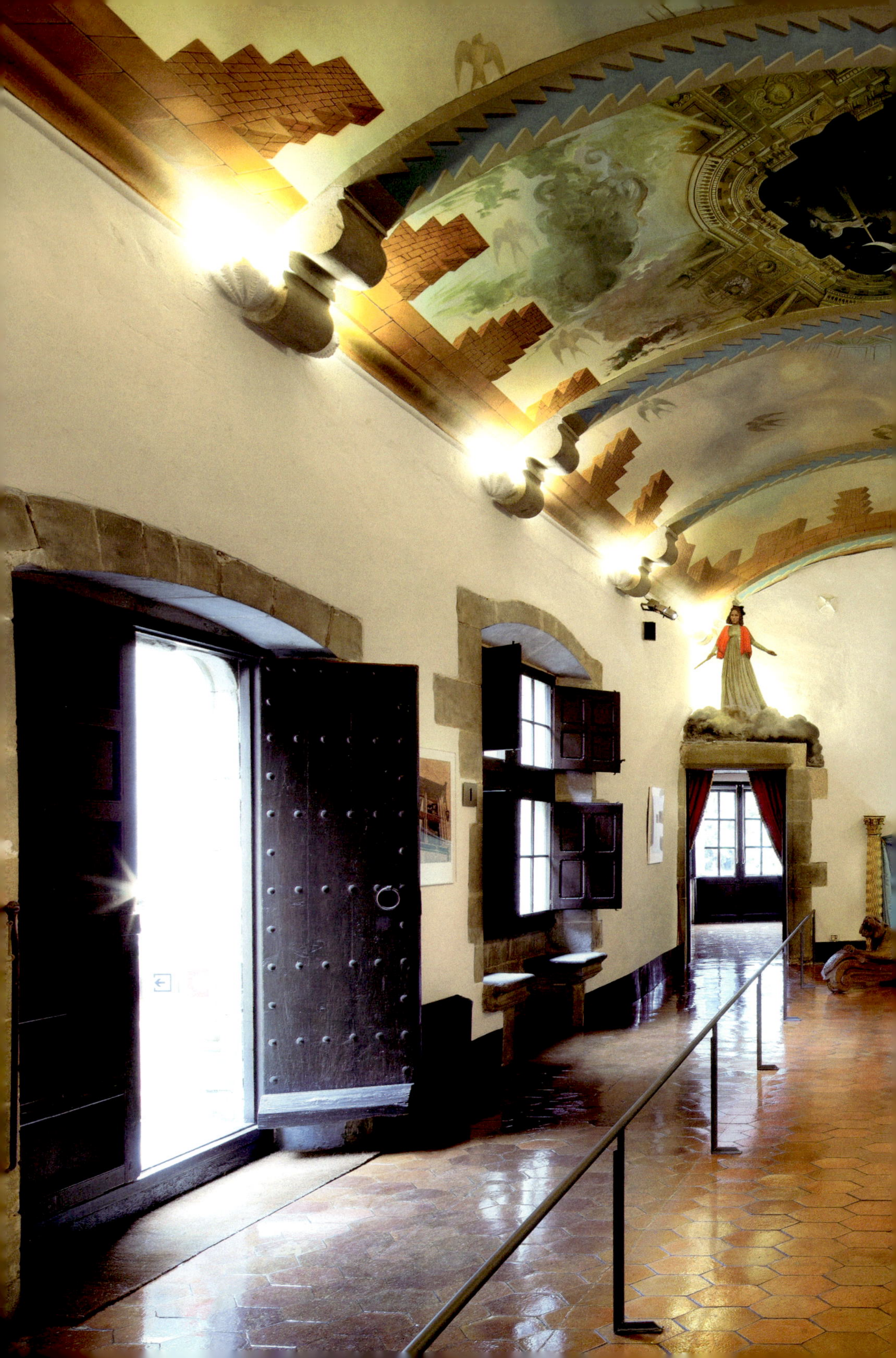

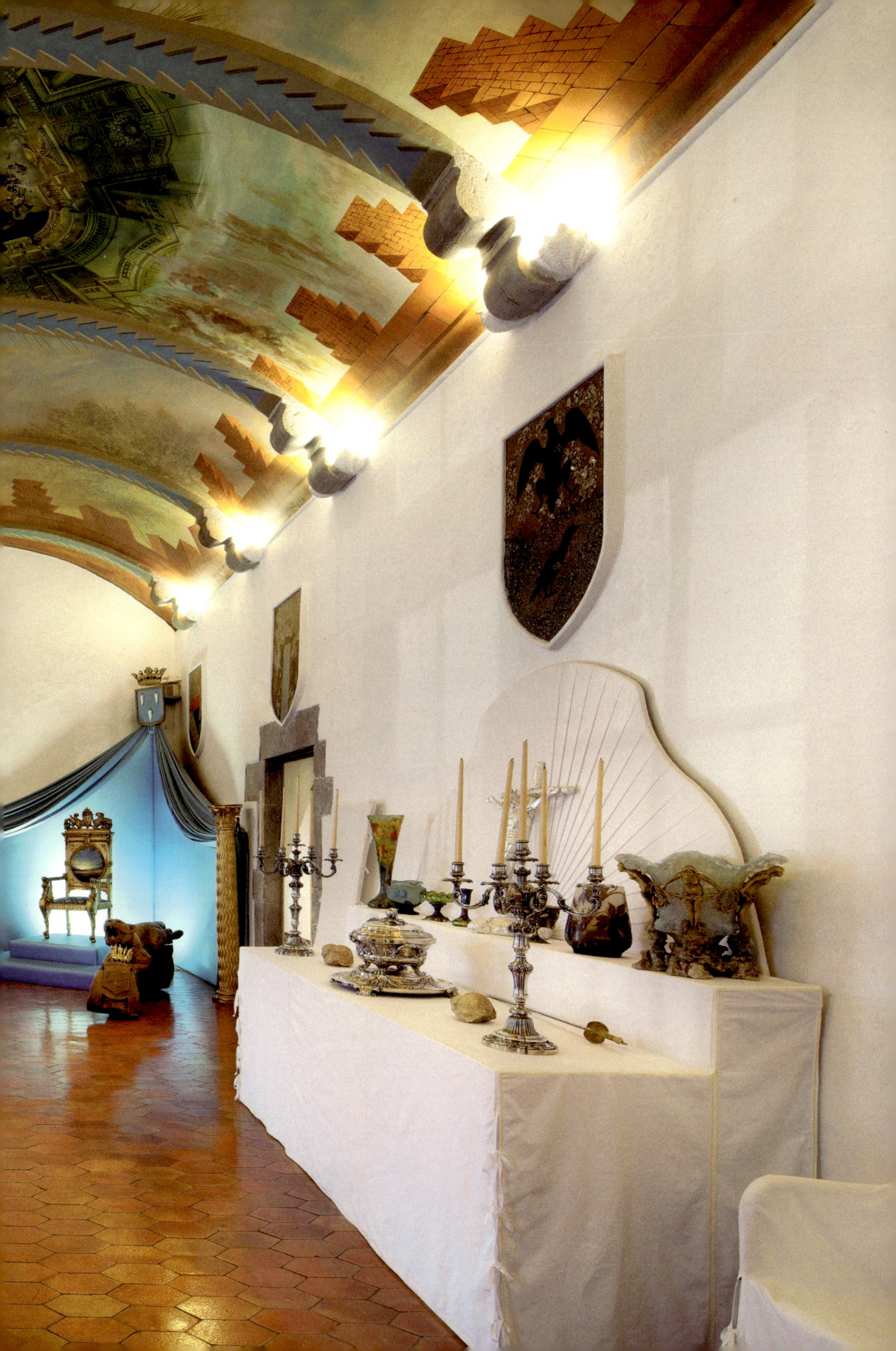

On entering this room, just like entering the "Palace of the Winds" room in the Theatre-Museum of Figueres, visitors are surprised and amazed. On the ceiling, a large painting covers the entire vaulting. On the opposite wall, there is an item of furniture and some chairs lined with white fabric, with knots in the style of the Dior label, like the costumes that are in the Theatre-Museum that the Dalí couple wore for the Beistegui ball in Venice, and which Pierre Cardin remembered in all detail recently on his visit to the Dalinian triangle. The furniture is adorned as if it was an altar and features a pair of five-armed candelabras worked in silver with their respective white candles and a wooden sculpture, the work of Salvador Dalí, of a Christ on the cross supported by crouton bread.

The two shelves are full of various objects: a large soup tureen and a silver tray with plant decorative elements; a gilded metal sword with a three-edged blade, which has the inscription VIVE LE ROI engraved on the handle; several glass paste vases, two in particular by Daum Nancy and Emille Gallé, respectively, with brown leaves over a white background, repositories of a totemic spirit; a slice of mineral; a shell of fossilised snail; a chalice of gilded metal; a fruit bowl of green glass. We see, then, the accumulation of typically Dalinian objects, which we can also find in the other two centres of the triangle.

Of special note in the room is the presence of six shields, which were already there when the Dalí couple bought the castle and must have represented the coats of arms of the diverse nobles who had lived there. They had to be restored, and despite the fact that some of the original elements were conserved, other details and esoteric emblems were added that demonstrate Dalí's intervention.

There is one exception, the shield situated on the left-hand wall and on which almost nothing could be distinguished, had been left full of splashes of the painters who worked on the rehabilitation of the space. Dalí said that it was the most authentic and asked them to leave it just as it was: two halves can be made out, one of brownish shades, and the other dark blue, in homage to the painters. In the case of this spattered shield we should consider the respect that Dalí had for the sign of the accident, always considered sacred on taking part in chance. In Portlligat he also liked to keep an outside door just as the fishermen who had dried the brushes they used to paint the boats with had left it. They did it over long winter days when, due to the bad weather, they could not go out to sea. Dalí, on returning from New York, would find the surprise each spring on the outside door with the best action painting of popular natural wisdom.

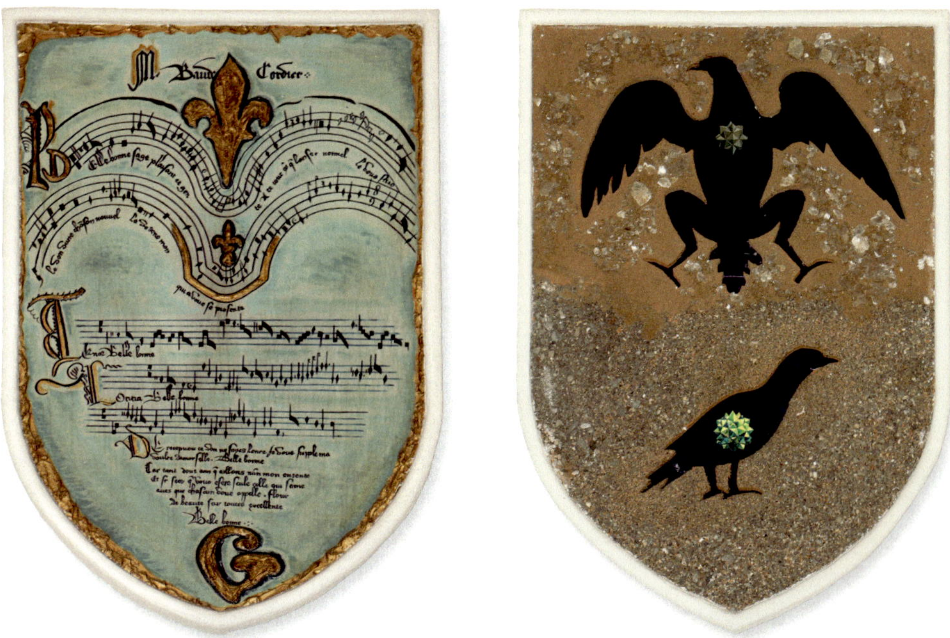

Coats of arms reinterpreted by Dalí

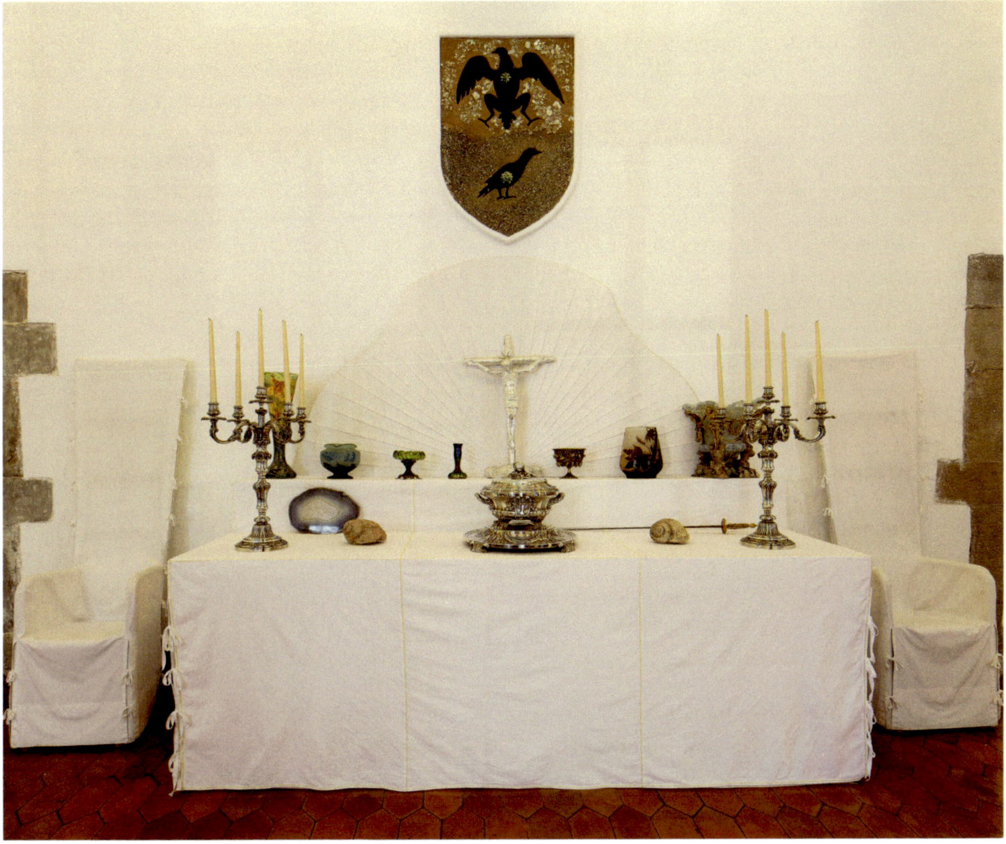

Furniture-altar

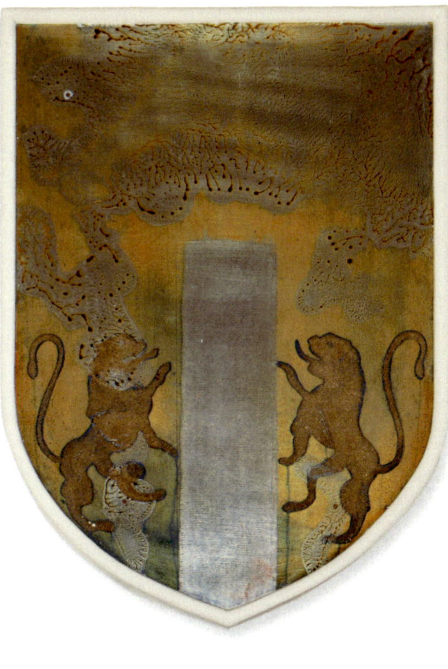

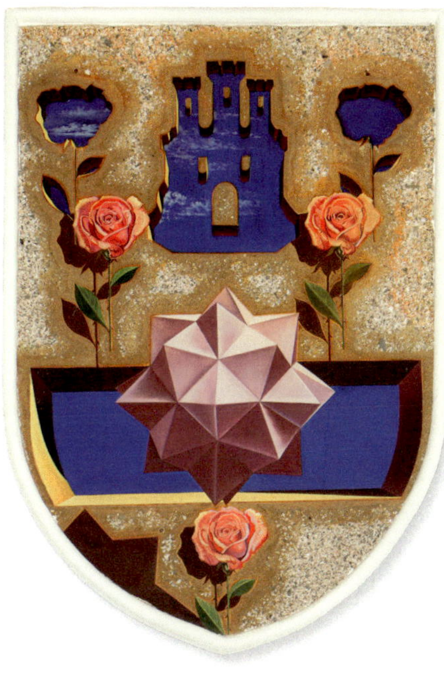

On the right-hand side of the room there is a completely renovated shield, with a musical score, a fleur-de-lis and a G (of Gala) over a green background. Perhaps the most Dalinian of all is the one that has the silhouette of a castle of bluish shades, in the upper part, and a dodecahedron below, with three red roses on the sides. Over this kind of profane altar there is a shield that represents a crow with the wings open and another in profile, though in a posture that does not coincide with that of the heraldry of the Corbera family. A third shield shows three fleurs-de-lis in the upper part over a red background (it might correspond to the coat of arms of the Miquel family, with a crossed band on the lower part over a black background). The last one that is still to be described has a strip in the centre (heraldic sign of the Campllongs) and two rampant lions on either side. Finally, of note is the heraldic coat of arms of the Marquis of Dalí of Púbol, made up of a crown of the marquisate and three white ermine tails over a blue background. We should remember that, in 1982, King Juan Carlos I named the painter Marquis of Dalí of Púbol, a title of which he always felt very honoured.

On both sides of the altar we come to both doors, but the one on the left is fictional, it is a trompe-l'œil from 1972 painted by Dalí (oil of 220.5 × 115.7 cm), framed by authentic stones, since before there had been an opening. This simulated door in the wall is half open and represents, with great credibility, that the paint is coming away.

As we have mentioned before, Gala was the one who defined many ornamental aspects of the houses and especially in Púbol. On this question the chairs really stand out. The ones we find on either side of the room are covered with white fabrics tied with some side bows, according to Gala's desires and which are also repeated in Portlligat. Nevertheless, we can highlight two chairs: one is the *Chair of spoons*, in bronze, a sculpture (111 × 36.5 × 46.5 cm) of which no more than 12 examples were made between 1960 and 1974. It is the cast of an original that they found in Portlligat (an old wicker chair, with ten large wooden spoons stuck on and some legs, at the front, that look like lion's paws). The chair in Portlligat was integrated into a montage that Dalí had called *Chair with vulture's wings* (1960). In Púbol, the sculpture has one more piece than the others of the series: it includes as a back a diadem that according to Dalí had belonged to the French dramatic actor François-Joseph Talma (1763-1826), known for his interpretations of characters of Shakespeare, Corneille and Molière, and admired by Napoleon. This actor was also known for his defence of the use of historical costume in the performance and popularised a long cape, which he always wore,

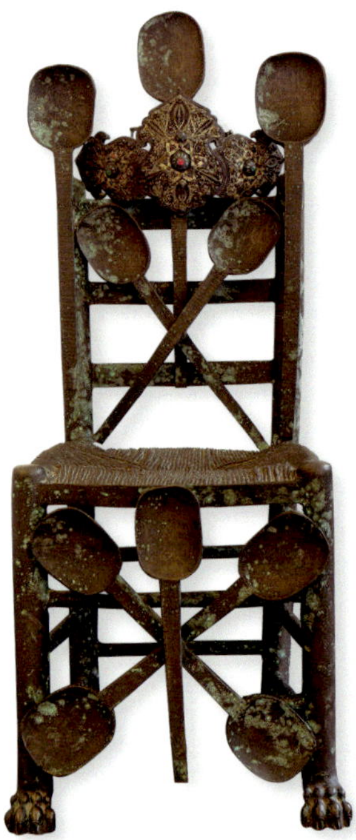

Chair of spoons

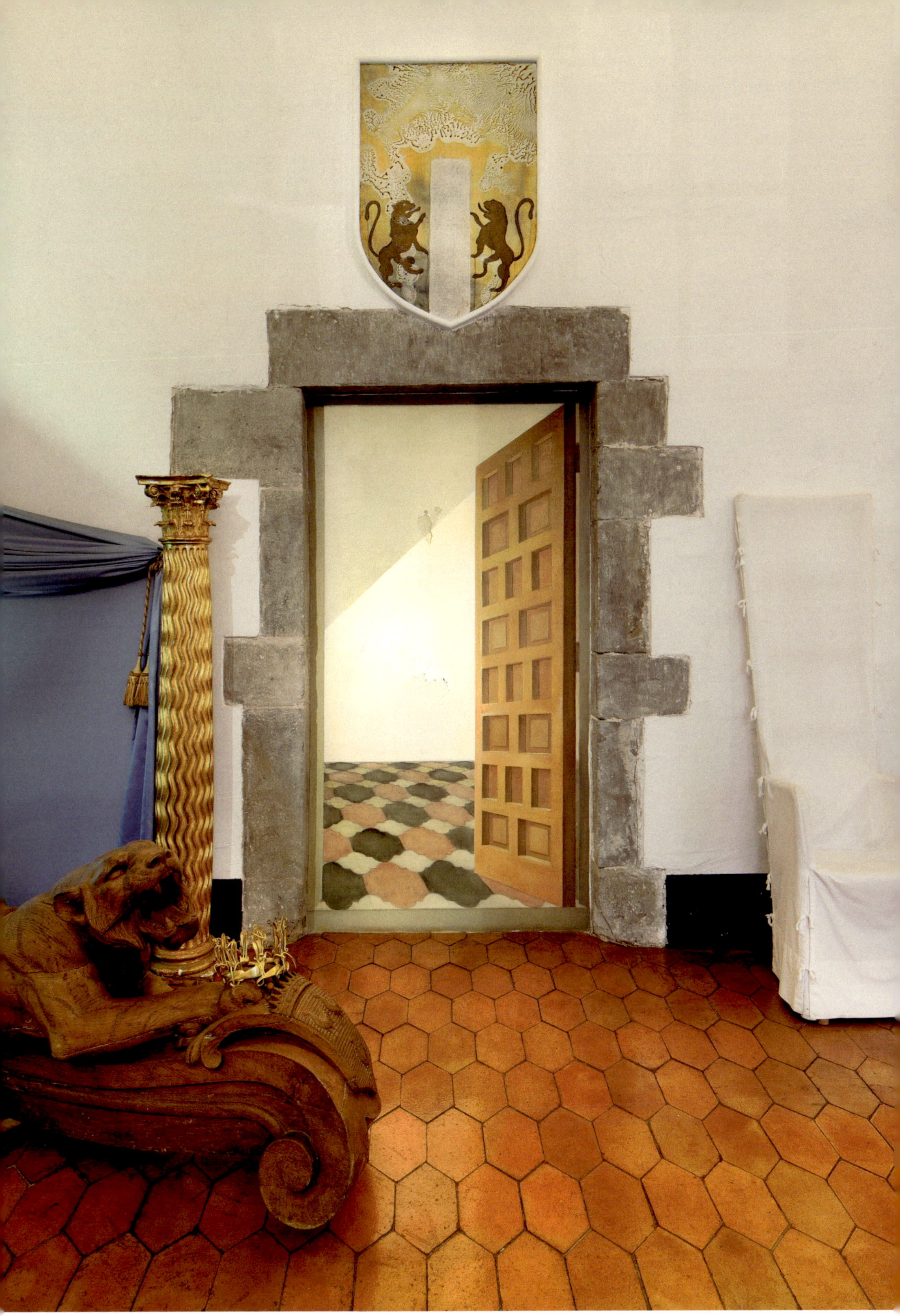

Trompe-l'œil painted by Dalí

and was given the name of 'shoulder cape'. Dalí was particularly interested in this diadem for what it symbolised in theatrical representation. We cannot forget, as visitors, our condition as spectators as well.

On the left part of the room, strengthening its heraldic air, is Gala's throne, a montage used as the seat for receiving special visits. It was designed by Salvador Dalí in 1974 and a drawing is conserved of the initial idea, where Dalí worked from the chair of teaspoons, and an autographic note clarifies the function: *Trone petit pour olivone petitone* (sic). Finally, however, the central piece of the montage ended up being the current chair with old arms crowned by two gryphons that support a shield where the artist simulates an engraved G; although it is on the back where we discover an interesting intervention of the artist who painted a dawn landscape in the central circle, a space of spiritual depths, where we see an open window to an indeterminate, idyllic place, like the Kythera to which the characters of Jean Antoine Watteau go in the oil painting *The Embarkation to Kythera*, one of the mythical works of art history according to Dalí. The throne, strictly speaking, situated over a dais of two steps, is flanked by two wooden lions, which according to Dalí were from Provence, in a defensive pose, to which Dalí added some riding stirrups. One of them guards the crown he made with intertwined forks and gold-plated. The seat of honour is framed by a structure of blue curtains in the form of a small canopy, decorated with two gilded columns and crowned by the coat of arms of the Marquis of Dalí and Púbol, created by the painter himself from the royal blue of Gala's bedroom and three ermine tails. Dalí, as we have mentioned, was proud of this appointment made by the King of Spain, who was also a personal friend.

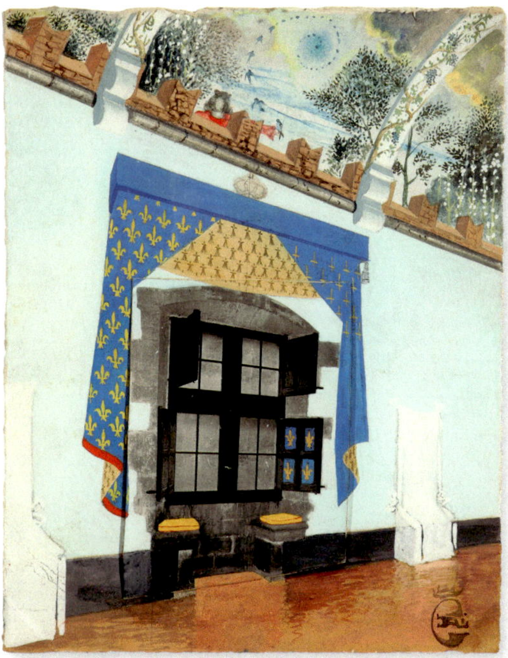

Intervention by Dalí on a photograph

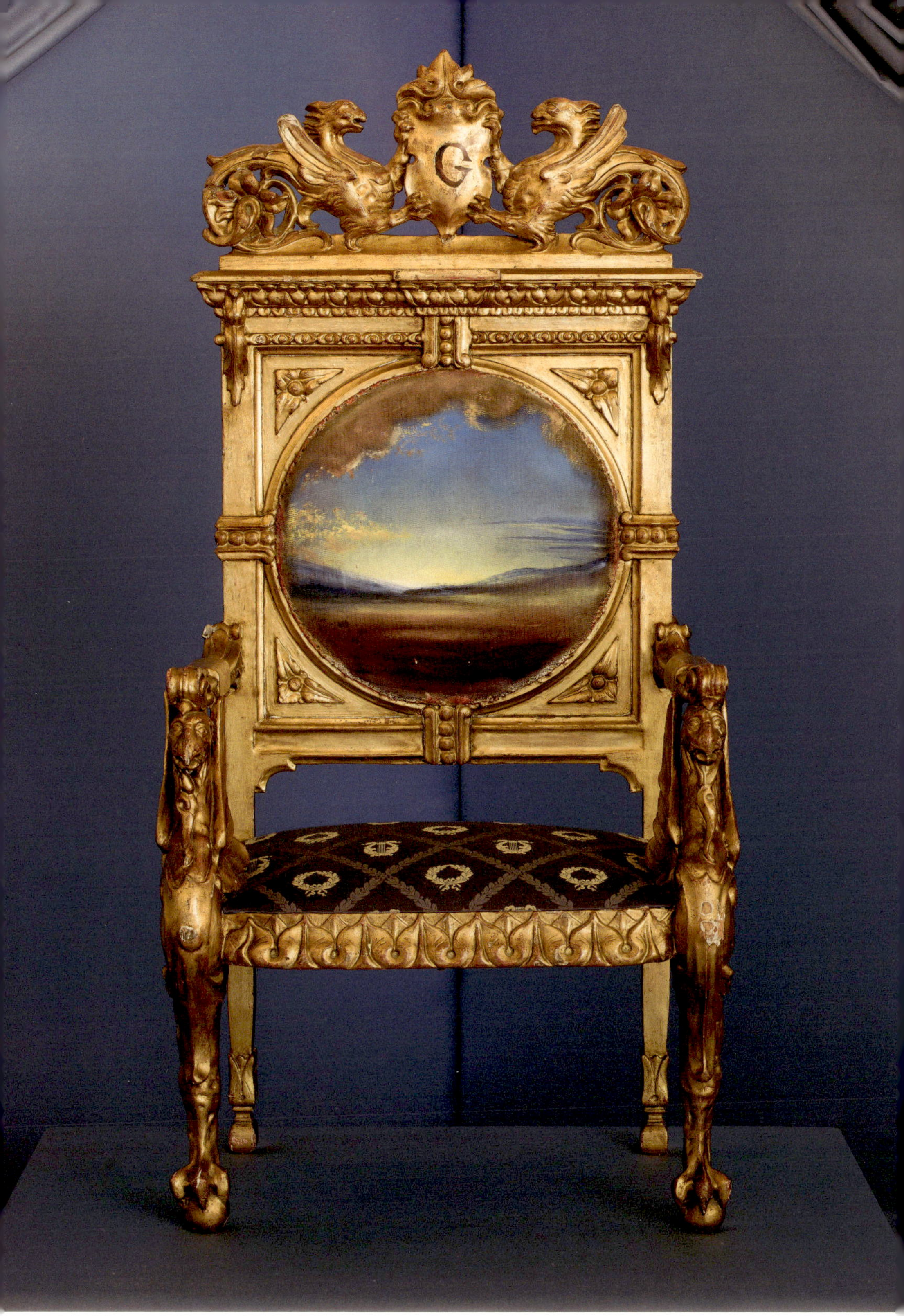

Gala's throne with painting by Dalí

THE CEILING PAINTING

Between 1969-70 the painter's studio was basically dedicated to the execution of diverse interior design projects: the ceiling of the Albéniz Palace in Barcelona; the ceiling of the main room of the Theatre-Museum that would be opened four years later and the painting that decorates that of the castle of Púbol that we deal with here.

According to the declarations of the master to *Vogue*[27] magazine, Gala made a list of requests for her castle, where it included the realisation of "a ceiling of 15 metres representing a nocturnal hole in the Mediterranean sky from which will fall surrealist treasures"[28]. And later she also ordered "in a purely friendly capacity a soffit of 20 metres for the Dalí museum in Figueres where, for the same price, Dalí and Gala will be totally opened by magical drawers with the aim of pouring over my home people the treasure that we are"[29].

A preparatory watercolour for this painting is conserved. The ceiling represents a yellow sky with plant elements, swallows flying and a night scene within a false architecture, all surrounded by castle battlements. There are also six arches decorated with blue fish bones. Here Dalí males a clear allusion to the *Camera picta, la camera degli sposi*, which Andrea Mantegna created (1465-1474) for the private stay of Ludovico Gonzaga in the Ducal Palace of Mantova. Dalí expressed his admiration for Mantegna, as in the ceiling of the "Palace of the Wind" room of the Theatre-Museum of Figueres where he expresses his homage to Michelangelo and the Sistine Chapel. Mantegna was a specific, defined painter, a grand master of perspective and, both to him and Dalí, symbols were transcendent. On looking up, on seeing the skylight, we see a fiction in which both the red terracotta battlements of the castle and the flight of the swallows around it are represented. We should recall that Dalí always represented what is ephemeral —such as clouds or sea waves— with precision and in a way worthy of Mantegna.

The portrait of Gala painted by Dalí over the doorway that leads to the next room also confers ritual and solemnity to this space. Gala, sword in hand, is, like the lady of the castle, a symbol of authority. The trompe-l'œil gives us the illusion of fiction and projects the presence of its resident, Gala, with more intensity. The world of the imagination is translated into fiction, at the service and for the pleasure of the person on the receiving end. Dalí applied fiction to his art to seduce Gala.

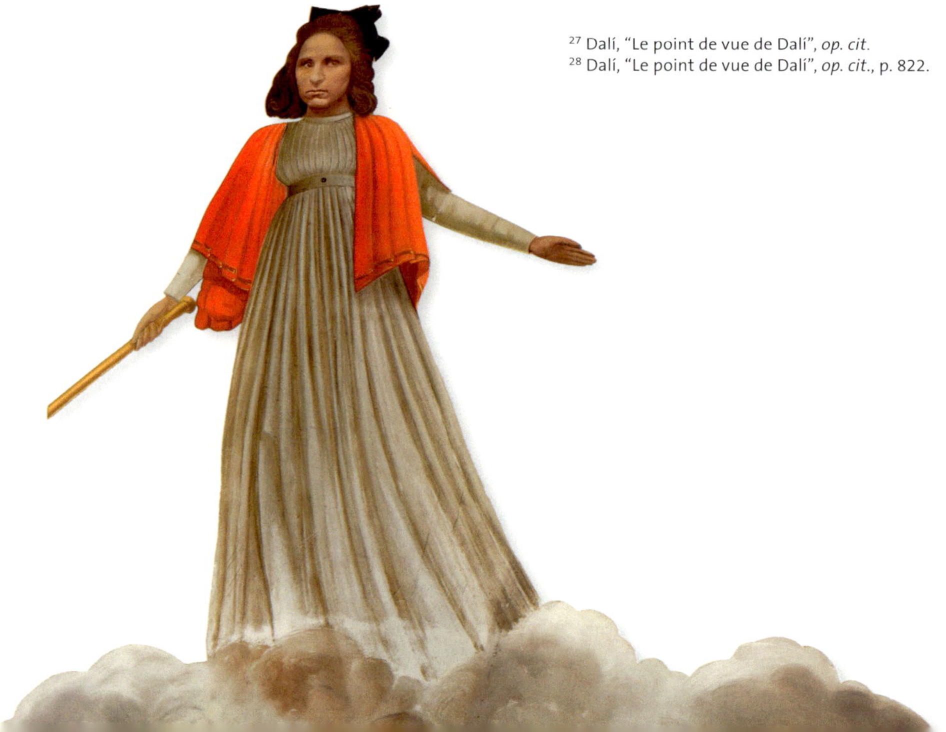

[27] Dalí, "Le point de vue de Dalí", *op. cit.*
[28] Dalí, "Le point de vue de Dalí", *op. cit.*, p. 822. [29] *Ibid.*

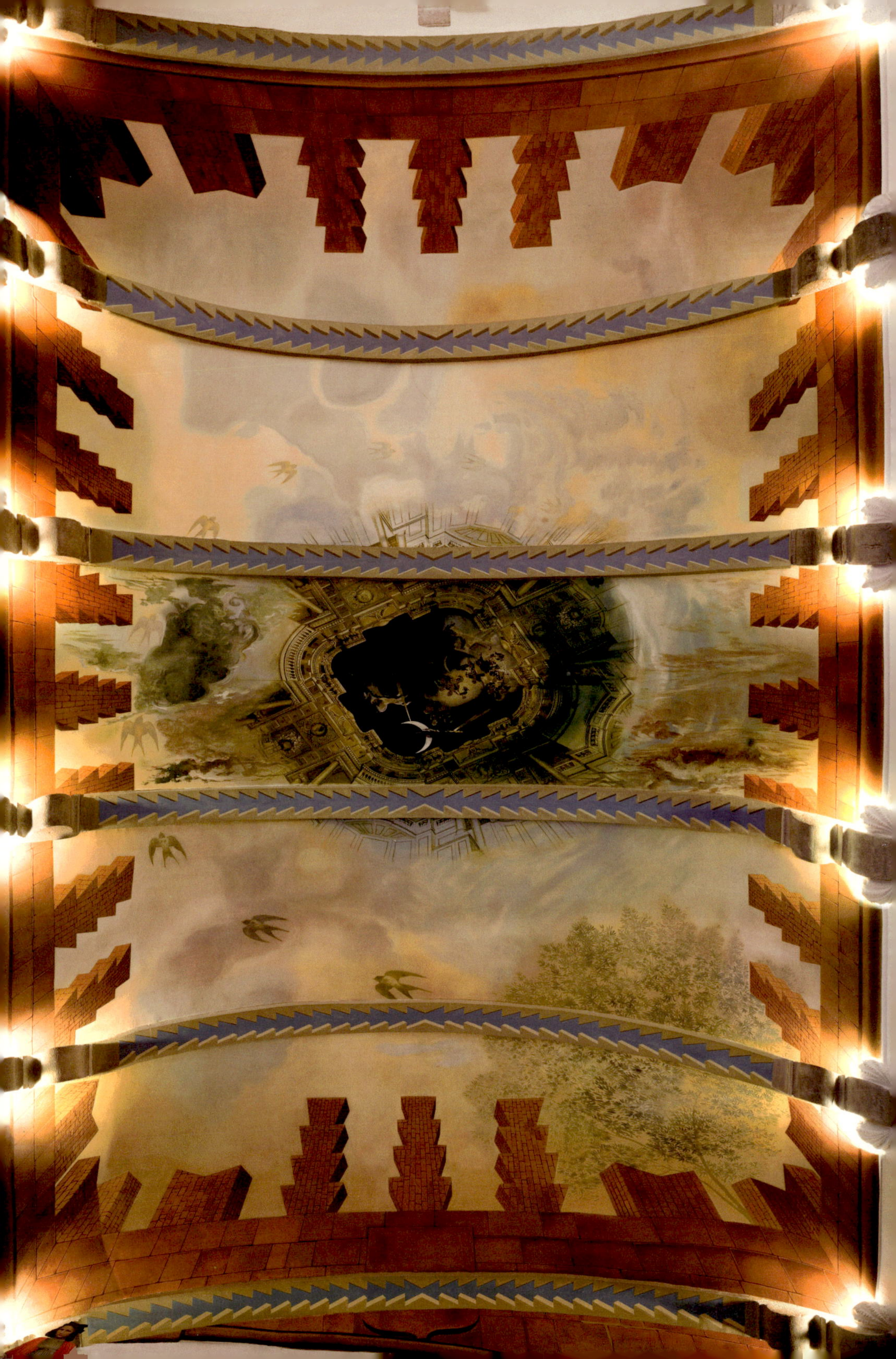

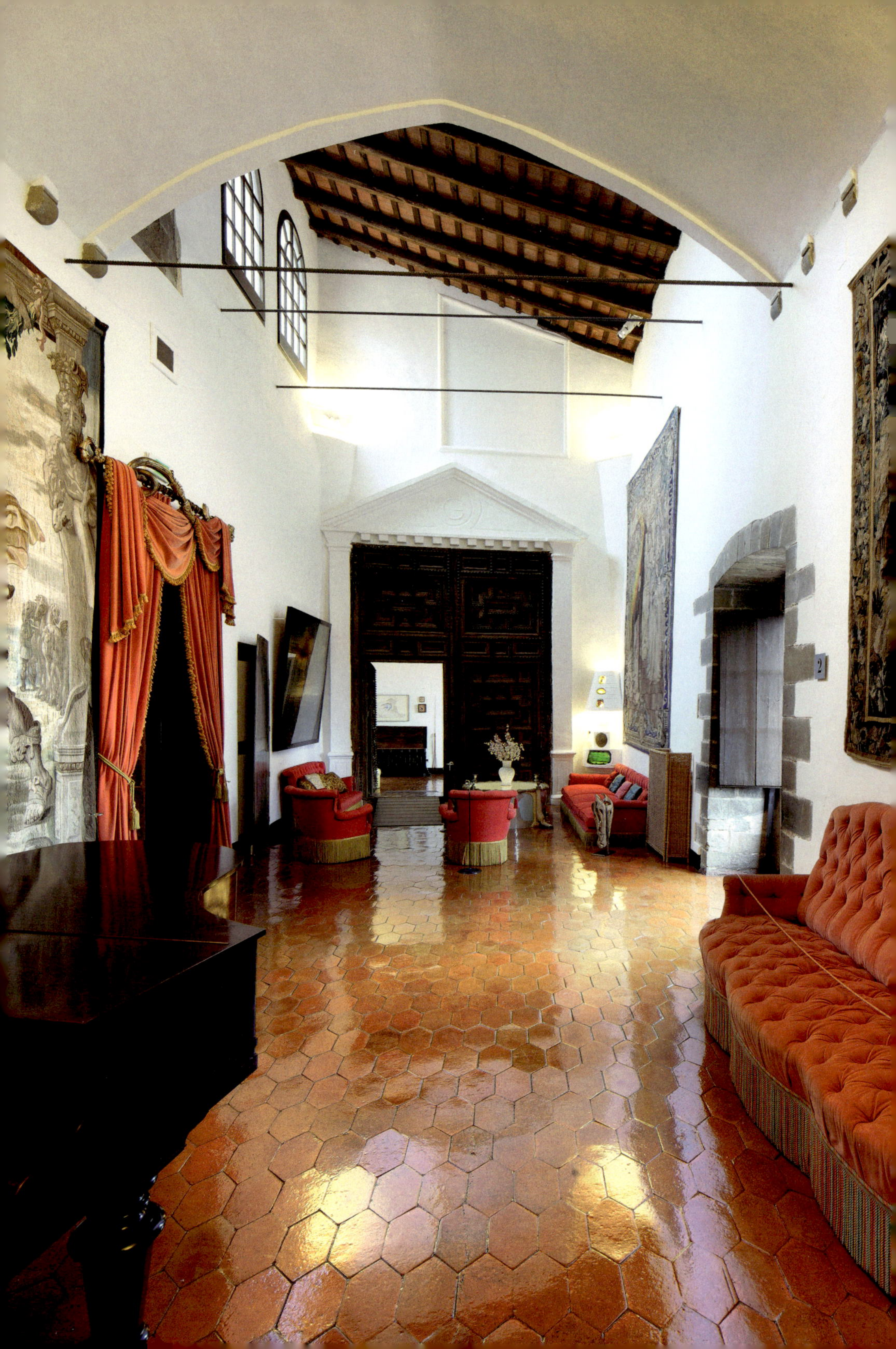
2

THE PIANO ROOM

To enter the piano room, we leave behind the figure of Gala, which reminds us that we are entering the private rooms of the lady of the castle, a space that reveals the bare squared rafters, since the roof had collapsed and had not been rebuilt. Dalí used this "accident" to design an interior that gives the sensation of amplitude and luminosity, in other words, a sensation of grandeur, a sensation that is strengthened by the imposing wooden entrance in Castilian style, with a plaster structure in the form of a tympanum that frames it. In the centre there is the G of Gala in relief, which leads us towards the sofa space. This is the space that, on entering, impresses us. Once again, Dalí knew how to make use of the ruin to create a different effect. The piano and the tapestries define the room. It is a place for resting, listening to music or chatting. We can talk of two areas: one more Baroque in style that corresponds to the piano area and, at the other end, the more Dalinian space.

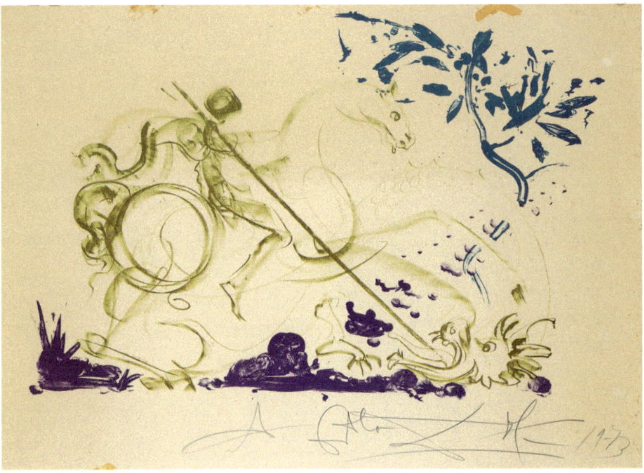

Saint George and the Dragon, 1973 (Lithograph / Arches)

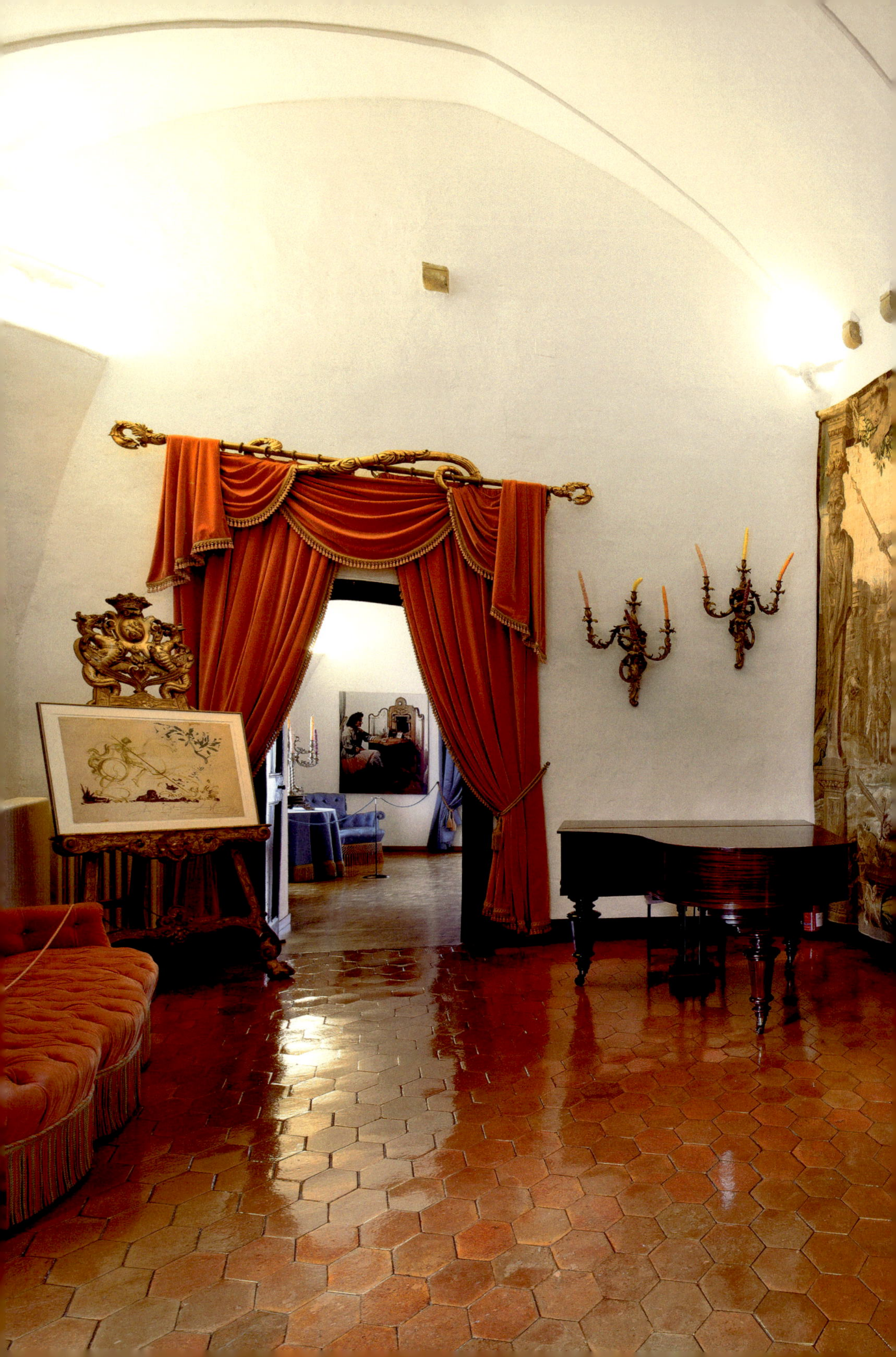

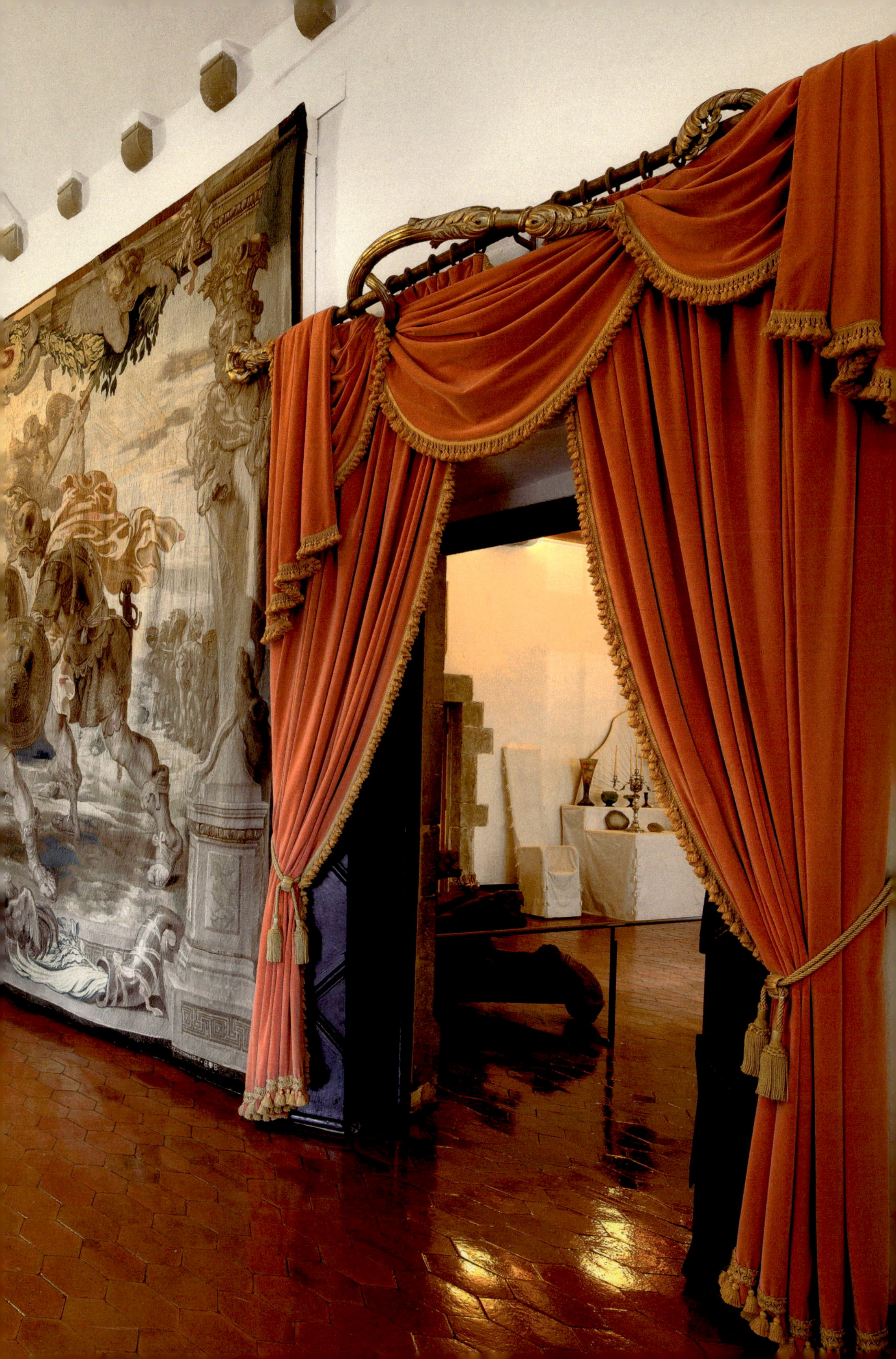

Standing out in the room is the grand piano manufactured by the Carl Bechstein firm. Bechstein was known as one of the best piano makers of the 19th century, special pianos decorated with gold and hand painted, commissioned by interior designers for royal palaces and aristocratic and elegant mansions.

The tapestries give a certain warmth to the room. We find three large tapestries. In the first, on the side of the piano, there is a scene of the Trojan War, which dates from the 17th century, signed by the master Daniel Eggermans from Bruselas. This craftsman worked from the original work by Peter Paulus Rubens, who produced a series dedicated to this mythical-historical episode from ancient Greece, a society from which flourished an immense cycle of legends and numerous poems (*Trojan Cycle*). Within the legendary Greek Cycle, several works (the *Cypria*, the *Small Iliad*, the *Taking of Troy*), of which only some summaries have survived, written in the 5th century AD by the grammarian Proclus, provide a great deal of data about this feat. According to these works, the cause of the war was the will of Zeus, who wanted to alleviate the earth of its state of overpopulation. Homer in his *Iliad* sings the feats of Achilles, the perfect hero, the bravest, strongest and fastest of all the Achaean and Trojan warriors. He fought in the Trojan War and his action was fundamental in the event. The tapestry shows the moment when the hero kills Hector, the Trojan prince. Other tapestries by this craftsman can be found in the Ducal Palace of Vila Viçosa in Portugal or the Boijmans van Beuningen Museum in Rotterdam. According to the testimony of Antoni Pitxot, while Gala was being buried, Dalí contemplated the tapestry, alongside him, both of them seated on the sofa facing the piano, and he compared the events represented on the tapestry with those of his own life. He pointed out the presence of Hector, wounded by his own destiny, as well as the presence of some Greeks that are similar to the emblem of the German swastika, even though they are long before Nazism. He also liked to contemplate the battle of cockerels that had been represented in the lower part, as well as the symmetry achieved with the position of the two fighters.

We can see the other two tapestries on the wall opposite the entrance to the room. The first, placed over a reddish velvet sofa, is also an old tapestry, dated in the 17th century, from the workshops of the city of Aubuson, where a hunting scene is reproduced with a hunter holding a bow, some arrows and with a dog. Due to the marks it has, we can deduce that it must have been much bigger originally. It is also interesting to know that its first Dalinian destination was the house in Portlligat, where it was used as a rug in the oval room, which, we should remember, was Gala's space.

The final tapestry is perhaps the most interesting, since Dalí himself intervened in it. It is a theatre curtain that represents Solomon and the Queen of Sheba and in the centre of which the artist painted a giraffe in flames: an iconographic element present in the painter's work, particularly in the nineteen-thirties. The following inscription appears on this curtain: Ramon Batlle. Stage Designer. Barcelona. (We should remember that this stage designer had worked for the Gran Teatre del Liceu in Barcelona). Once again the connections with the Theatre-Museum are made clear: the presence of the background curtain of a theatre, which underlines the expressly theatrical character of the construction.

If we continue the visit, through some red curtains, we reach the threshold of Gala's room, which on her death became that of the painter, where a profusely decorated gilded wooden easel stands out. On the upper part, there is a coat of arms made up of a crown, and two dragons that frame the letter S. Leaning on it, we find a lithograph, *Saint George and the Dragon* (1973, lithograph / Arches paper, 56.4 × 76.1 cm), which the painter dedicated to Gala in 1973. This is, in fact, the place where the drawings that Dalí gave Gala on some of his visits were kept. Curiously, also in Portlligat, in the library, we find a gilded easel. This easel matches the 15th-century style candelabras of four arms and gilded wood, adorned with plant motifs that we find on the walls.

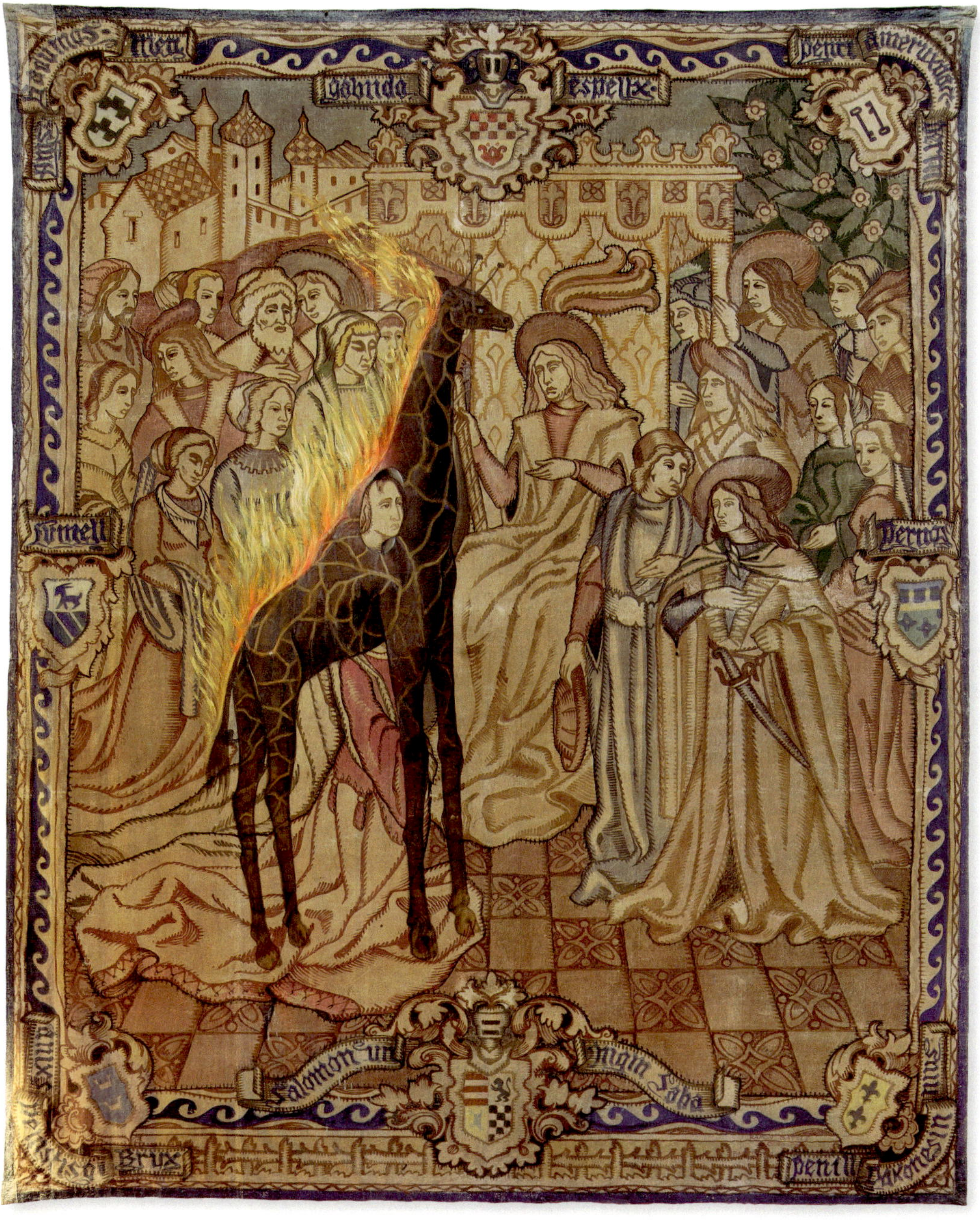

Theatrical curtain that represents Solomon and the Queen of Sheba in the centre of which Dalí painted a giraffe in flames. c. 1970. Oil and watercolour on canvas (320 × 402.5 cm).

We have already mentioned that Dalí undertook several projects to decorate the castle. Retracing our footsteps, we once again go to the most Dalinain area of the space. The tapestry worked on by the painter is in the living room area, with the sofas upholstered in red fabric and golden fringes. The designs by Dalí for this area are interesting, above all those made for the unusual table-skylight. This is built in, with the upper part in glass, so that we are able to see the room below. It has four ostrich feet embedded —which previously, in the house in Portlligat, had been used as candelabras— two are preserved and the other two of plaster. On the sides of the table are framed the four parchment cups: *Swallow, Fleur-de-lis, Crown of milk* and *Púbol of Gala*, the originals of which can be seen on show in other parts of the castle. This skylight, in this case, is not used to provide more natural light to the room, but to show us the horse that "lives and watches over" the lower part of the castle.

The horse was a gift from the painter Joan Abelló to Dalí. Abelló had bought the horse from the bull-fighting businessman Pere Balañá, also known by the painter from Portlligat, since he had "devised" a bullfight (which never took place) in 1953. Once preserved by the taxidermist Joaquim Jover, it was presented on the fifth floor of the Hotel Ritz in Barcelona, amidst great media expectations. The next day, before moving it to Púbol, Dalí called a press conference in the room and had himself photographed on the horse, which had religious images hanging from it. Although today the horse is exhibited in its natural place, in the old stables, while Dalí was living in Púbol it was placed at the foot of the stairs that go down to the crypt, as if it were the guardian.

Of the watercolours that decorate the table, the most interesting is the one that could be considered the heraldic coat of arms of Gala's castle. It is inspired by the upper part of the stone coat of arms of the main door and represents half a body of a lion that rises from the interior of a crown and with one of its paws raises a bunch of red flowers. The Dalinian version replaced the warrior's helmet of the coat of arms of the doorway with a crown of pearls (or tassels) and added a G to the lion in the centre of the body. Beneath the drawing, within a square, figures the title: *Púbol of Gala*. The watercolour is signed "Petit Daris", one of the affectionate names with which Gala called Dalí. On the side of the drawing there are some notes, written in pencil, that are directed at "petite olivone" (another of the affectionate names that Dalí used for Gala [30]) instructing her how to place the parchment behind the glass of the table. These notes were signed "Salvador Dalí of Figueres".

A second watercolour represents a brick wall in the form of a fleur-de-lis that suggests an olive tree with its roots. The fleur-de-lis is an emblematic element for Dalí that is found in several spaces in the castle. This watercolour could be an initial sketch for the decoration of the garden, specifically for the bench that is currently there, even though the final design is quite distinct.

[30] "I call my wife: *Gala, Galuchka, Gradiva* (because she has been my Gradiva); *Oliva* (because of the oval of her face and the colour of her skin); *Oliveta*, diminutive of olive; and its delirious derivatives: *Olihuette, Orihuette, Buribetye, Burihueteta, Sulihueta, Solibubulete, Oliburibuleta, Cihueta, Lihuetta*. I also call her *Lionette* (little lion), because she roars like the Metro-Goldwyn-Mayer lion when she gets angry; *Squirrel, Tapir, Little Negus* (because she resembles a very lively little forest animal); *Bee* (because she discovers and brings me all the essences that become converted into the honey of my thought in the busy hive of my brain). She brought me the rare book on magic that was to nourish my magic, the historic document irrefutably proving my thesis as it was in the process of elaboration, the paranoiac image that my subconscious wished for, the photograph of an unknown painting destined to reveal a new aesthetic enigma, the advice that would save one of my too subjective images from romanticism. I also call Gala *Noisette Poilue*-Hairy Hazelnut (because of the very fine down that covers the hazelnut of her cheeks); and also *Fur Bell* (because she reads to me aloud during my long sessions of painting, making a murmur as of a fur bell by virtue of which I learn all the things that but for her I should never know)". Dalí, *The Secret Life...*, op. cit., p. 647 (English version p. 248.)

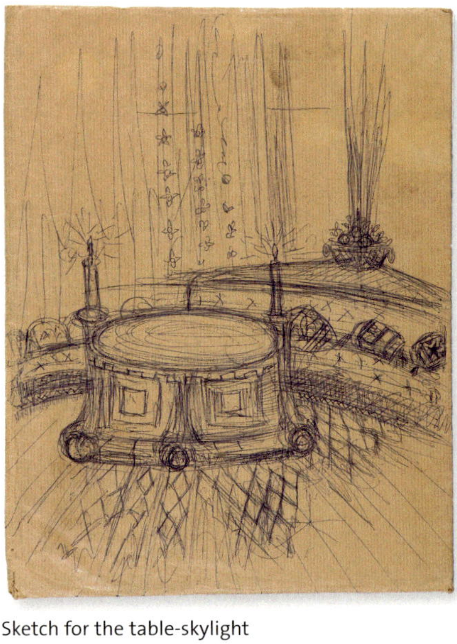
Sketch for the table-skylight

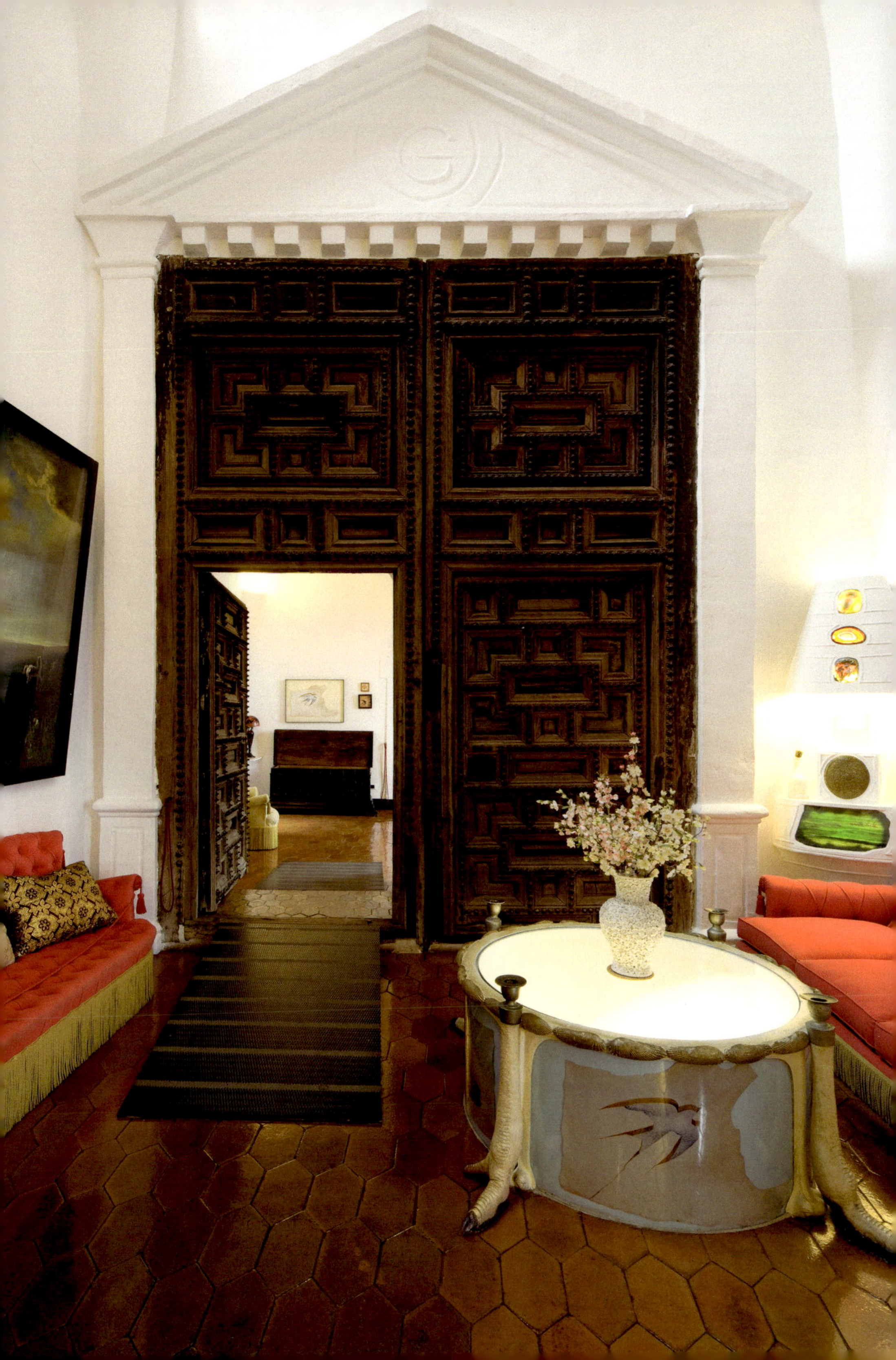

The *Crown of milk* (signed "Salvador Dalí, 1971"), the third watercolour, is a piece of work realised just when the restoration work on the castle was completed, but linked to much earlier concerns regarding the law of gravity and microscopic discoveries. In 1939, in the invitation for the exhibition in New York's Julien Levy Gallery, Dalí had already used this image. It involves a type of photography called stroboscopic (done at a very slow speed) of the impact of a ball on the surface of milk and the result is the formation of a crown of splashes, something that interested Dalí and which he used on more than one occasion; we could even say that the small crown with a cross, which he sometimes placed on the signature of his surname, is a smaller version of this.

The fourth parchment, *Swallow*, as the title written in pencil suggests, is, however, found in the library. It is the representation of a swallow that, in the way that it seems to be represented, could also be a sketch for some decorative project.

Additionally, in this room, in the corner on the side of the sofa, our attention is drawn to the original lamp, designed by Dalí, with a metallic plaque in the centre and erotic motifs in relief which, from a distance, seem like a floral decoration. The painter inserted decorative elements from minerals or imitations of minerals, through which light filters. Once again Dalí enjoys himself with this true/false game. We can contextualise this lamp, both the plaster shade and the base, with Dalí's creations of the 1970s.

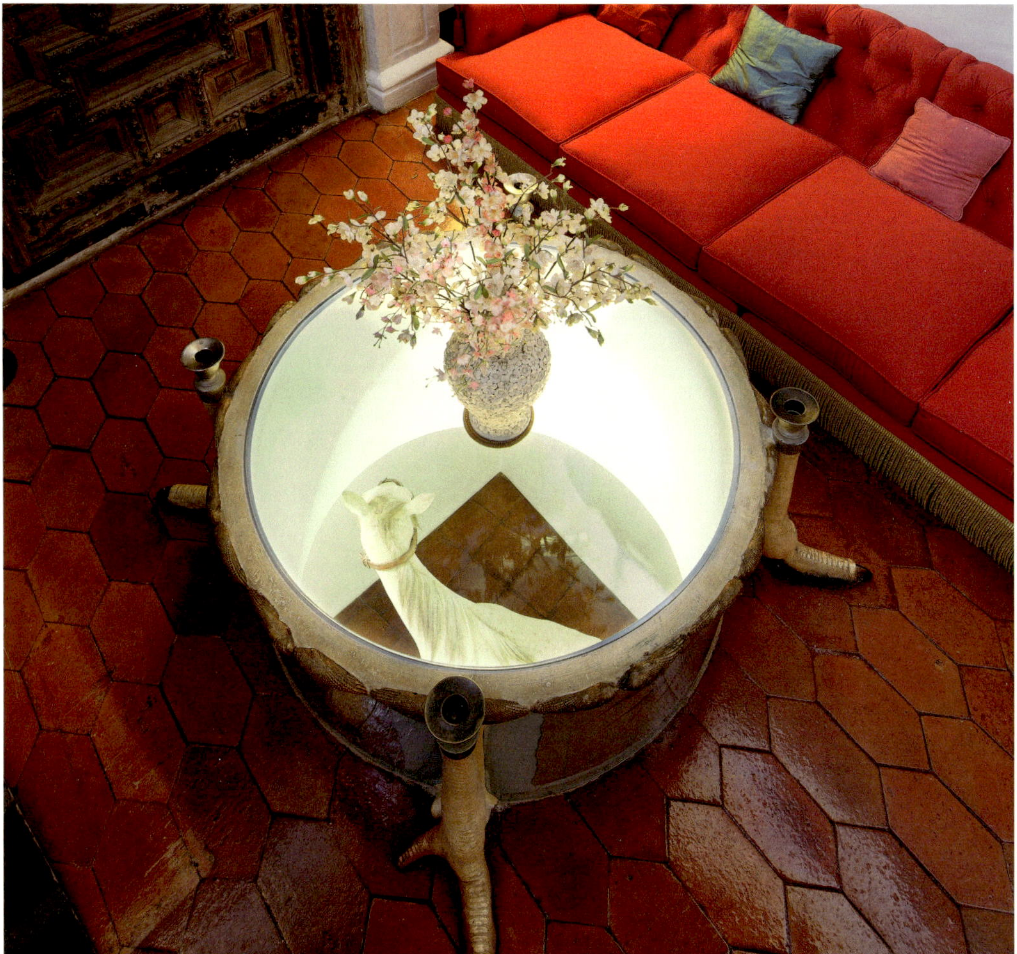

The horse seen through the table-skylight

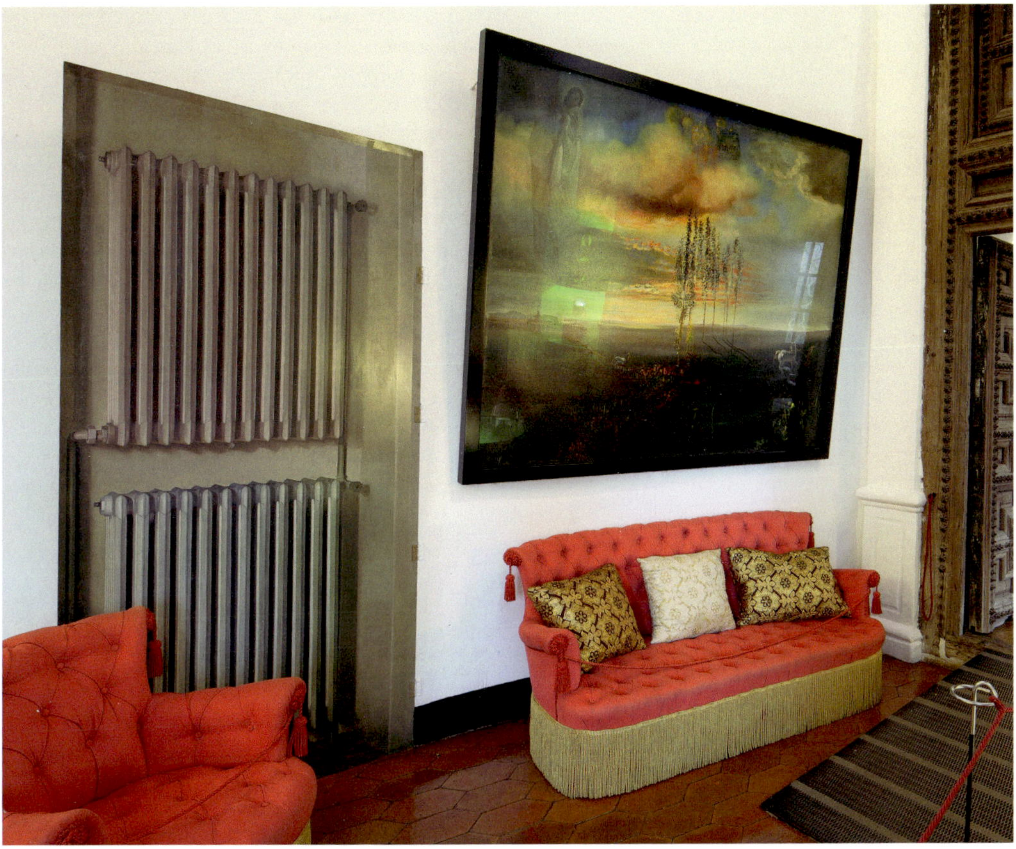

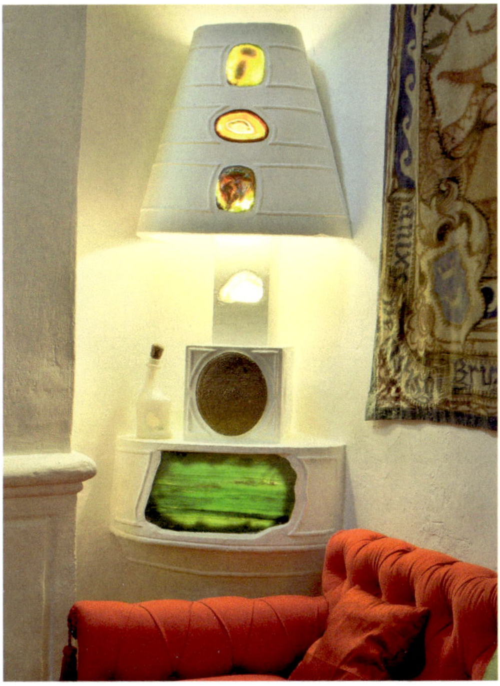

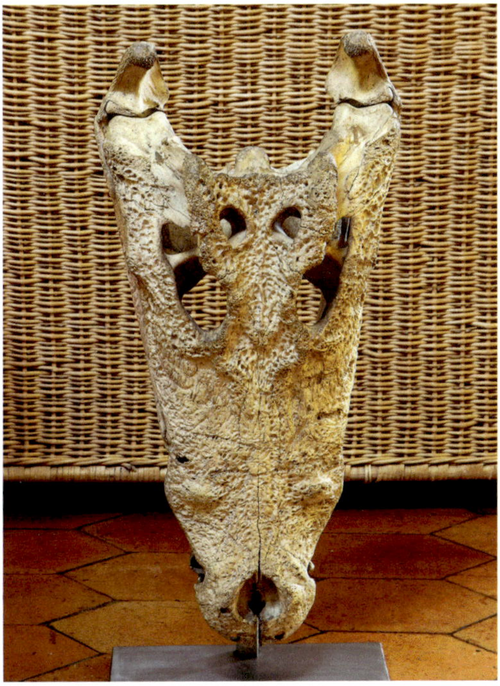

Trompe-l'œil of the radiators and *The Path to Púbol* | Lamp designed by Dalí | Cranium of crocodile

Before going through the doorway that connects the piano room with the library, we must admire the two paintings by Dalí that decorate this space. The larger one of the castle, titled *The Path to Púbol* is impressive. It is also the work by Dalí where the landscape of Púbol has such an outstanding central role. Painted in the early 70s, to be precise, certainly between 1971 and 1973, it is an allegory to Gala, a rising Gala, who appears in the upper left part of the canvas, framed in a banner, just as she also appeared in another oil painting, *The Discovery of America by Christopher Columbus*, from 1958.

The second work that we refer to is the trompe-l'œil found beside *The Path to Púbol*. As Gala did not like radiators, in most places she had them covered with wicker screens. Dalí offered to cover the two in this room, set into the wall, and to conceal the sheet metal door that covered them he painted other radiators (oil of 229.1 × 105 cm). The painting conceals yet represents reality. Again, although at another level, we can speak of the Dalí-Mantegna relationship. The radiator is a curious representation of what is rougher and more everyday, that does not want to hide reality. If you want to cover a radiator, it must be done in a way that the same object, the radiator, is painted, with the utmost realism. There is a phrase by Raymond Roussel, admired by Dalí, which gives a good idea of this: *"L'art de l'imitation rejoint l'imagination puisqu'il se âgit á fin de comptes par des moyens artificiels de donner l'illusion complete de la realité"*. One could establish an aesthetic-philosophical triangle between Mantegna, Roussel and Dalí. Moreover, in the special issue of *Vogue* that we have already mentioned on several occasions, in the list of jobs that Gala gave Dalí for the castle, she makes very clear: "Windbreakers painted in optical illusion representing heating radiators to conceal them"[31].

[31] *Ibid.*

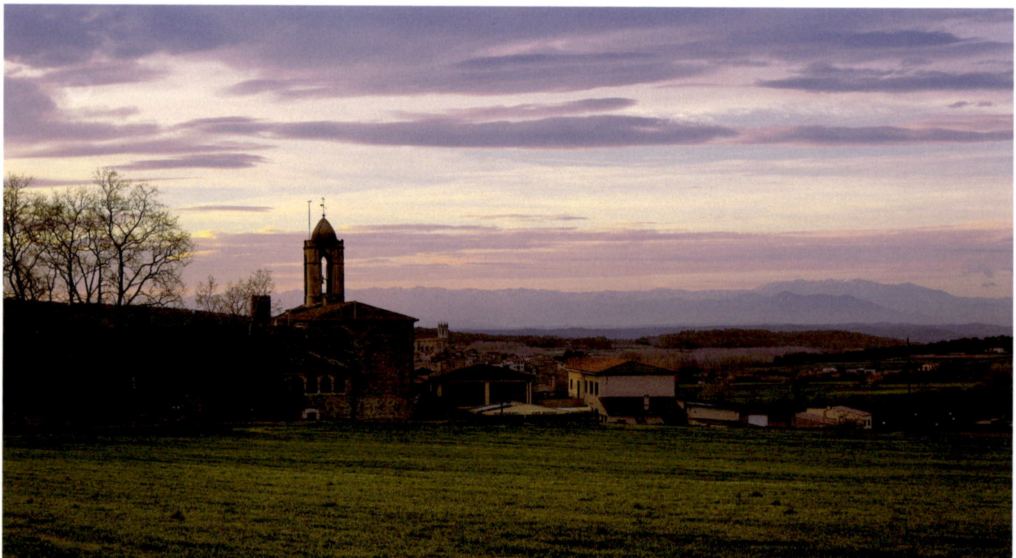

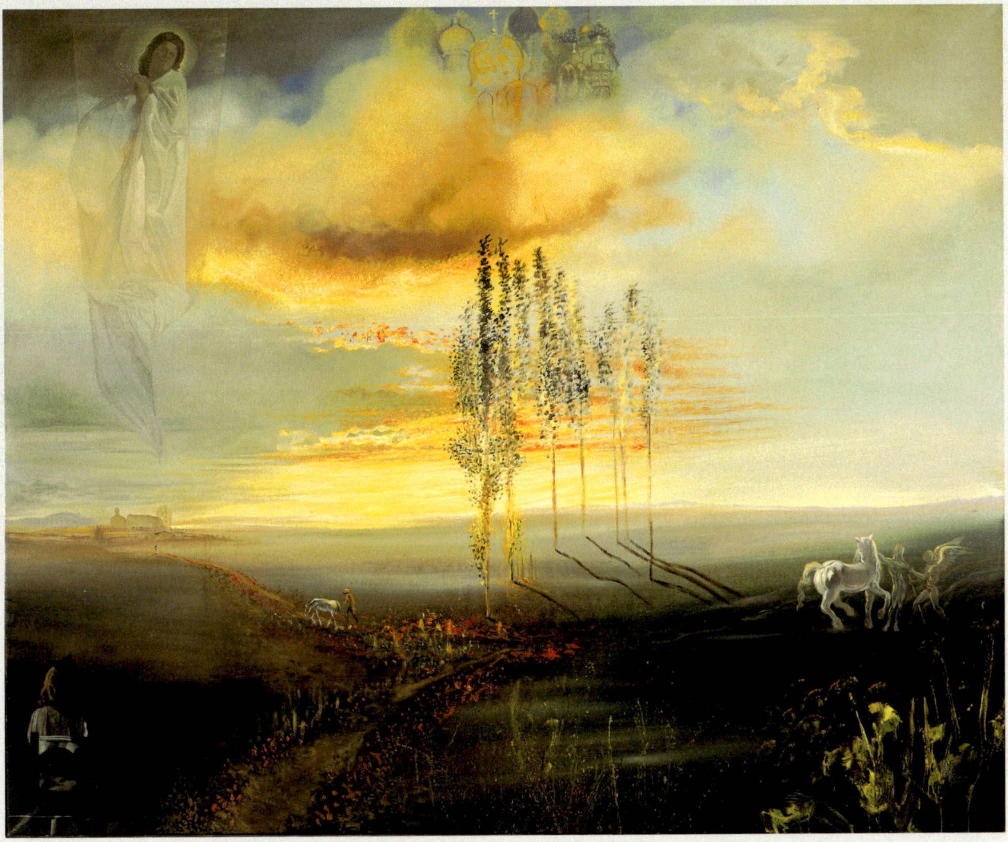

THE PATH TO PÚBOL, 1973
Oil on canvas (160 × 189,7 cm)
House-Museum Gala Dalí Castle in Púbol Piano Room

In this oil painting, we can see, through the magic of art, the whole journey from the beginning of the path, with the first presence of a Gala from the back wearing children's sailor's clothes just as Gala and Dalí himself often appear in his own iconography. The route of the path, narrow and tortuous, is bordered by a flourish of poppies, a sign of spring and illusion. In the setting that leads to the castle of Púbol and its church, the magical number seven is shown very clearly to us. All important things are seven, repeated Dalí; seven black poplars, or rather *púbols*, which make up the name of the village. Also present along the long path are figures relating to farm work: farm labourers, horses, one with the head down. On the right side, we are shown a scene with more mythological meaning: an elegant white horse with a knight, who is being given a type of special payment in the form of a staff by an angelical being, perhaps Mercury, the messenger of the gods. Everything culminates, in the upper part of the canvas, with the glorification of the image of Gala, between radiant shades of carmine, installed in her origins of oriental spirit, with Byzantine cupolas that vouch for it. It has something of the rising spirit, as in the *The Burial of the Count of Orgaz* by El Greco, which really impressed the young Dalí on his first visit to Toledo.

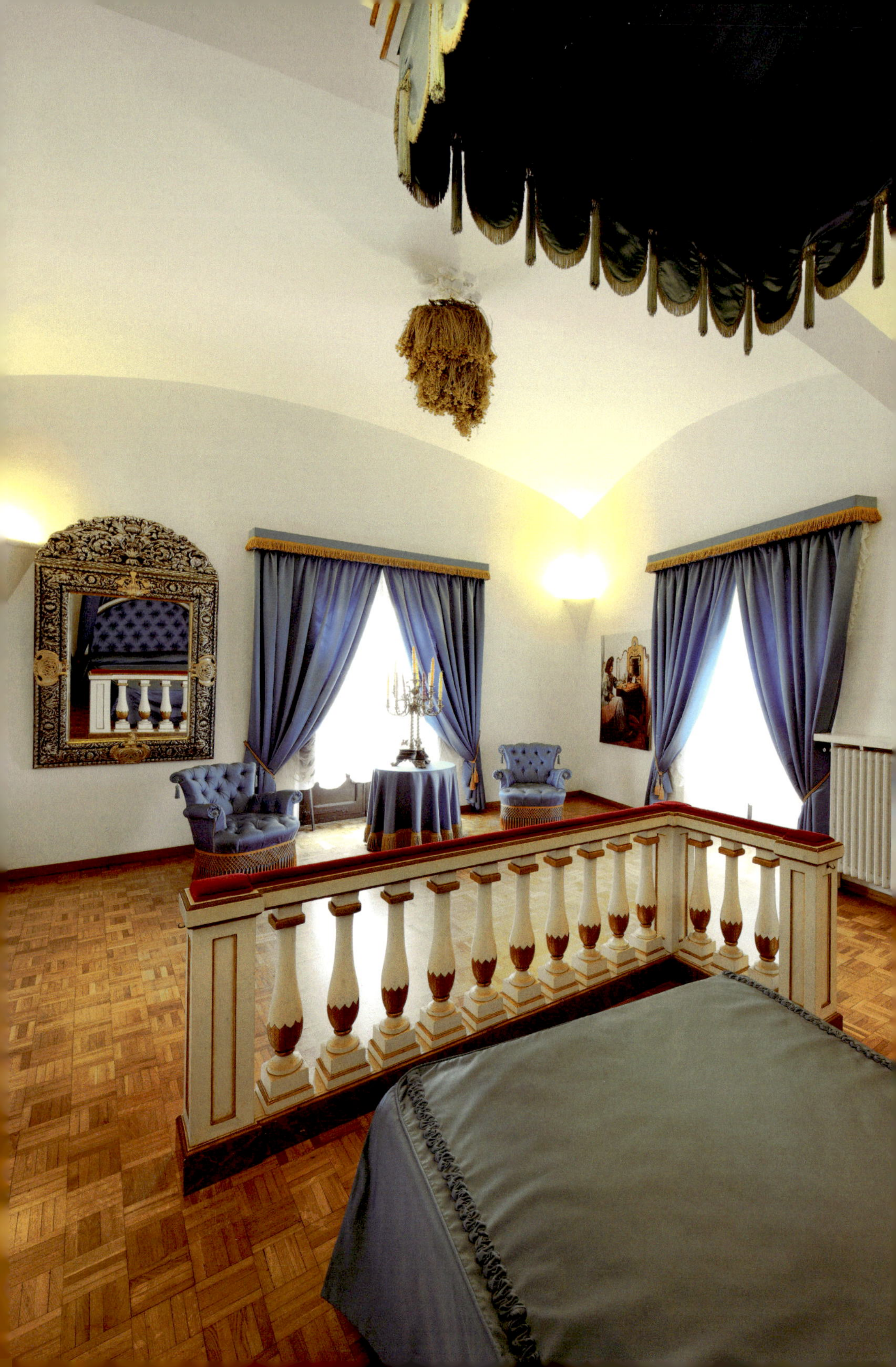

GALA'S BEDROOM

In Gala's bedroom which, later, on his wife's death, the painter occupied, we find a sumptuous bed with canopy, protected by a balustrade of white and gilded wood, with the handrail coated by red velvet.

The design of the space is inspired by a room in a castle on the Loire, the Château de Maintenon, an elegant castle, where medieval and Renaissance styles are mixed, which conserves the 12th-century square tower. It is known because it belonged to Françoise de Aubigné, future lady of Maintenon, first the favourite and then the secret wife of Louis XIV. Unlike the bedroom of Madame de Maintenon's castle, here the predominant colour is blue: the curtains, the bedspread and the upholstery of the two armchairs. It is also the colour of the material covering the round table.

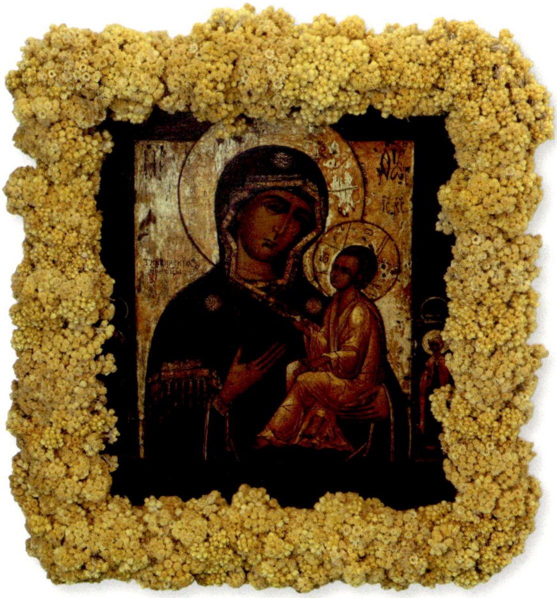

Virgin Hodegetria, with frame of houseleeks

Gala and Dalí would share the room, but in different times. Remember that on Gala's death in 1982, Dalí, who was living in Portlligat, moved to Púbol, where he continued painting until 1983, in a space in the castle dining room. They were years, however, in which physical discomfort and the pain for the loss of Gala were evident. The painter's state of health gradually worsened; he was old, tired and the circumstances did not help him. On the 30 of August 1984, the room caught fire. It was a fire caused involuntarily due to the insistence of the painter of calling the nurses who were looking after him. He called them with a bell installed by his bed, a simple apparatus popularly known as "pear", which, on not being designed to be pressed constantly, caused a short circuit. The fire destroyed the whole room and Dalí was rescued with serious burns. Finally, a specialist determined that he should be admitted to a hospital, despite the painter's refusal. He slept one more night in the castle, on this occasion, and for the first time, in the guests' room and, finally, accepted being admitted to the Clínica del Pilar in Barcelona. He did so, however, on the condition that he could visit his Theatre-Museum in Figueres beforehand. In the middle of the night, in a wheelchair, accompanied by Antoni Pitxot, he made this emotional, ritual visit to his work, his last great creation.

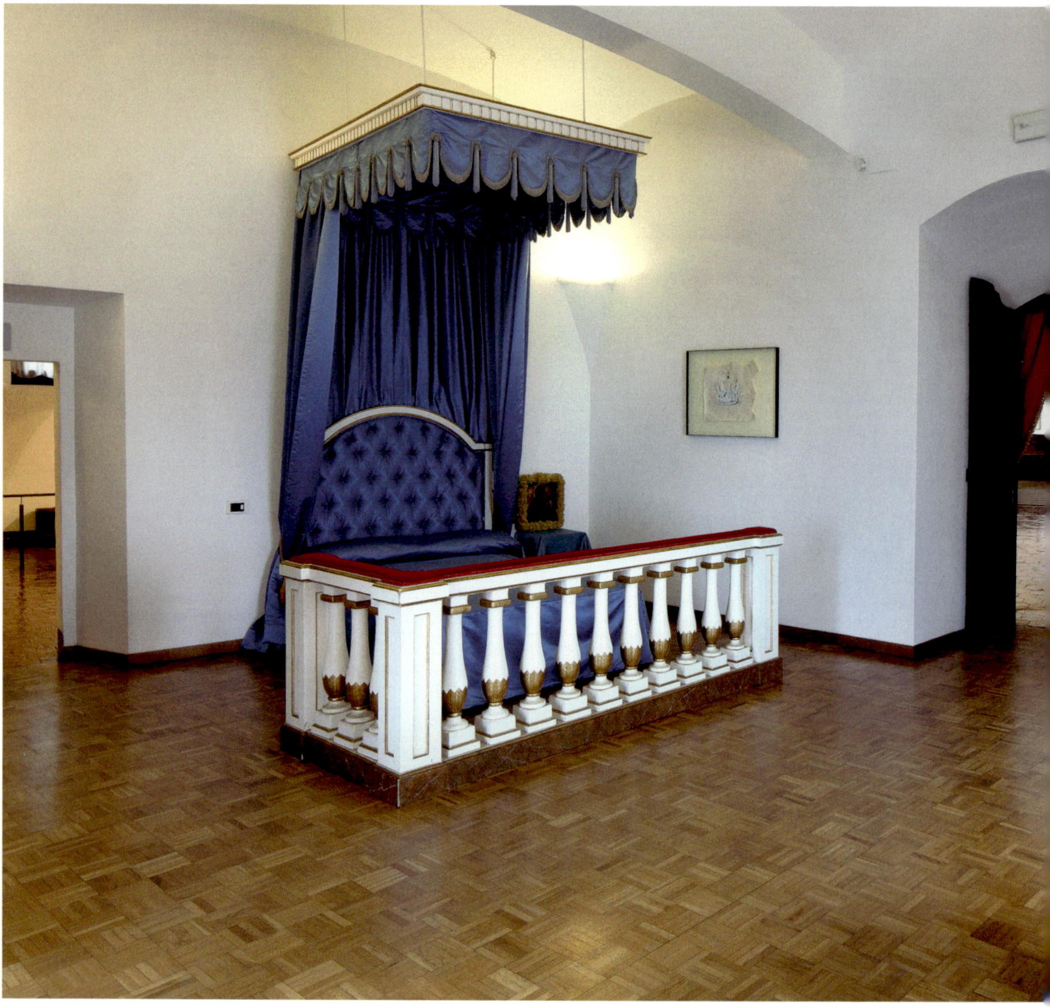

Gala's bedroom

Dalí immediately ordered the rehabilitation of the room, since the fire had destroyed some decorative pieces that could not be restored, such as a profusely worked dressing table that we can admire thanks to the images taken by the photographer Marc Lacroix. Also a special gift from Dalí to Gala: the delicate angel with the golden hair —a small drawing on paper, slightly coloured—, as well as an icon of Russian origin, in a silver frame. The rehabilitation involved recovering the metallic elements. The rest of the furniture was also damaged and affected by the smoke, but a mirror of Portuguese origin in florid Gothic Manueline style could be restored, as well as a silver candelabrum. This candelabrum, made up of ten candlesticks with plant motifs and three winged horses on the base, has the identification of a silversmith who worked in Birmingham in 1875. One of the icons of Gala's collection was also replaced; a Hodigitria virgin from around the late 18th century, with a frame made of houseleeks, also present on the ceiling. This plant, which we usually find in dry and sunny soils, was picked every summer in the olive grove of Portlligat. The custom is to dry it since the bright yellow colour of its petals remains unaltered for a very long time. The idea of prolonging in time, immortality, was one of the great interests of both the painter and Gala.

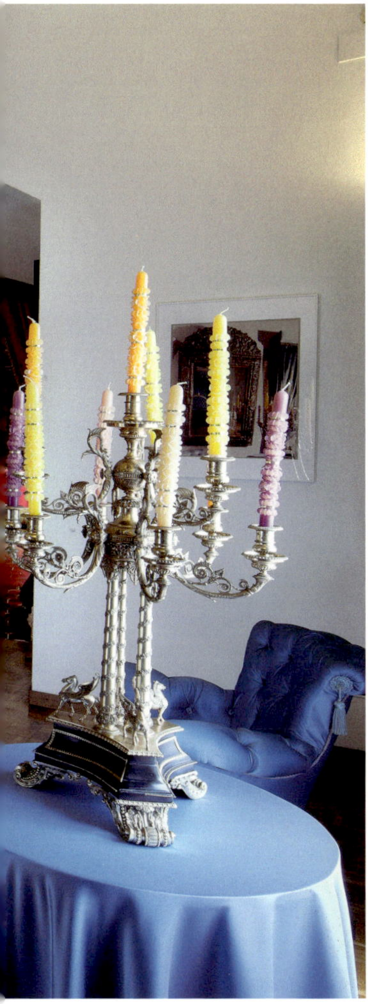

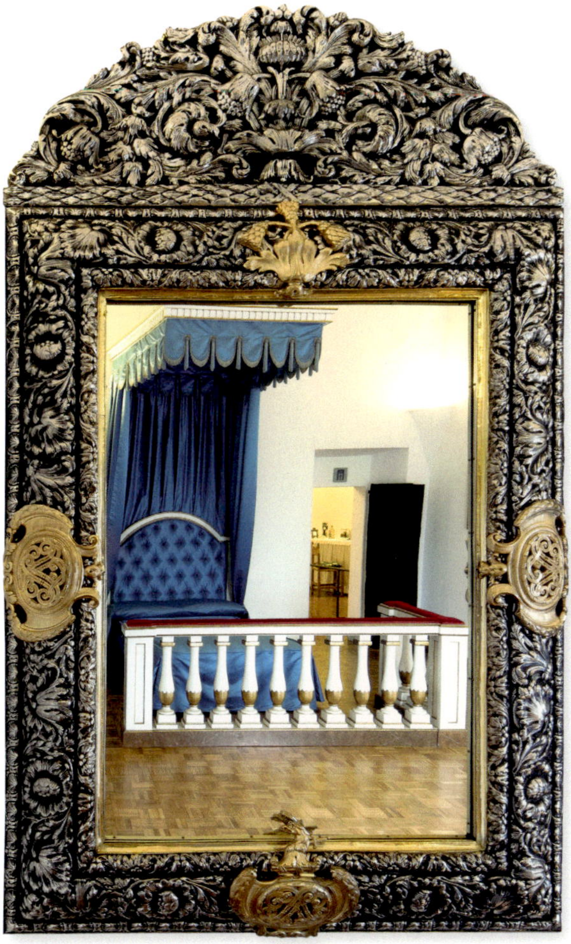

Mirror of Portuguese origin

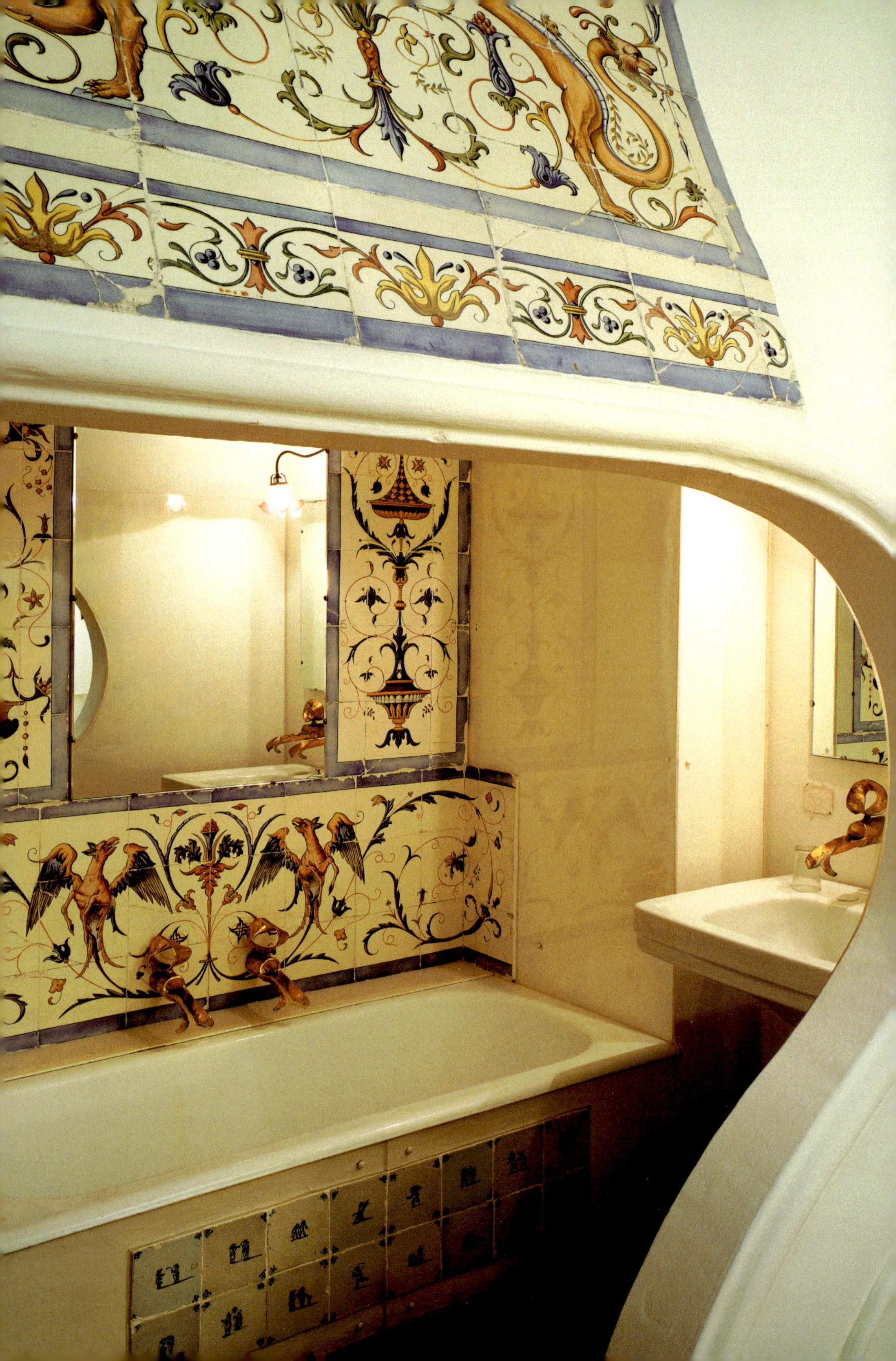

BATHROOM AND DRESSER

Through a small door, situated at the side of the bed, we reach a room that had once been the castle kitchen. Gala decided to transform it into a bathroom with dresser. Gala, from the time she was very young, had had health problems and was always concerned with her physical appearance —the image she gave was very important to her—, of the fragility of the body, of ephemeral beauty, that is, with the personality she wanted to transmit.

Although we owe the peculiarity of this space to Dalí, Gala specifically wanted to hide the stove with some small curtains, following the style of her dresser in Portlligat. Above, we can see elements befitting a dresser such as the boxes to keep jewellery, a special ceramic jar, a plate that forms part of a crockery set designed by the painter and a collage in the form of a fan with a photograph of Dalí, Gala and a young lad. At the base of the card reads the following inscription:

« *Sur cet or japonais*
expés pour aquarelle
Aquarelle que je te peindres
quesque doncs ne feire pas pour quil
soit contente son olivone
Enbase le NAI petit Daris » (sic)

(In this Japanese gold / expressly for watercolour / Watercolour that I paint you / that I would not do for her / my little *olivone* would be happy / *Enbase le NAI* petit Daris) which ends with the signature that Dalí often used when he wrote to Gala.

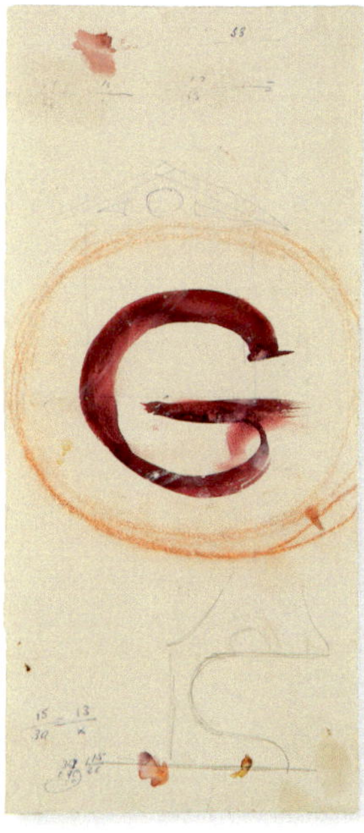

Project for chimney and bath, 1969

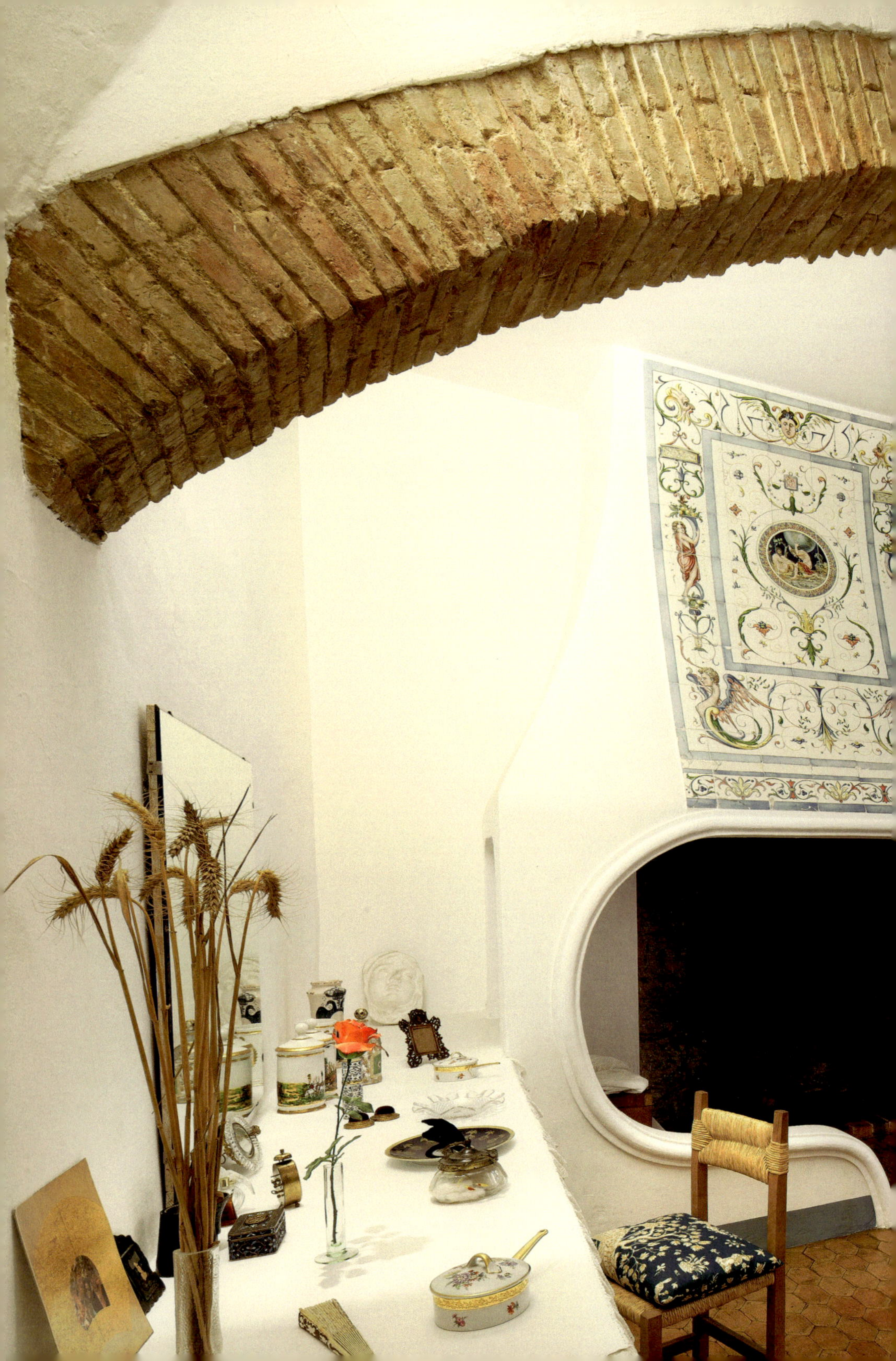

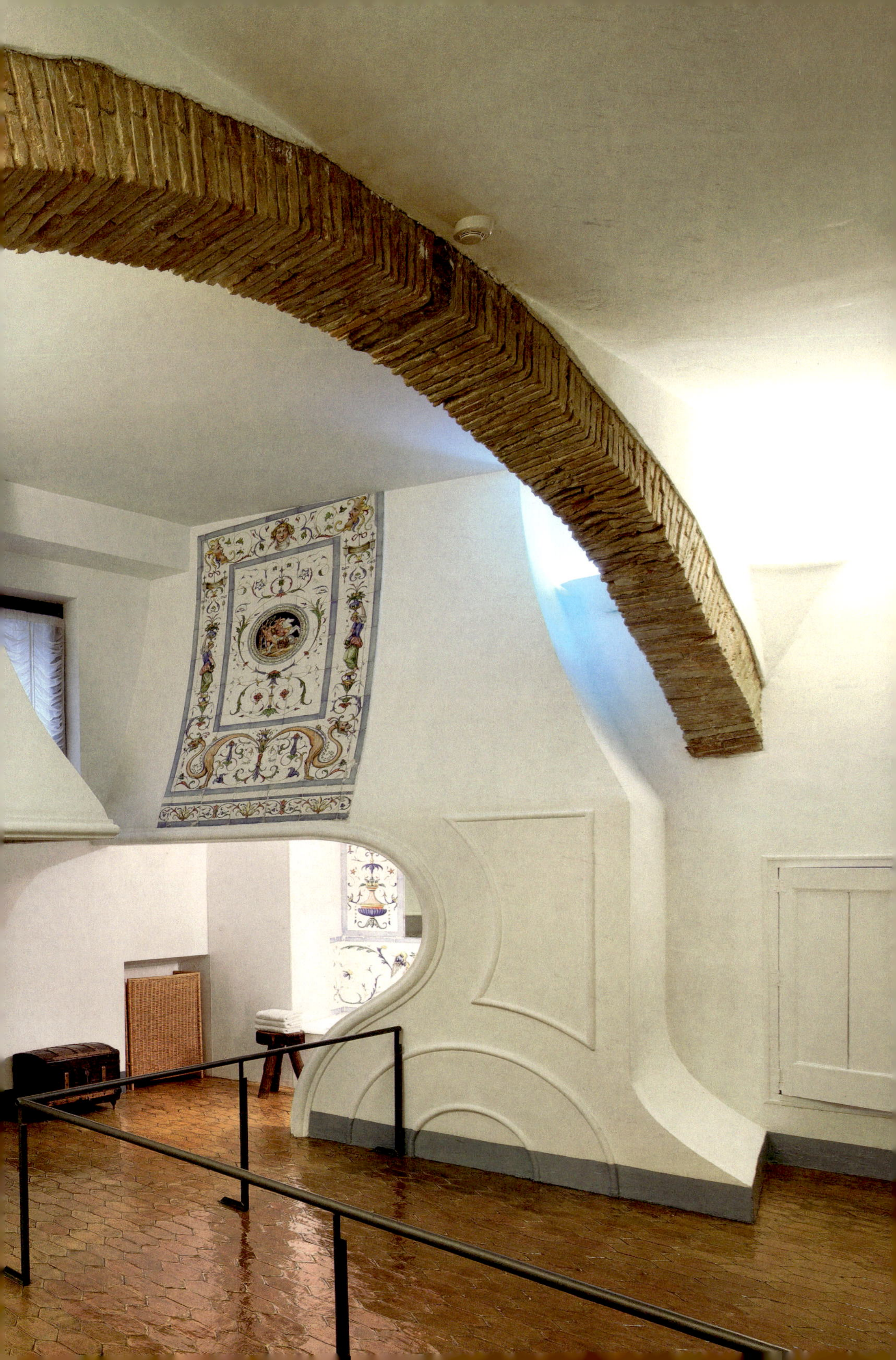

The dresser also features a bottle of Imperiale eau de cologne from the Guerlain firm, of glass with gilded decorations. In the lower part, there are reliefs of flies, and the upper part, a floral network. There is also a vase with a rose, which always had to be, according to Gala's instructions, from the castle's garden. In each room there is the presence of Gala, she is constant, the leitmotiv, the central theme that gives unity and meaning to the castle as a whole.

Dalí designed two extractors, one for the chimney and another for the bathroom, which are once again hidden. Both suggest the G of Gala and are decorated with glazed tiles from the Cartuja of Seville, with scenes of the work of Hercules, a gift from Ignacio de Medina, Duke of Medinaceli, Count of Empúries, and, therefore, as Dalí stated, "my natural lord". On the chimney hood, we can see a bench with the cases that Gala used. Regarding the bath, the front part features decoration with tiles from Delft, which represent scenes of children's games. Dalí liked to explain that on these walls were represented, through the ceramics from Seville and Delft, its two great masters admired for their painting, Velázquez and Vermeer de Delft. The taps of the washbasin, designed from the Möbius strip [32], and the bath are painted in golden tones, although they are not solid gold as Dalí had stated on several occasions.

[32] Möbius strip: a non-orientable surface, in other words, that has only one side. Discovered by A. F. Möbius, it can be built attaching a flat strip, twisting one its ends 180° and joining it immediately to the other end.

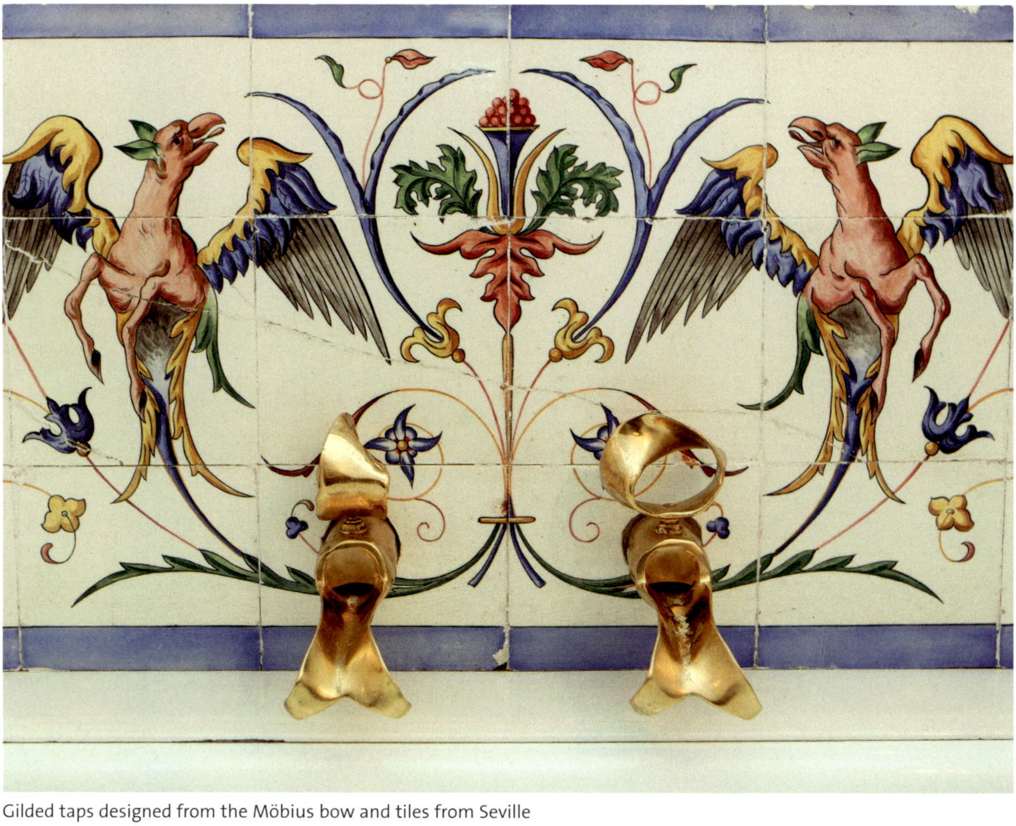

Gilded taps designed from the Möbius bow and tiles from Seville

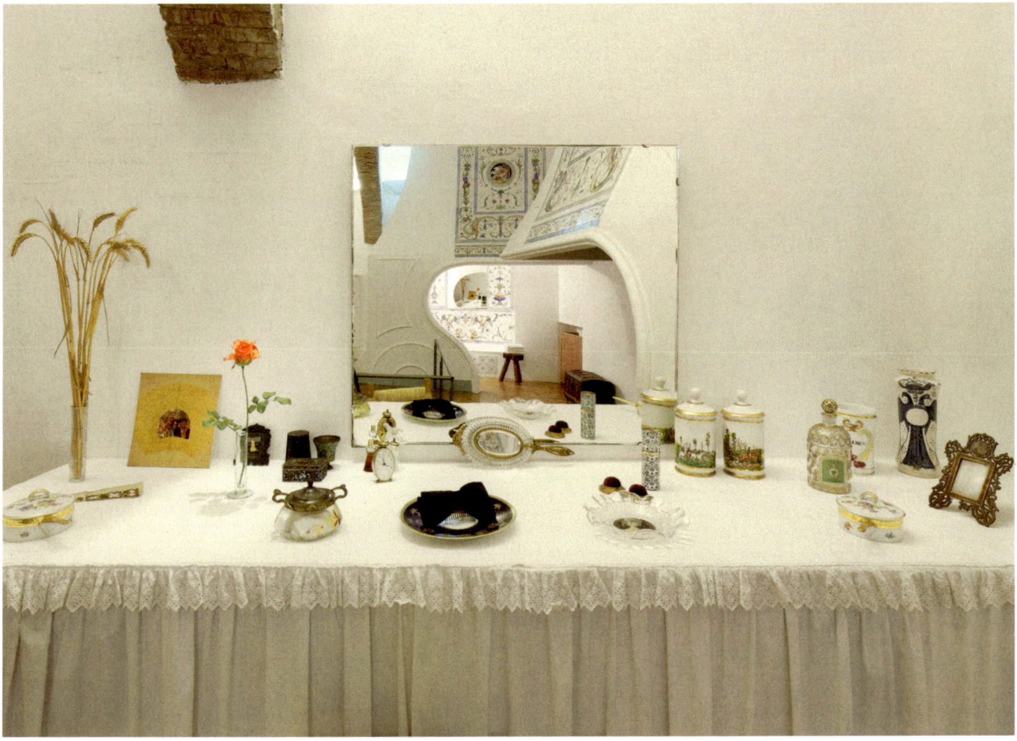
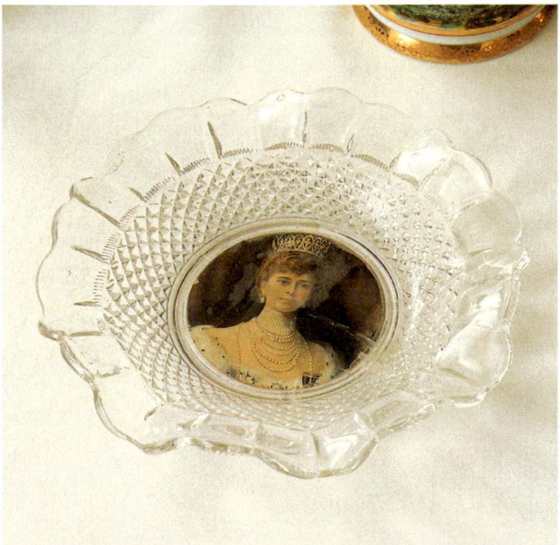
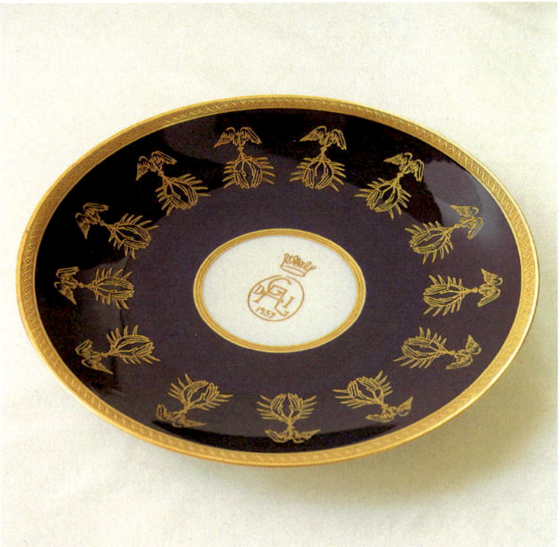
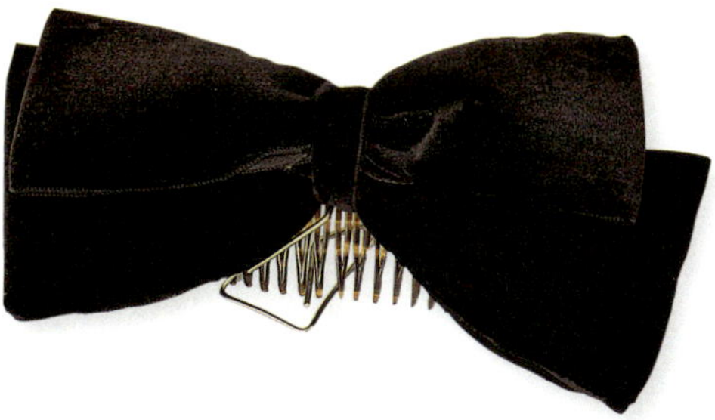
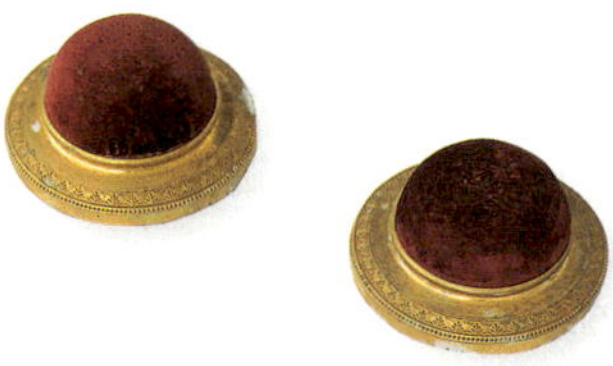

Gala's dressing table and details

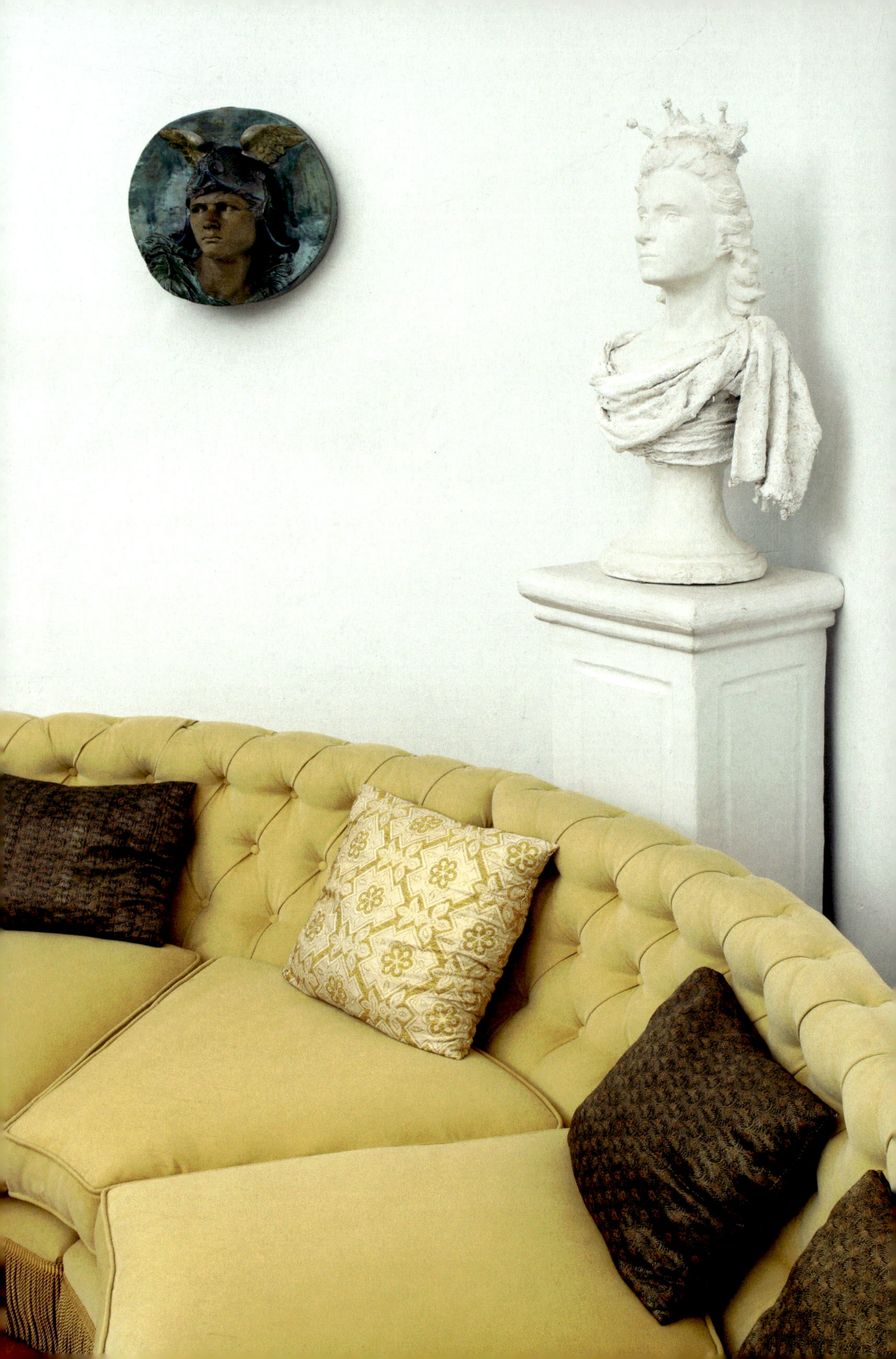

THE LIBRARY

We cross the piano room again and, through the opening of the large doorway, we enter a living room that in Gala and Dalí's time had been used as a library. If in Gala's room blue is the omnipresent colour, here yellow had overall domination, represented by the corner sofa. It is a Naples yellow, each colour having a special description for Dalí, such as Parma violet or royal blue.

Music and books were, despite everything, the main features of the space. In the room we can see a record player, the sound of which reached the piano room, dining room and the library itself.

There are also two chests in the room. In the large one, possibly a large chest of a Catalan bride from the Tarragona area, there are the records and cassettes, the chessboard, a magic lantern —reminiscence of the interest that everything related to optical illusions always aroused in Dalí from an early age—, and a camera. There are also two gilded legs, corresponding to a frustrated project of the artist for high backed chairs. If we look inside the chest, we can discover some of the music that Gala and her guests listened to while they were in the castle. It is basically the work of the German composer Richard Wagner, a musician also admired by the painter. Among the records of course are *Tristan and Isolde*, *Lohengrin*, and the *Tetralogy*, the series of four operas based on the Scandinavian legends that led to the Song of the Nibelungs (titled as a whole *Ring of the Nibelung*): *The Rhine Gold*, *The Valkyrie*, *Siegfried and The Twilight of the Gods*. There are also works by Tchaikovsky, Stravinsky, Handel and three small records with poems by Paul Éluard, Federico García Lorca and Arthur Rimbaud, in a cardboard sleeve *Eluard dit par Gérard Philipe*.

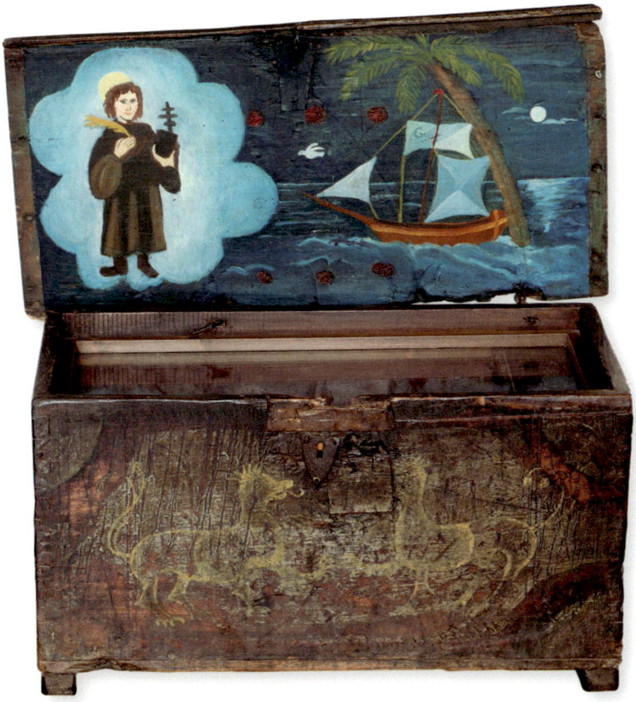

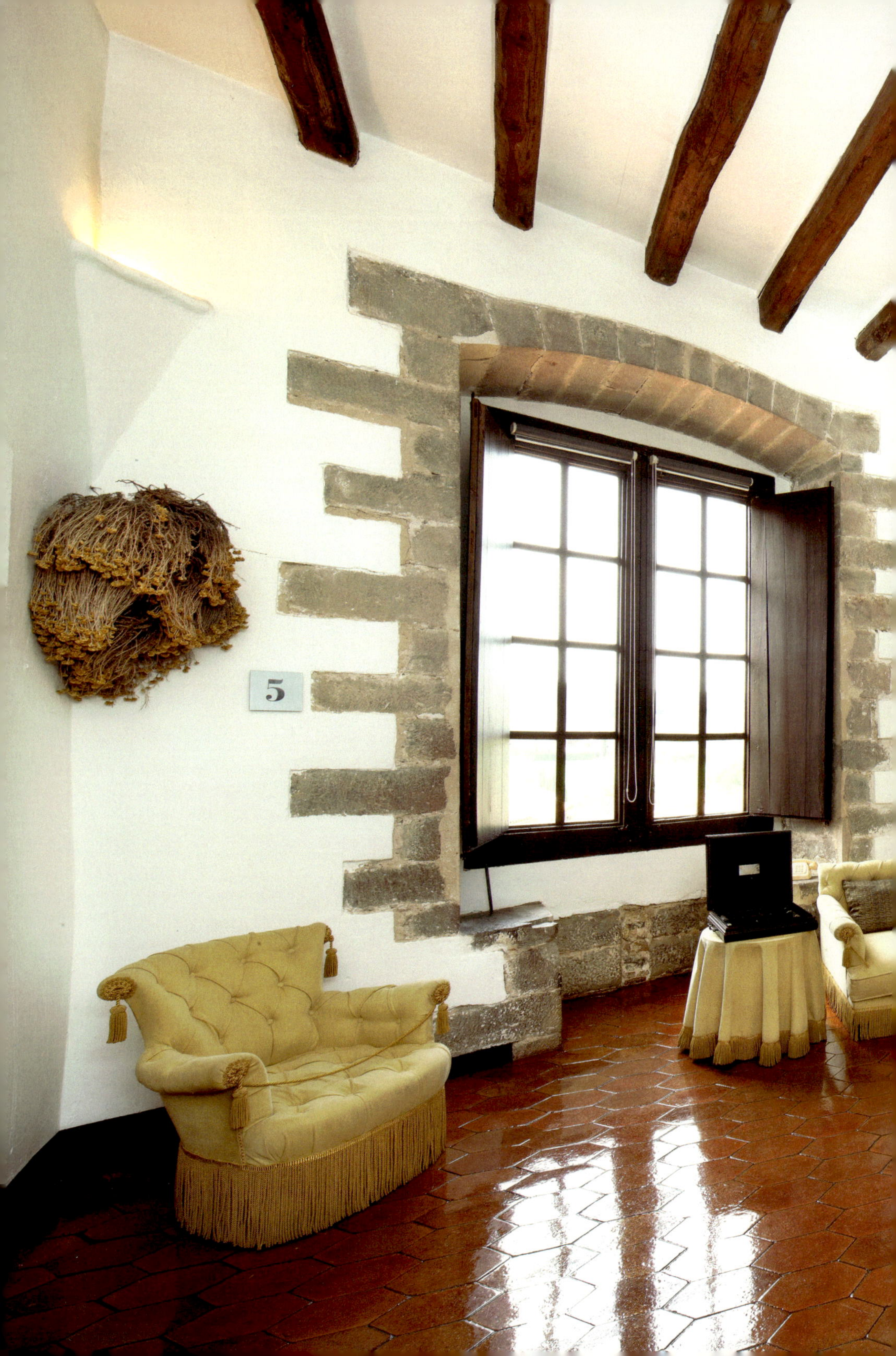
5

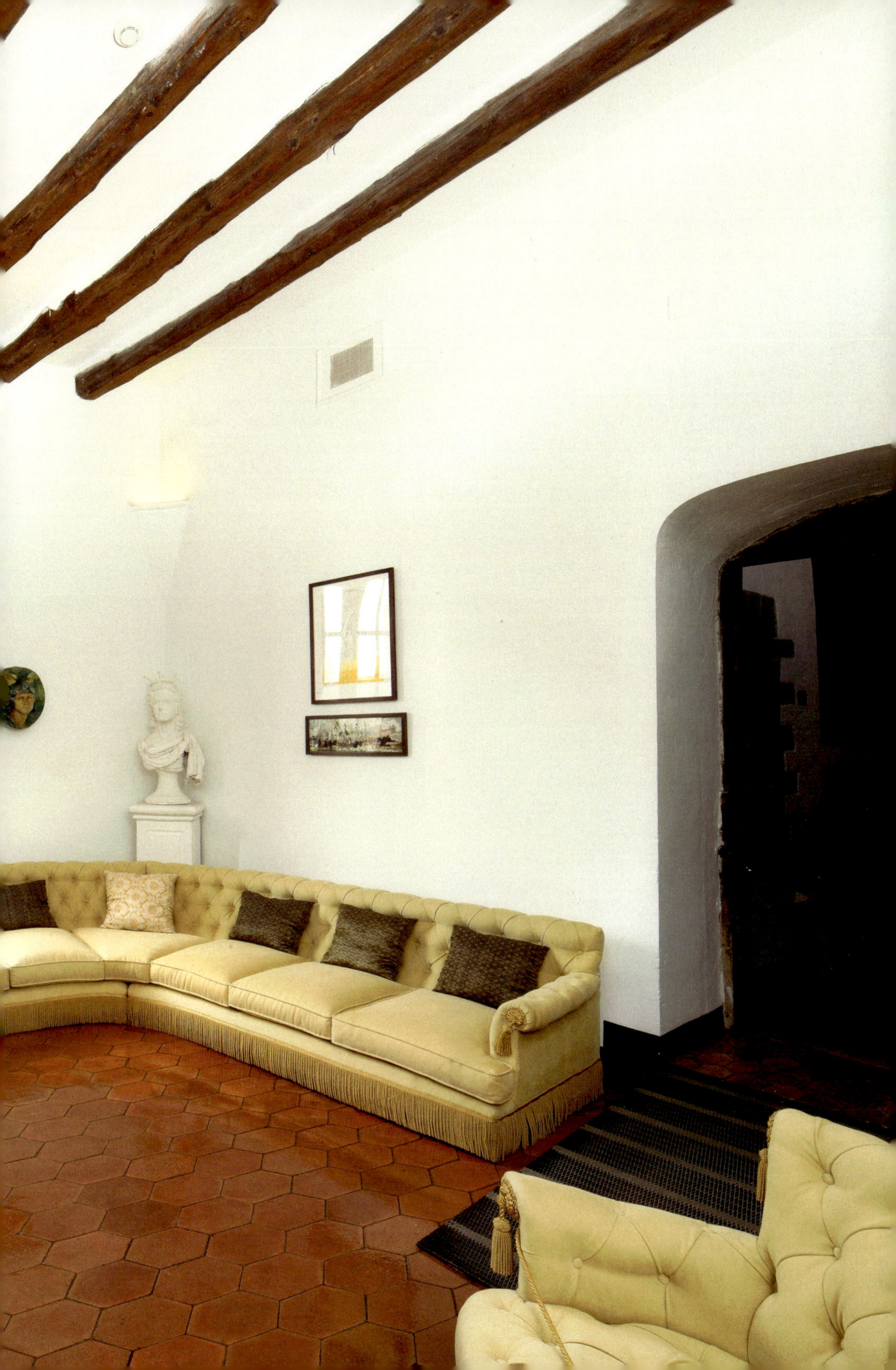

The second, which recalls a sailor's chest, is profusely decorated. It contains old photographs of Gala, board games —of which she was a great fan and, in fact, games in general—, invitations to the castle and a soft toy elephant (remember that soft toys are also very present in the oval room —the one used by Gala— in the house in Portlligat).

Gala was a person who was passionate about reading and would read aloud to Dalí. In Gala and Dalí's library, currently placed in the Centre of Dalinian Studies of the Gala-Salvador Dalí Foundation, we find great masters of Russian literature, basically from the 19th century, such as: Alexander Alexandrovich Blok (1880-1921); Ivan Alekseyevich Bunin (1870-1953); Fyodor Mikhaylovich Dostoyevsky (1821-1881); Konstantin Alexandrovich Fedin (1892-1977); Nikolai Vasilievich Gogol (1809-1852); Maxim Gorki (1868-1936); Mikhail Yurevich Lermontov (1814-1841); Alexander Sergeyevich Pushkin (1799-1837); Lev Nikolayevich Tolstoy (1828-1910); Anton Pavlovich Chekhov (1860-1904)... there is also a volume of memoirs of one of her childhood friends, Anastasia Tsvetaeva, who writes this dedication to Gala: "To my dear Galocha, as Marina called you, to the friend of adolescence, the book of our young and old Moscow. With affection, Asia Tsvetaeva (in the year of my 80th birthday). 6-12-74", which provides us, as does the autobiographical diary-text written by Gala, *Gala Dalí, The Secret Life. Unpublished diary*, until very recently unpublished, with information, real and fictitious, about her childhood and adolescence in Russia. It is important to know that these manuscripts, along with some texts by Dalí, where found in Púbol, in the castle.

Gala was also a great chess fan. She had played with the painter and with Marcel Duchamp, who left painting to devote himself to this *art*. Marcel Duchamp was probably the only friend from the surrealist

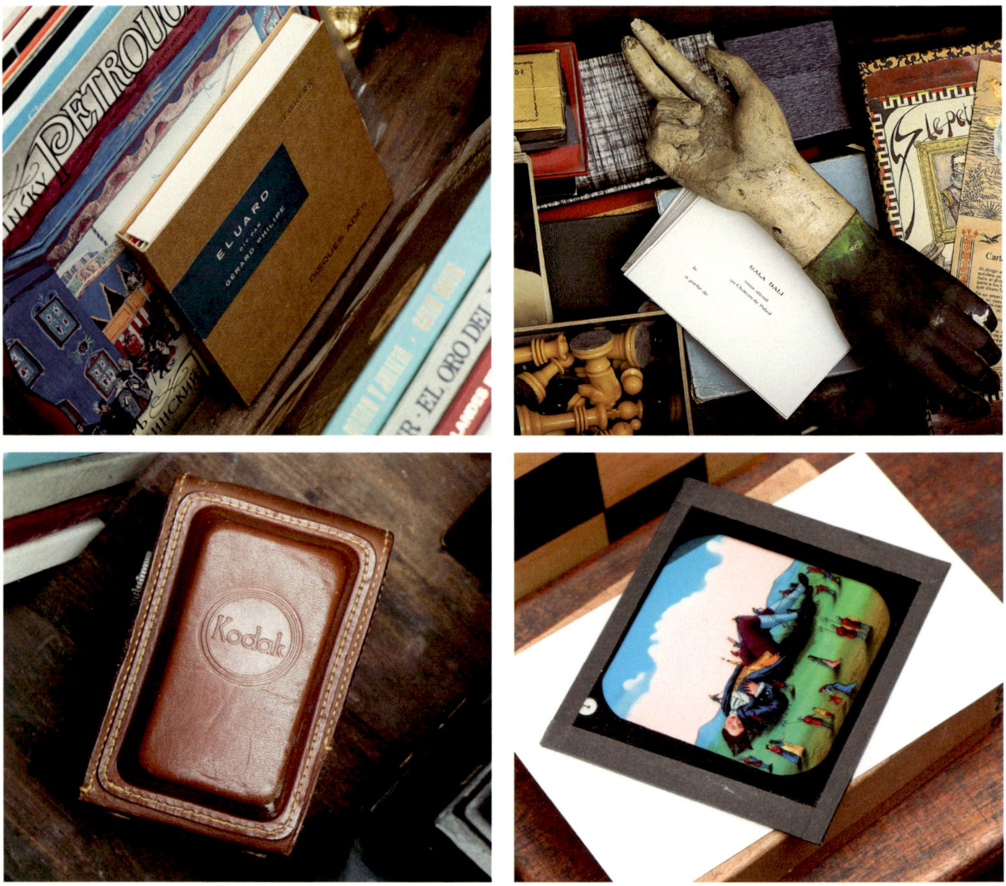

Personal objects of Gala and Dalí, kept in the chests

period with whom Dalí maintained a good relationship. Both coincided in diverse exhibitions of the surrealists, with who Duchamp —with being a member of the group— maintained an involved distance. After the war, once Dalí had broken with his old colleagues, the two maintained the thread of their relationship, perhaps because it was stronger than the merely personal link. Apart from the artistic affinities, they shared geographies: Paris, New York, but also Arcachon and Cadaqués, the latter town where Duchamp spent periods until his death, and where he and Dalí kept up their contact [33]. A result of the friendship and collaboration was the chess set designed by Dalí, which is in the middle of the room, beside the sofa on a small table. The small plaque accompanying the box states that it was "created by Salvador Dalí in honour of Marcel Duchamp for the American Chess Foundation" and produced by the jeweller F. J. Cooper Inc. of Philadelphia.

Dalí presented this set at a press conference in New York in 1971 and stated that the cost of the entire set, with 32 silver figures, would be 4,000 dollars. Douglas Cooper, the producer, announced the set in the following way:

"We bet you've never seen a chess set quite like this before. The pieces are cast from Salvador Dalí's fingers in solid sterling silver. Dalí created the set in honour of his late friend, Marcel Duchamp, and in tribute donated it to the American Chess Foundation. F. J. Cooper was commissioned to produce a limited number of sets.

Both the King and the Queen (the King is Dalí's thumb, the Queen is Madam Dalí's) wear a tooth as a crown. Mr. Cooper, in a moment of unrestrained curiosity, asked Dalí why a tooth. Dalí fielded the question brilliantly and asked Mr. Cooper why not a tooth. (Mr. Cooper went on to other things.)

[33] Aguer, Montse; Fanés, Fèlix, *Salvador Dalí. Àlbum de família*, Fundació Gala-Salvador Dalí, Fundació "la Caixa", Figueres, Barcelona, 1998, p. 32-33.

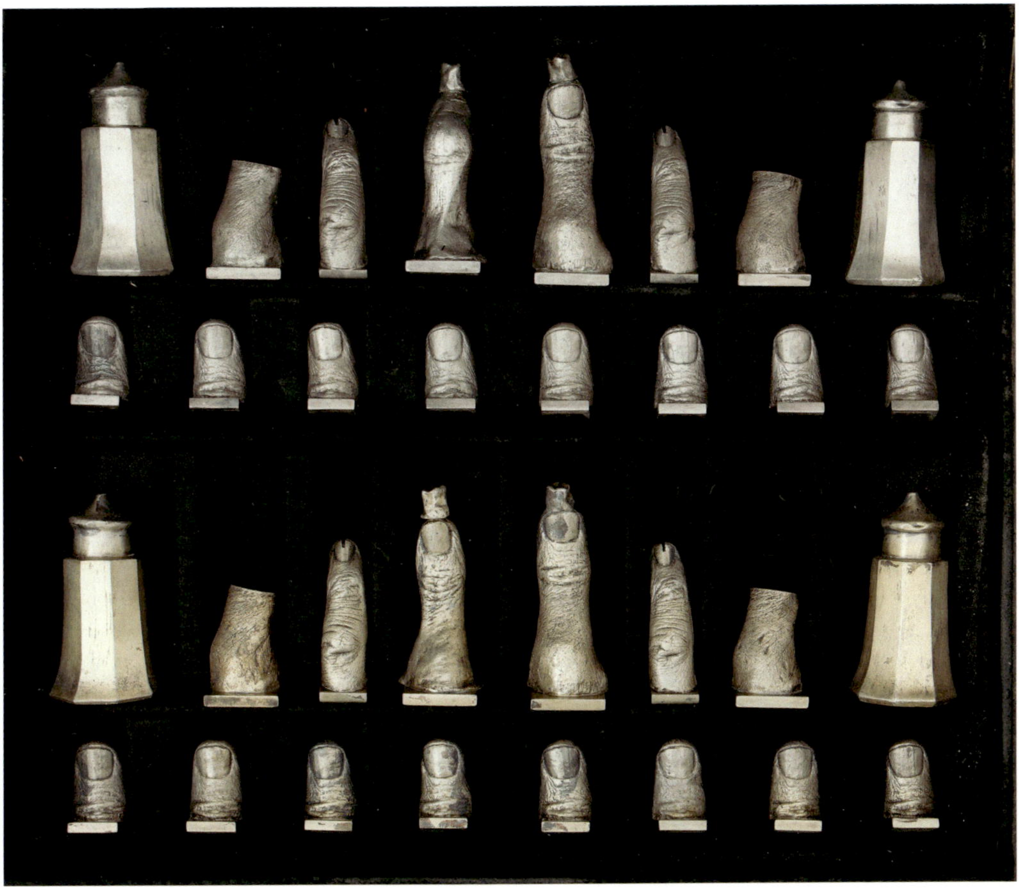

Chess set designed by Dalí, in homage to Marcel Duchamp

As to the reason why Dalí created a set using his own fingers, he said, 'I had a precise and yet symbolic concept. In chess, as in other forms of human alchemy, there is always the creator, above all, the artist as the creator. It is this that I wanted represented: the hand of the artist, the eternal creator. How better to express this vision than by sculpting my own hand, my own fingers?'

Each piece is signed by Dalí. Each set is numbered (Dalí owns set number one) and comes in its own oaken chest. Four thousand dollars. (...)

P.S. One collector we know bought a set and gave different friends different pieces. Now thirty-two people have a signed Dalí sculpture. Not a bad thought"[34].

The figures, then, are inspired by the artist's fingers, except the castles which had the salt cellar of the Hotel Saint Regis in New York as a model, where Dalí spent long periods of time, above all in winter.

This room is one of the most packed in terms of the number of works. The smallest is one that frames a dried four-leaf clover, on the back of which Dalí wrote an eloquent "Pour Gala", since, as we have mentioned before, Gala was superstitious and believed in luck and chance, and had a genuine obsession in finding in the countryside, in the long walks she loved so much, the rare four-leafed clovers, which she conserved between the pages of her most cherished books. From a photograph from 1971, which we can see in Gala's bedroom, we know that this piece had been on her dresser before. Small in size, it is also the ink and watercolour drawing on paper from 1957 called *Swallow* (16 × 15 cm).

On another wall there are two etchings that are among the most well-known by Dalí: *La grande Place des Vosges, du temps de Louis XIII.* (56.7 × 76.5 cm, Published by Duplesis-Orengo, 1958) and to its left *Saint George and the Dragon* (56.8 × 45.5 cm, Published by the Print Club of Cleveland, 1947). There are also reproductions of the latter in the house in Portlligat and in the Theatre-Museum.

We should also point out the presence of the work *View of Púbol* (Mixed technique / card, 20 × 56.3 cm, from 1971), a vision of the church and castle of Púbol, also present in other works from the same period. This composition is the result of Dalí's passion for the use of accidental or intentionally caused marks, and this reminds us of the film by *Dalí Impresiones de la Alta Mongolia*, which has the same structural intention. In the case of this watercolour, Dalí reinvents amidst the suggestive greenish forms, two fishermen, one of them in the boat rowing, and a hunter.

Placed right above this watercolour we come to an etching, *The desert with its footprint* (62.6 × 44.9 cm, Ed. Skira, 1973), which forms part of the *Roi, je t'attends à Babylone* series (another etching, *Darius swears he would like to paint...*, from the same series is found hanging in the next room, the guests' room).

On a shelf, just beside the window that looks out to the inner courtyard, there is a Modernist light —a style, as we know, often vindicated by Dalí— by Émile Gallé (1846-1904), a French artist who worked in glass and who is considered one of the most important representatives of French Art Nouveau. The lamp is also adorned with swallows, a bird very present in the castle, since it was one of the ways that Dalí had of calling her affectionately, and two photographs of Gala: a reproduction, where a fragment of a photograph of an adolescent Gala with a cat in her arms appears, the original of which is found in the house in Portlligat, together with copies of works that represent a *Madonna* by Raphael and the *Ginevra de'Benci* by Leonardo. Dalí said the three had the same structure of the face, over which Gala wrote: "Tête a chateau".

[34] "[Publicity of F. J. Cooper Inc.]", *New Yorker*, New York, 1971, 3 April 1971.

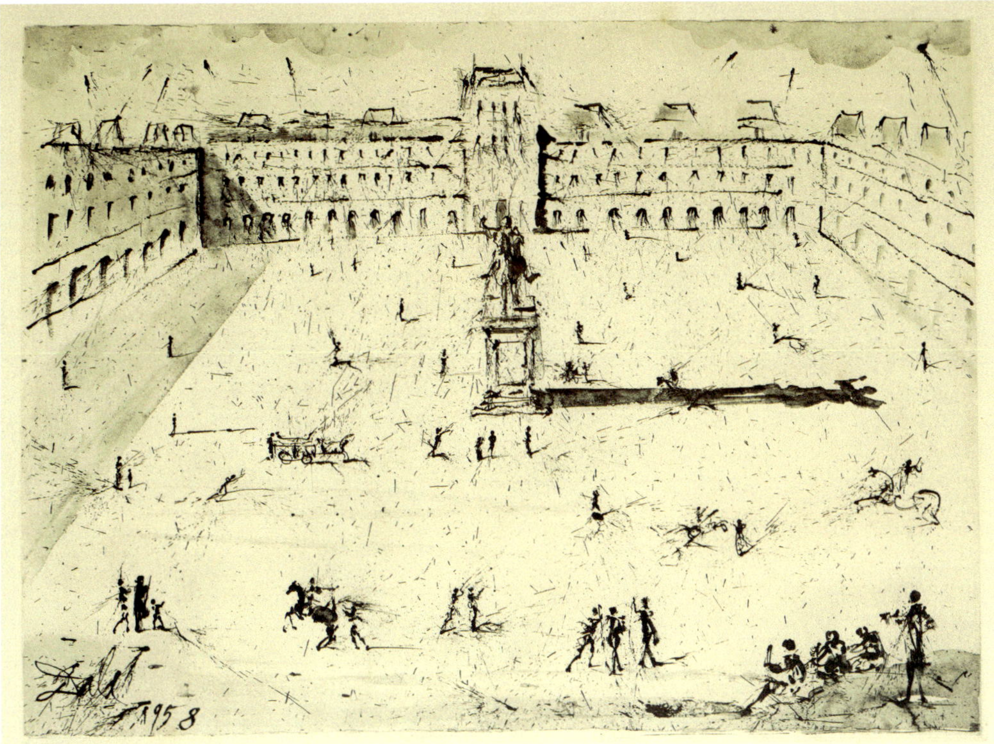

La grande Place des Vosges, du temps de Louis XIII, 1958 (Etching)

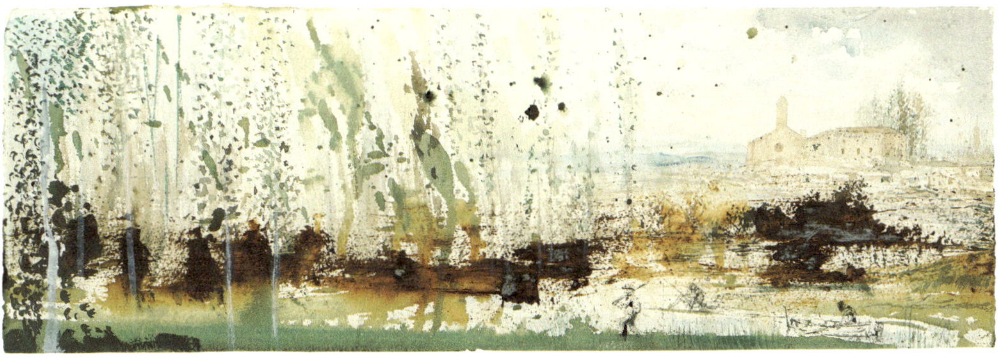
View of Púbol, 1971 (Mixed tecnique / card)

The second photograph, by Marc Lacroix, represents Gala's eyes that emerge from behind a stone in the garden of Púbol, eyes that surely transmit to those of *The visible woman* a look that, just as Paul Éluard expressed, sees through walls.

The decoration of the room is completed with a plaster bust that corresponds to Gala's face, with a crown that recalls her idea about the circle that the drop of milk forms on falling; it had been before the *Venus de Milo with drawers*, which corresponded to part of the inheritance of Cécile Éluard, her daughter and, finally a piece of painted ceramic (signed E. Muller) that reproduces the head of a deity, with winged helmet, an allusion to the myths of Hermes and Mercury.

Additionally, in this room there had been a small bookshelf furnishing, with no more than forty books, some bound by Gala herself. They were mainly Russian and French literature, although they also shared space with other books that had been given to Gala. Of course there were the works of Paul Éluard and other contemporary authors who had dedicated their books to her. Dalí conserved different copies, as one would expect, of *The visible woman*, our Gala. Both the shelves and the books and some personal objects were given to Cécile Grindel, daughter of Gala and Paul Éluard, as part of the legitimate estate. There is a large chest and the watercolour *Hirondelle de ciel* from 1971, which, as the title indicates, is a swallow painted in blue following the trace of a crack.

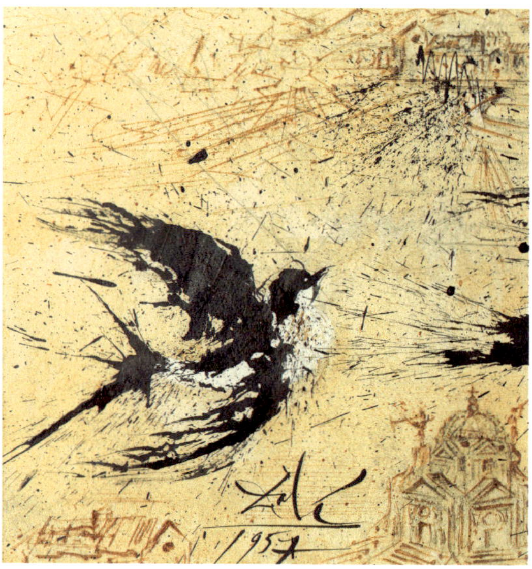

Swallow, 1957 (Watercolour drawing on paper)

Photographs of Gala and Modernist lamp by Gallé

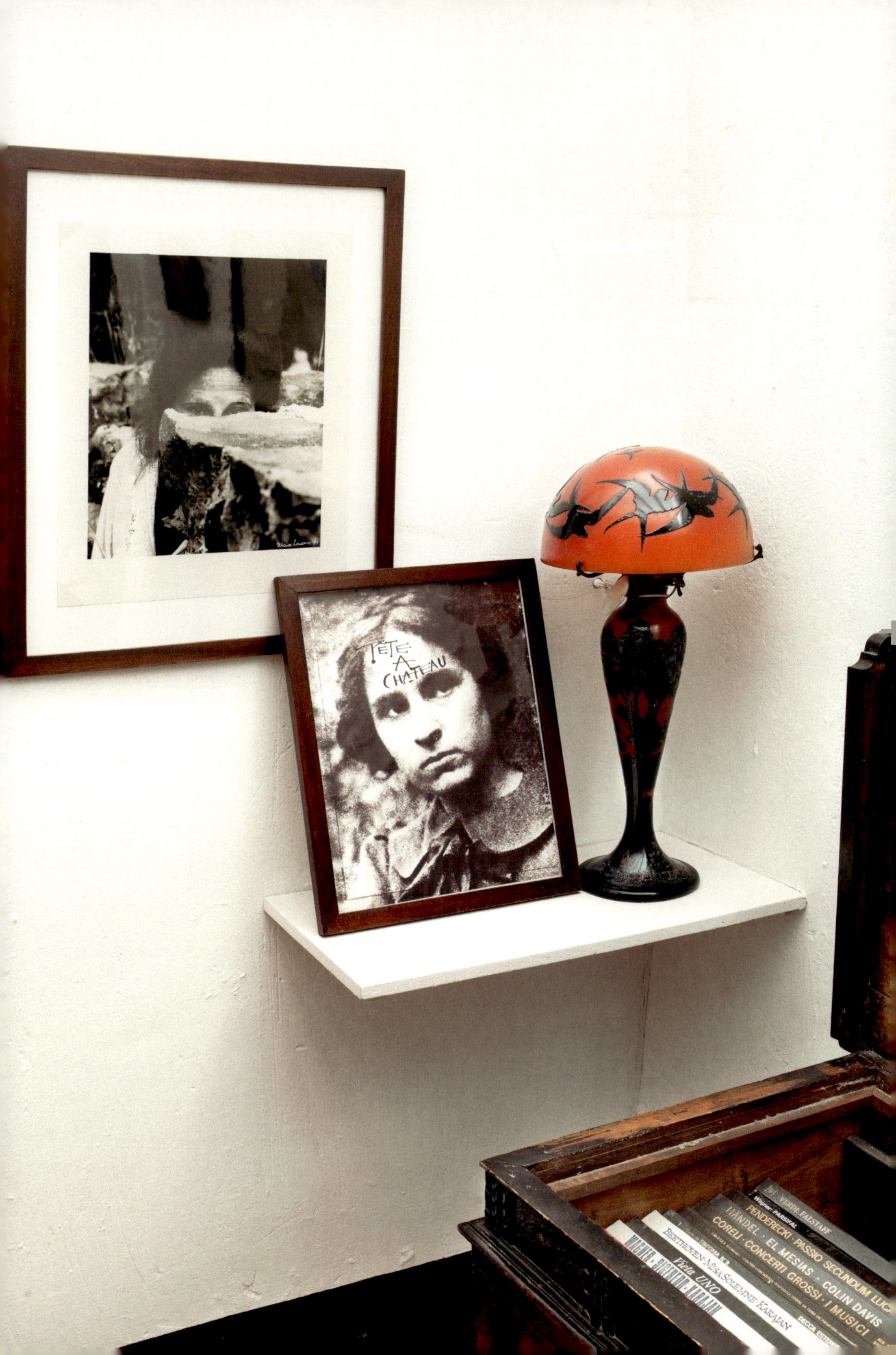
TÊTE A CHATEAU
VERDI FALSTAFF
Wagner PARSIFAL
PENDERECKI · PASSIO SECUNDUM
HÄNDEL · EL MESIAS · COLIN DAVIS
CORELLI · CONCERTI GROSSI · I MUSICI
BEETHOVEN MISSA SOLEMNE KARAJAN
WAGNER · SIGFRIDO · KARAJAN
DECCA

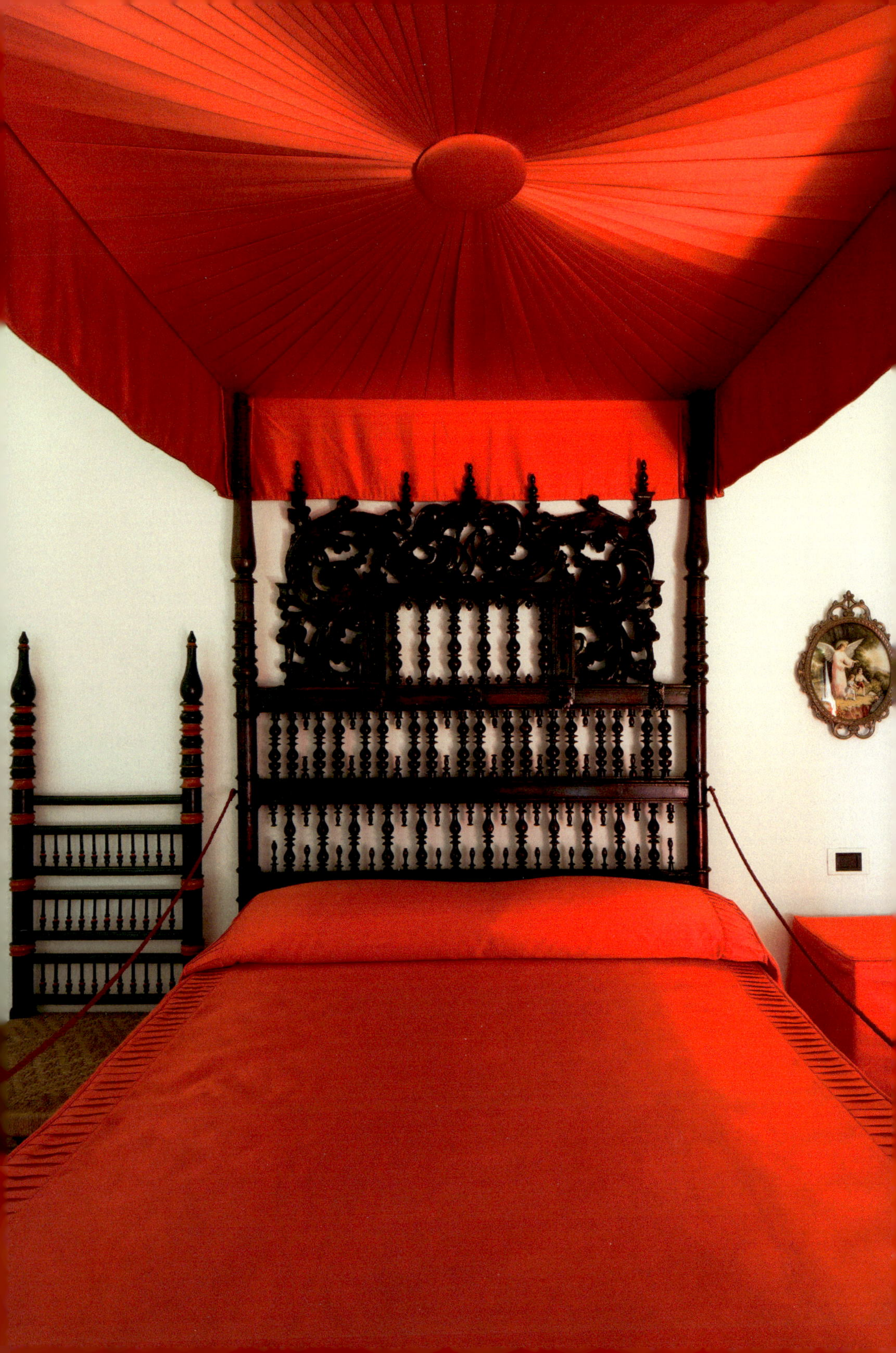

THE RED ROOM

We go through a small door that leads us to a room where red is the predominant colour. A horseshoe, placed over the threshold of the door, welcomes us to the room reserved, in Gala's time, for guests at the castle.

Of an austere character, like the rest of the castle, with a beautiful canopied bed, we find few ornaments: there are, of course, the houseleeks on the ceiling, an etching by the painter and a painting-lamp with an image of the guardian angel in painted glass. However, on the wall opposite the bed, we find on a shelf presented as a display cabinet an accumulation (remember that Dalí always said that one had to work by accumulation and never by selection) of diverse objects: curious bottles of spirits, one of them a reproduction of the Sagrada Familia for Bodegas y Destilerías Agustín Bofill of Badalona, the other two a bullfighter and a manola, a typical woman from Madrid (like those found in the swimming pool area of the house at Portlligat) of the Nogueras Comas company in Barcelona. A ceramic charioteer, a dish with hazelnuts, a tortoise that is also a reception bell; a couple of sweethearts; two porcelain ashtrays and a soft toy squirrel. Diverse religious images and, above all these objects, a sculpture *Clock hanger* (1971), made with *pâte de verre*. This is a very rare and old glassmaking technique that dates back more than 3,500 years. The current process involves the fusion of glass and the reproduction of forms by means of the method of lost-wax casting, a very different method to the traditional technique of glassblowing[35]. In 1878 the Daum family took over a glassmaking factory in Nancy, France, where they developed this art and made it famous across the world. Another generation of the Daum family took control of production and in 1970 decided to introduce *pâte de verre* and invited a series of famous sculptors, designers and glass craftsmen to design special limited editions for the company. Salvador Dalí was the first, creating among others, the object we can admire in this display cabinet.

[35] *Complete collection of sculptures in* pâte de verre *by Salvador Dalí,* Dau al Set, Art gallery, Barcelona, 1981.

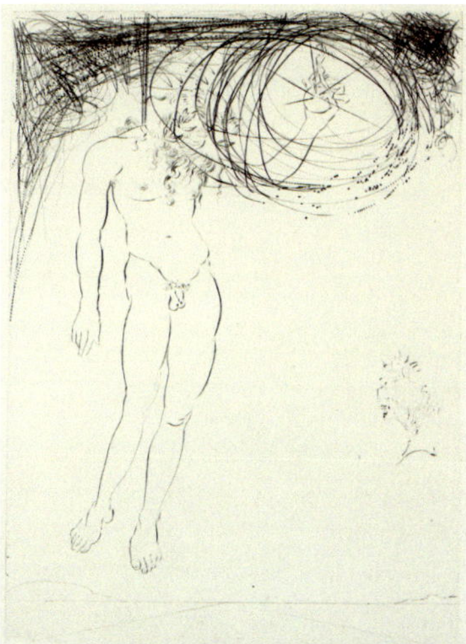

Darius swears he would like to paint..., 1973 (Etching)

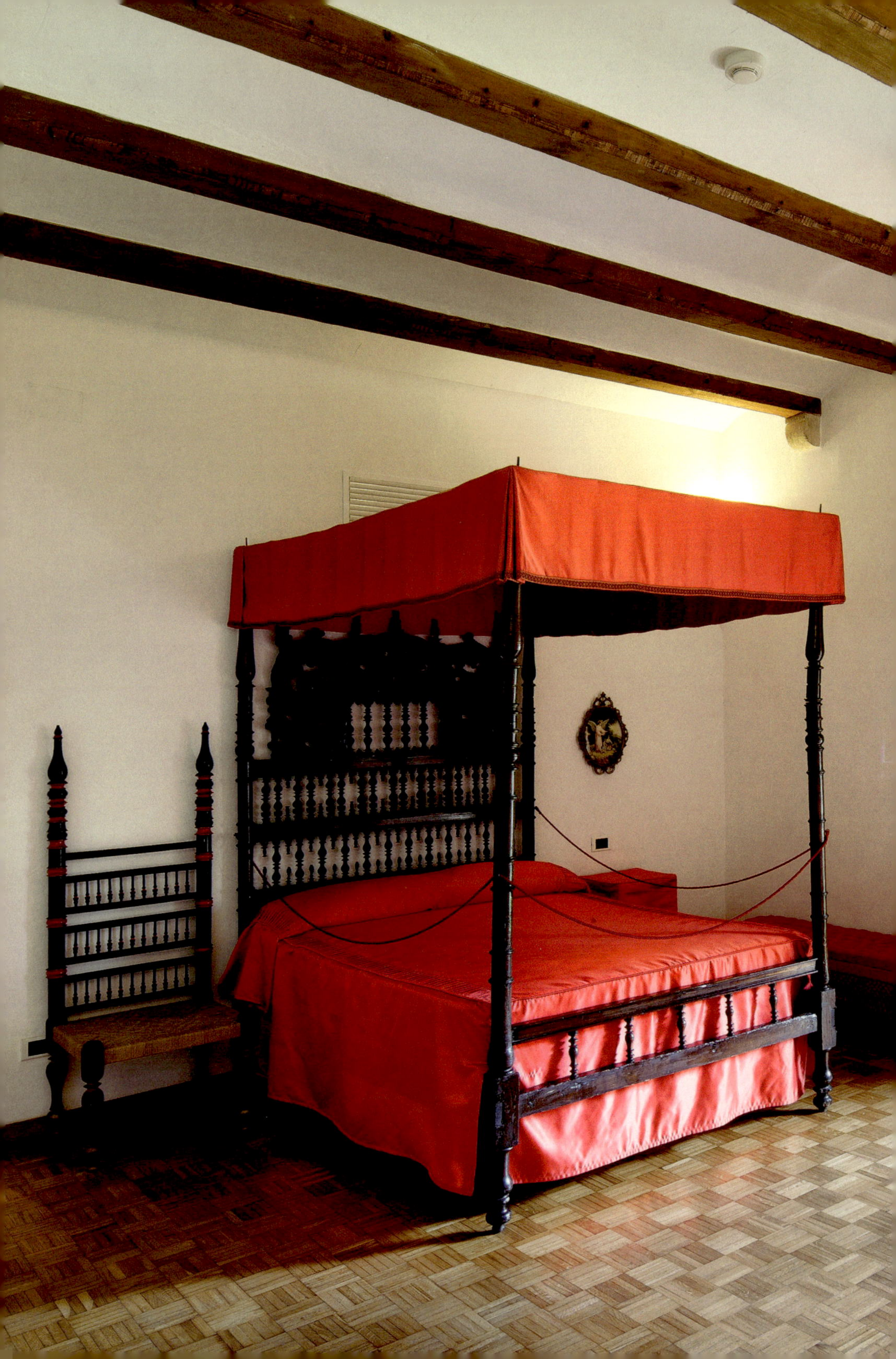

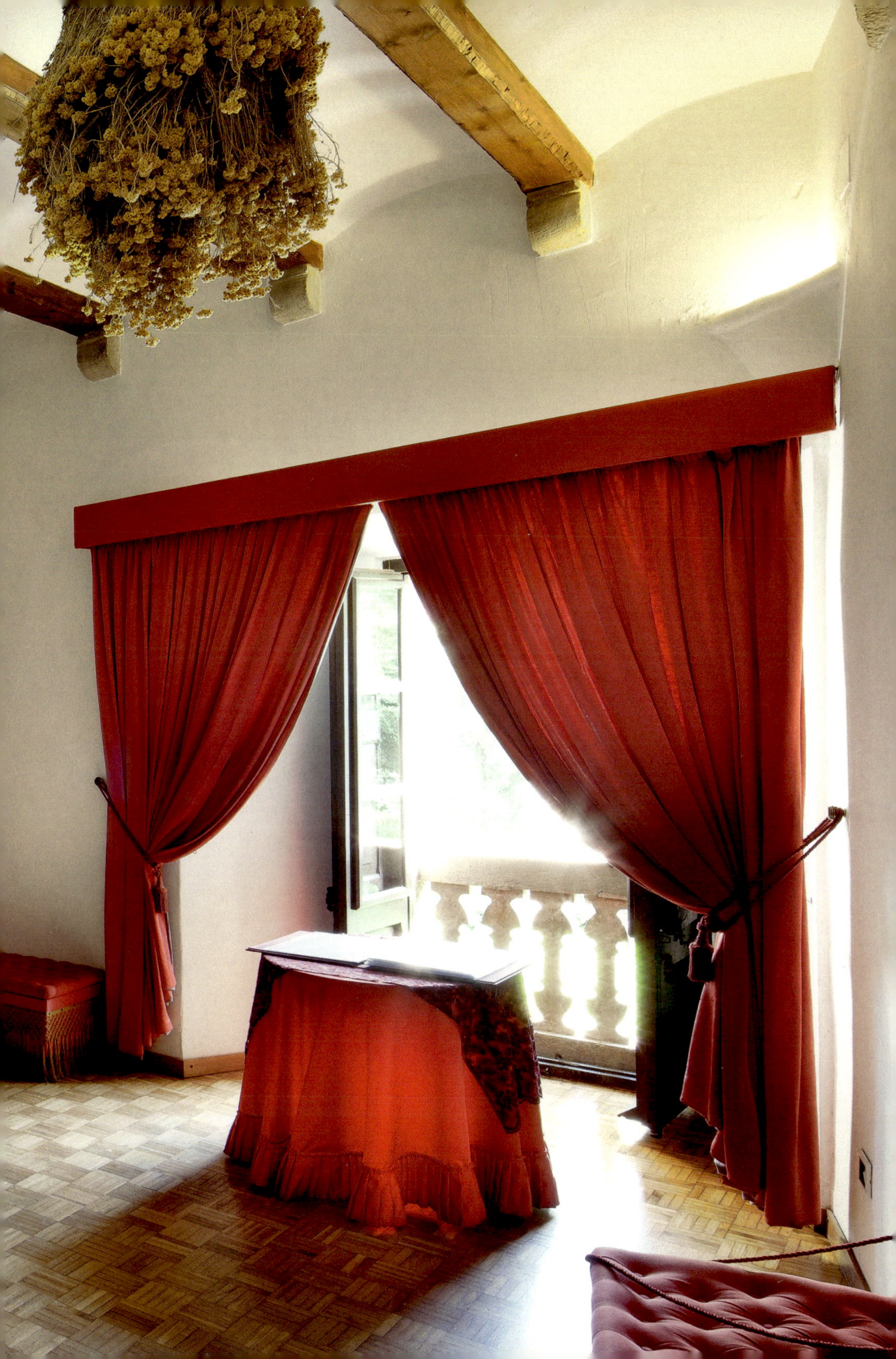

The surprising combination of objects of this display cabinet is certainly another reference to Marcel Duchamp, specifically the *Boîte en valise* and the *ready-made*, in other words, the act of giving artistic category to an object in accordance with the place or centre where it is placed. Of the religious images, we can highlight a couple of representations of the Virgin of the Carmen, patron saint of fishermen, a sacred heart and a polychrome wood carving that represents the Immaculate Conception from the El Arte Cristiano workshop of Olot. This carving is most likely based on the painting by Bartolomé Esteban Murillo, *The Immaculate Conception of Aranjuez*, painted between 1670 and 1680, which can be seen in the Prado Museum in Madrid.

Before leaving the room, it is interesting to take a look at the photo album on a table in front of the balcony, from where you can see the garden. This album is a compilation, in chronological order, of photos of Gala, through which we can follow the stages of her life. We can highlight images such as Gala with her brothers, one of her with her first husband, the poet Paul Éluard, and all those in which she appears with Salvador Dalí.

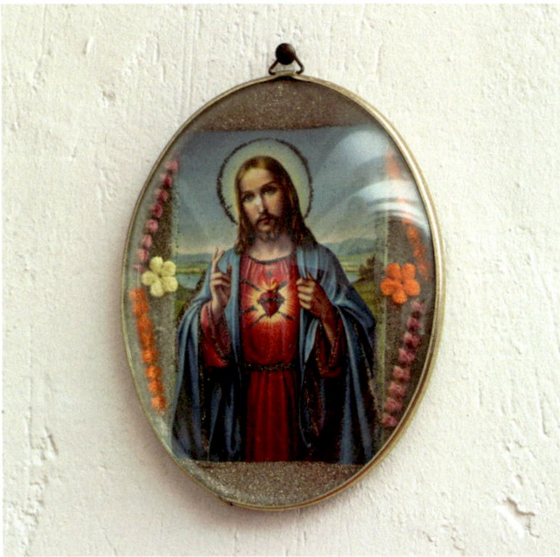

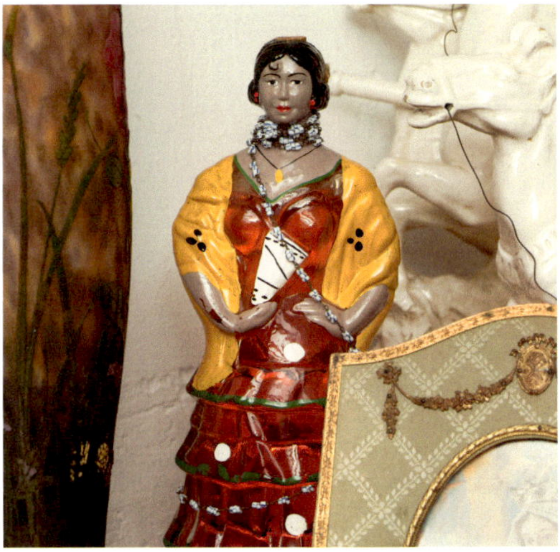

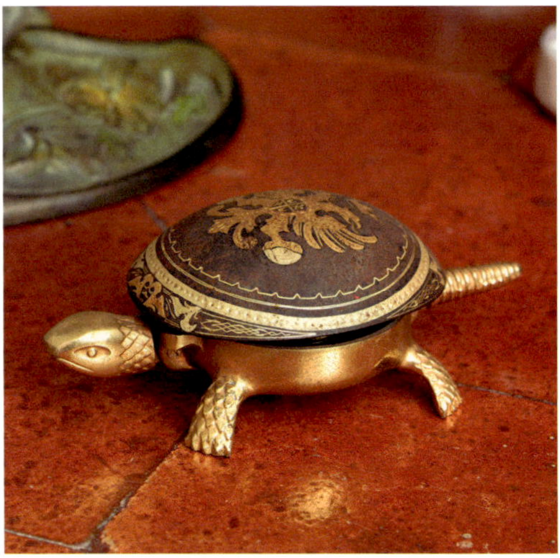

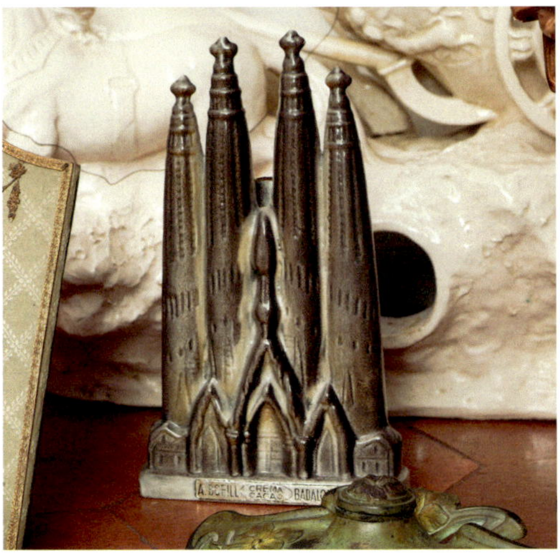

Display cabinet of the red room and details

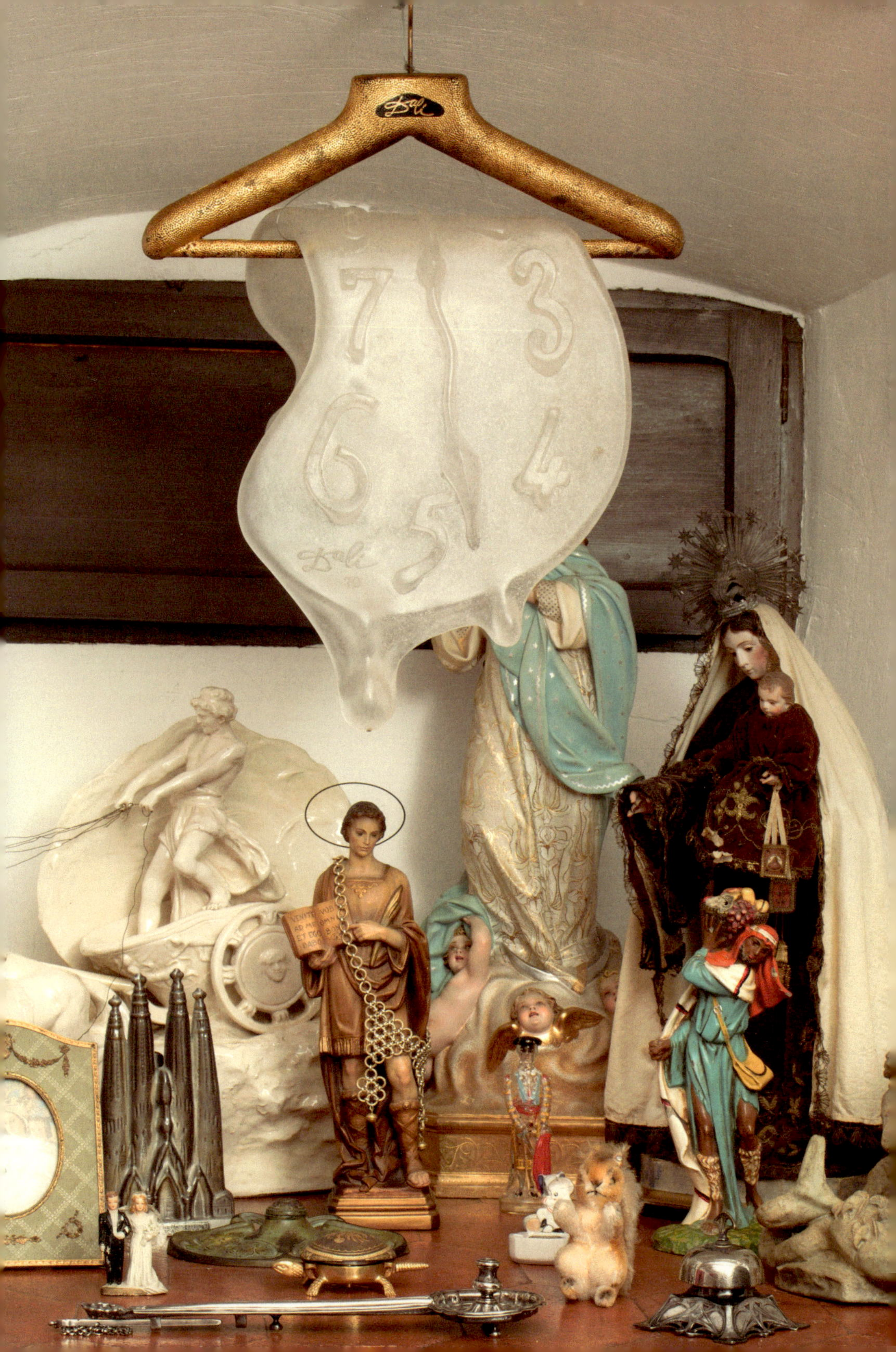
Dalí
Dalí

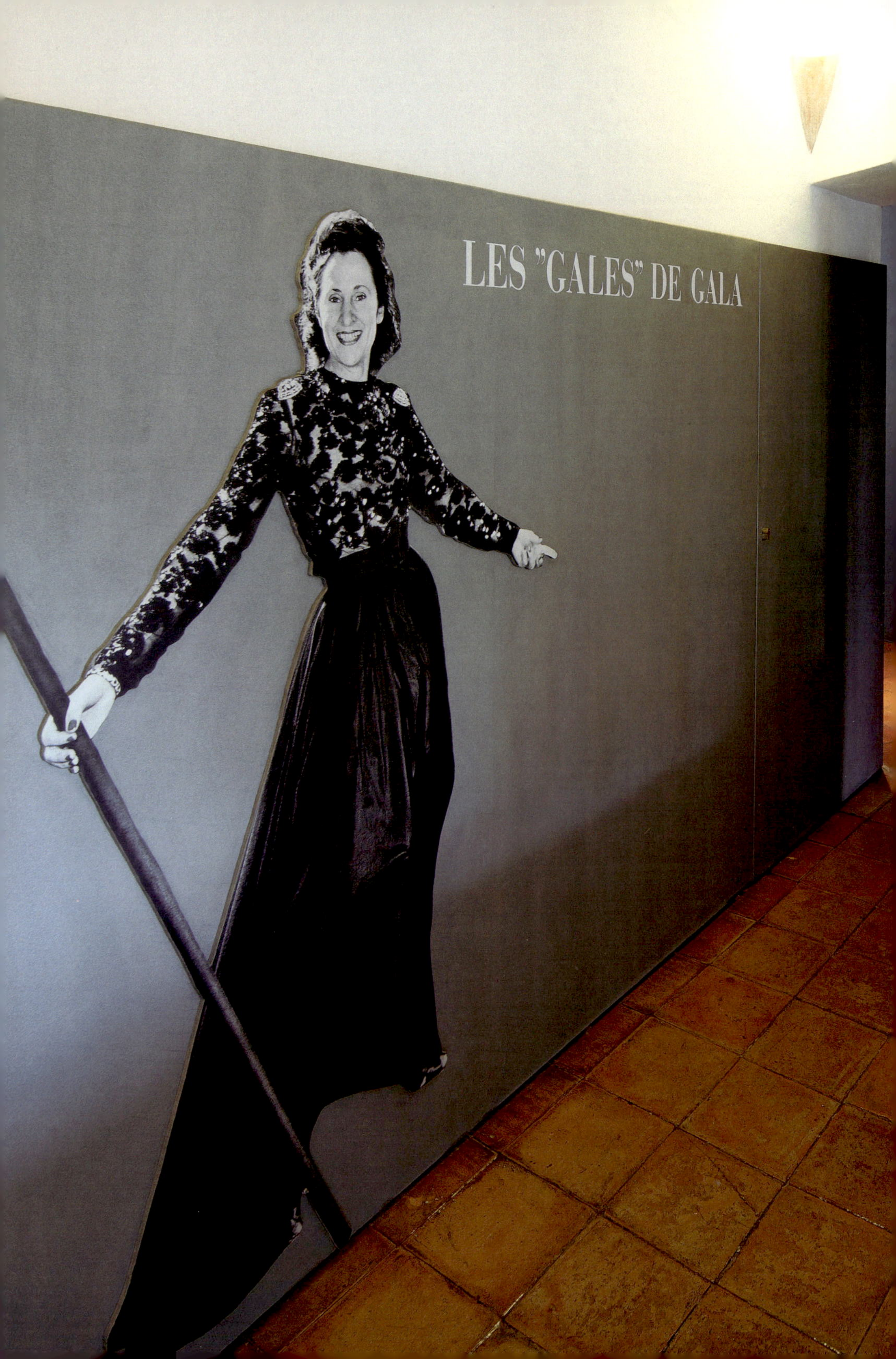
LES "GALES" DE GALA

THE "GALA DRESSES" OF GALA

This floor and its new uses were determinant for the Gala-Salvador Dalí Foundation, with a rehabilitation undertaken by a team led by the architect Oriol Clos. A new space was created, that has a magnificent large window with Gothic capitals, different from the rest of the castle in order to be able to present to the public the "gala dresses" of Gala: some of the haute couture dresses, worn by Gala in some of her public appearances. With the background music of Wagner's *Tristan and Isolde* (the same as Dalí wanted for his Theatre-Museum), the visitor can appreciate the dresses of Gala duly restored and in the best conditions of conservation.

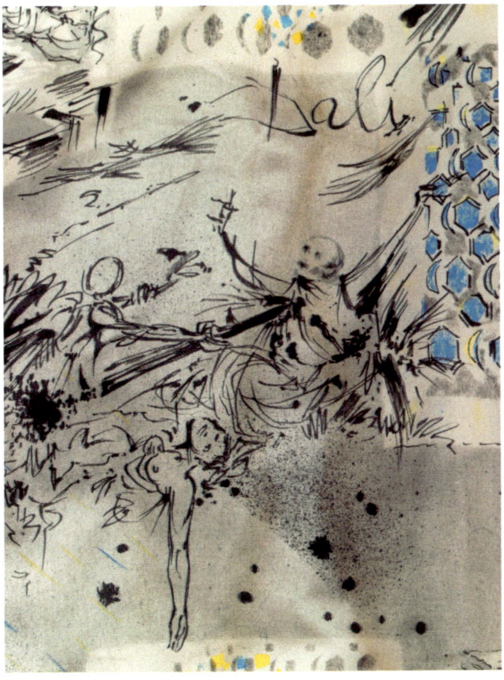

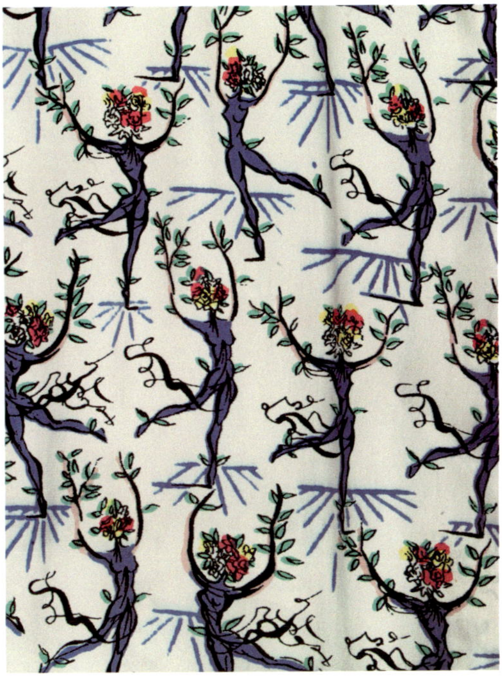

Dresses with patterns designed by Salvador Dalí

The upper floor had never had any precise use: when in 1982 the works that Dalí had stored in the United States were repatriated, it became an improvised storeroom. A greenish sofa, perhaps one of the first tests for the furniture in the form of lips in the Mae West room of the Dalí Theatre-Museum, welcomes the visitor to this room which is reached from the guests' room, always going around the inner courtyard, towards a corridor where there is a stairway that leads to the upper floor.

Apart from these dresses, this exhibition also shows clothes of the painter himself, such as an unusual blue denim shirt, with abundant embroidery, which he often wore in his private receptions in Portlligat. This shirt can be seen in a photograph that was taken, in its day, by the friend and photographer Melitó Casals, Meli, or Melicolor as Dalí cordially called him. It also features the *barretina*, the Catalan beret that he wore sometimes and a crown bearing the initials D and G.

We then come to a second display cabinet, with matching purple trousers and yellow jacket with black horizontal stripes, Gala's clothes, represented by Dalí in the stereoscopic painting *Battle in the Clouds* from 1979. It is a three-dimensional installation simulating the presence of Gala in the oil painting.

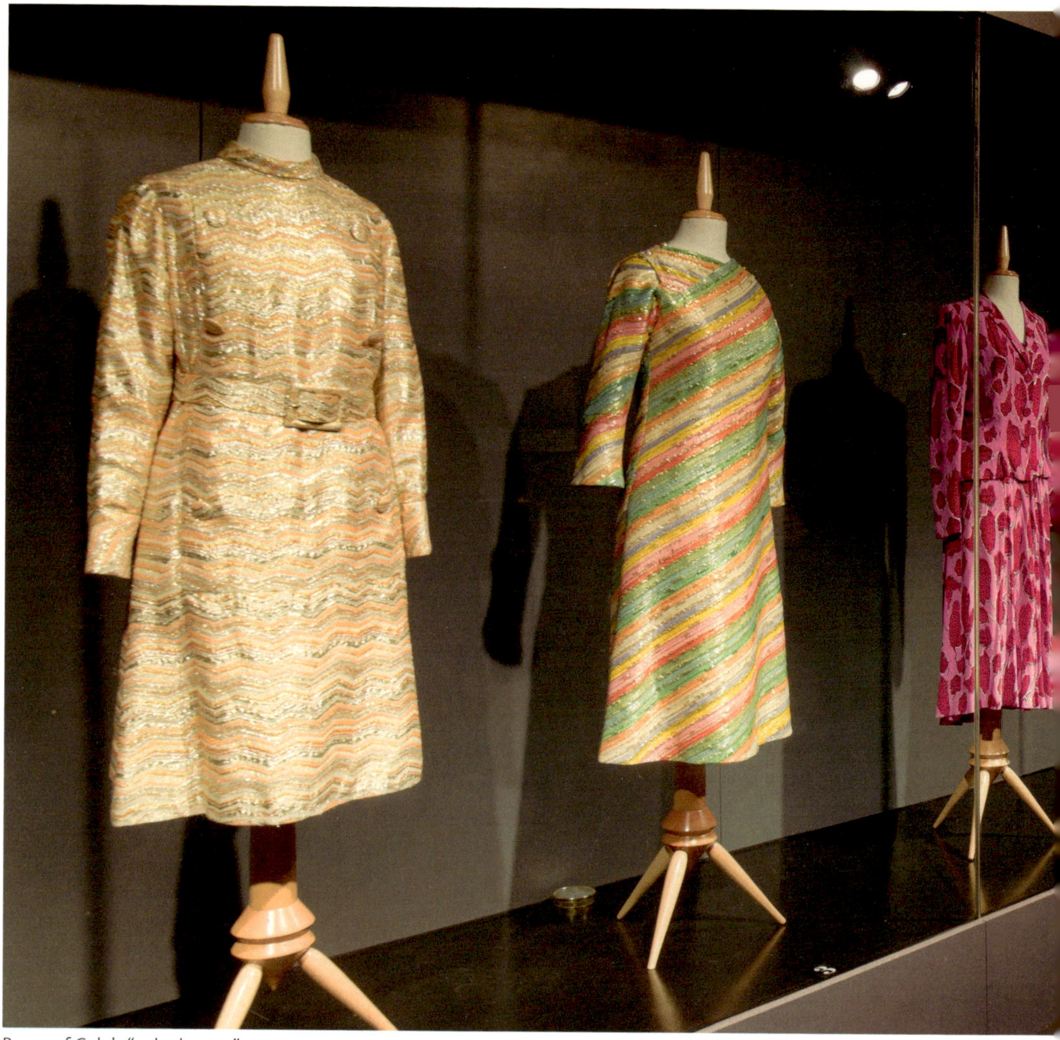

Room of Gala's "gala dresses"

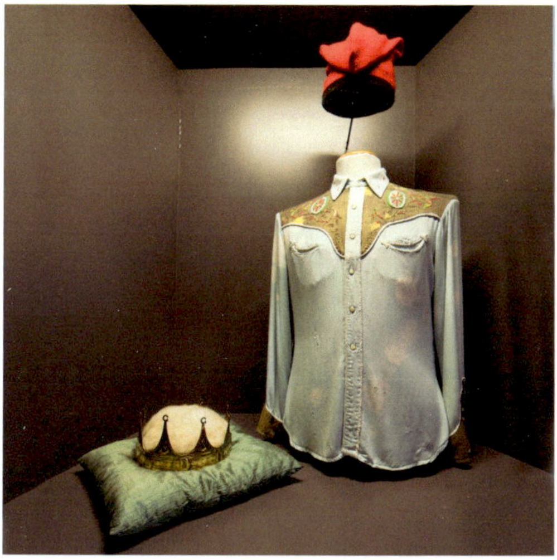

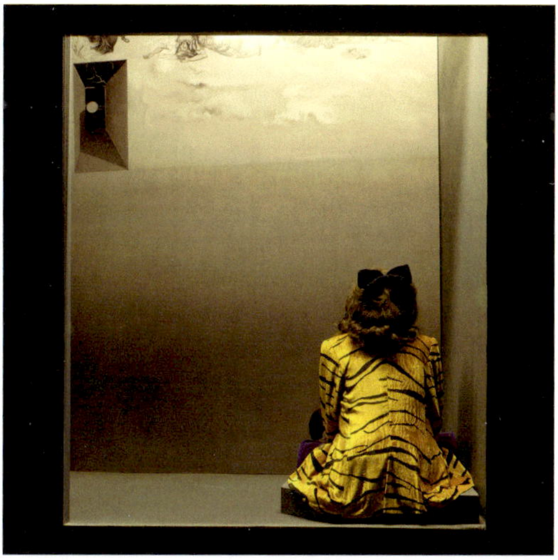

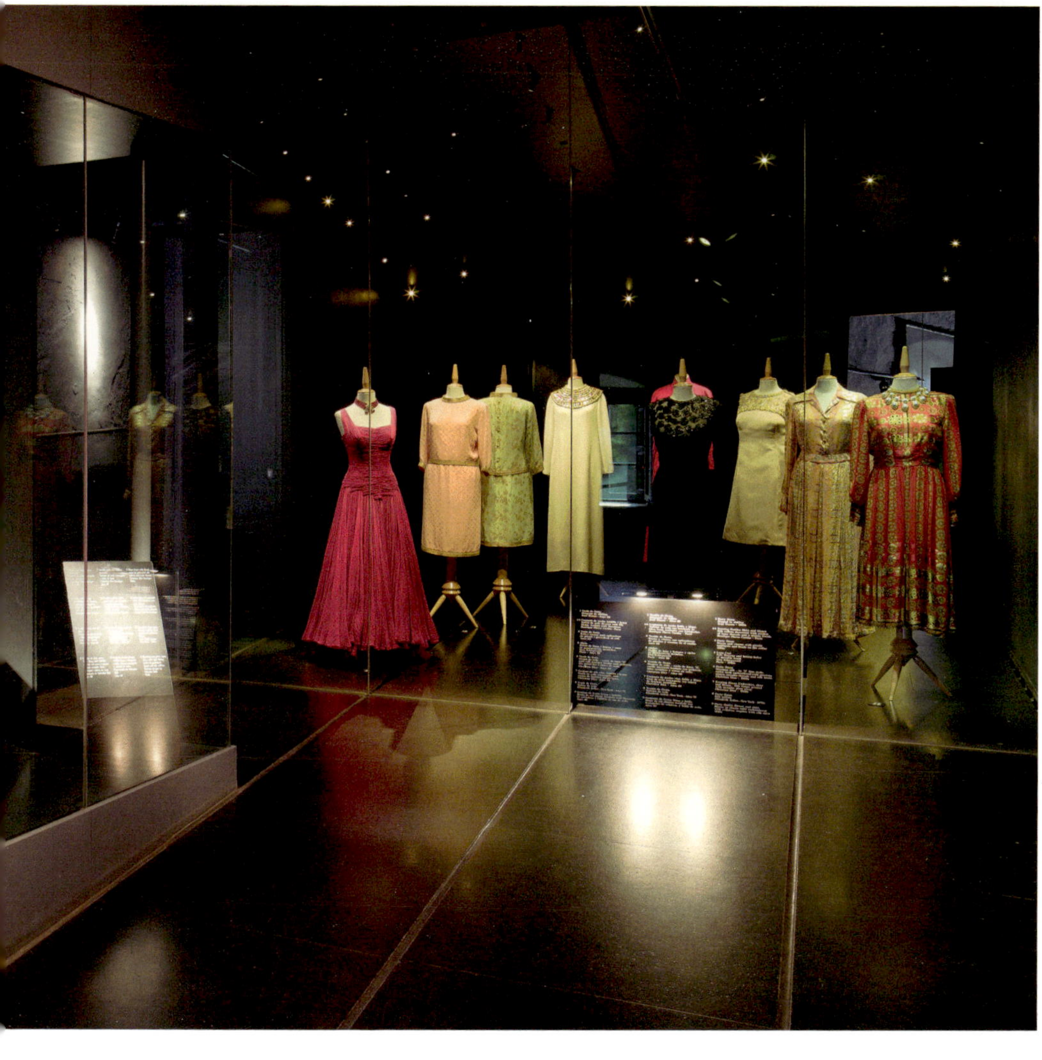

Next, and distributed among two large display cabinets, we come to the dresses by famous clothes designers that the lady of the castle wore.

By JEAN DESSÈS: Party dress, long and waisted, with full skirt in red. The design is by Jean Dessès (1904-1970), a leading fashion designer in the 40s, 50s and 60s. His designs reflect the influences of his travels. He specialised in creating evening dresses draped in gauze and muslin, based on early Greek and Egyptian dresses. This creation is made with silk and dates from the 50s. [1]

By CHRISTIAN DIOR: There are four matching sets exhibited.
A matching blouse and skirt made in lamé in the 60s. The blouse is short-sleeved with lapels and buttons. The skirt is ankle-length, and the lining silk taffeta.

A party dress in trapezoid shape, sleeveless and with rounded neck. It has a piece over the collar similar to a sailor's lapel. Made in the 60s with Ottoman silk and lined with organza silk. It has precious stones and metallic threads. [2]

A three-piece set: slip, skirt and blouse. Long slip with marked waist, with full skirt. The blouse is long-sleeved with shirt collar. It is made with patterned silk gauze and silk taffeta of reddish-golden tones. We date it from the 50s. [3]

Finally, a short dress, below the knees, with the waist marked by a wide piece. It is made with patterned silk taffeta in several colours and gold lame threads. We can place it in the 60s.

Christian Dior (1905-1957), especially known for what is called the "new look of 1947", a style of women's dressmaking that proposes turned shoulders, slender waist and skirt. It represents classical elegance

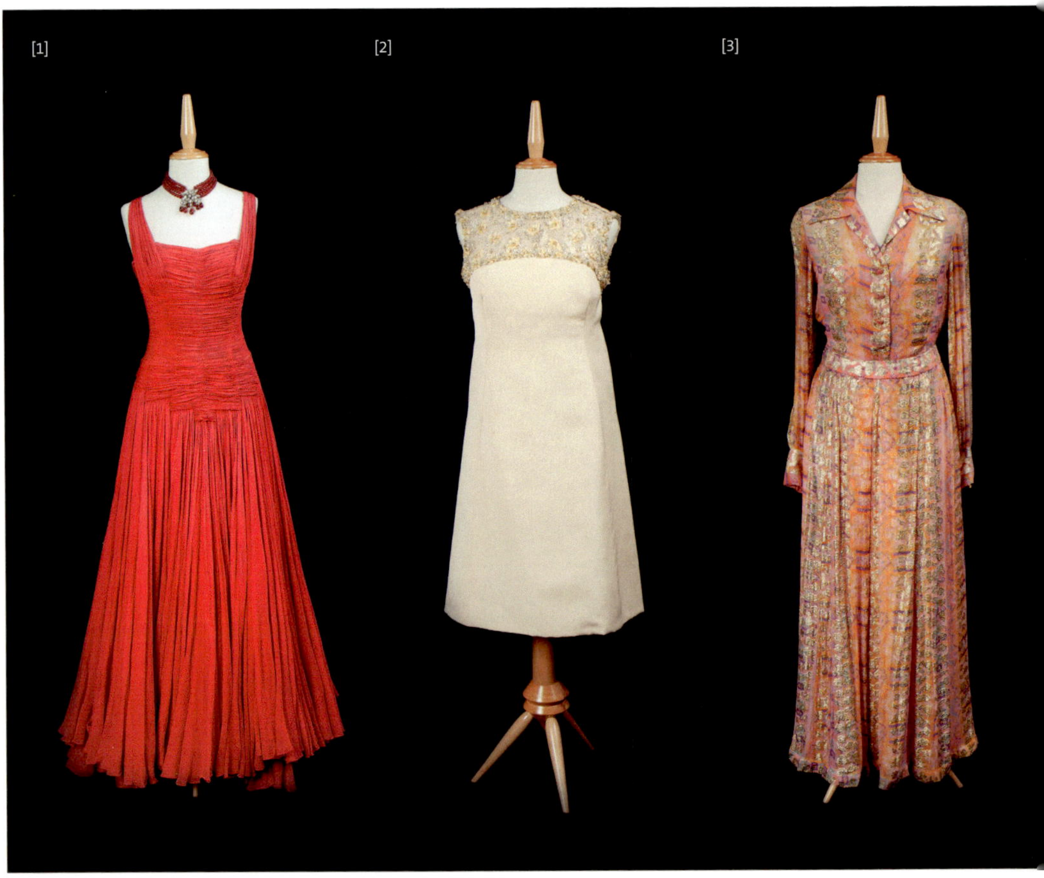

and the return to a feminine image, and represented the recovery of luxury and excess after the depression of the Second World War.

By PIERRE CARDIN: We come to two matching two-piece sets, tight-fitting to the knees, blouse with round neck with three-quarter sleeves. One in green and gold is made with silk taffeta and decorated with lamé threads. The lining is also in silk taffeta [4]. The other one has the same characteristics but is in pink and gold. They are two creations by the designer Pierre Cardin who worked with Elsa Schiaparelli until becoming the head of the Christian Dior atelier in 1947. When they did not allow him to work with the grand master Balenciaga he decided to found his own firm in 1950. This is how Cardin began in haute couture in 1953. He was known for his avant-garde style and his "Space Age" designs. He preferred geometric forms and motifs, often ignoring the feminine figure. He stood out for the innovation in designing unisex fashion. In 1954 he presented the "bubble dress".

By ELISABETH ARDEN: Better known for her cosmetic empire than as a fashion designer, this dress has a round neck, long sleeves and a tight-fitting waist. It is in five colours, red, yellow, green, blue and black, with red dominant. The fabric is silk made in the 70s in taffeta, trimmings and silk lining. [5]

By ELSA SCHIAPARELLI: We can see this fantastic long coat with a high neck, tight-fitting, with a narrow waist and skirt in trapeze form. Made with red felt and fastened from top to bottom with gold buttons, the coat, as well as the collaboration of this designer with Dalí, dates from the 30s [6]. Elsa Schiaparelli (1890-1973), along with Coco Chanel, her maximum rival, is considered one of the leading figures of

[4]

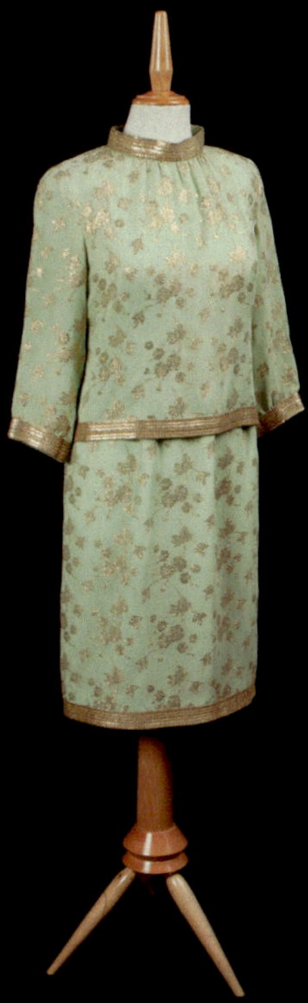

[5]

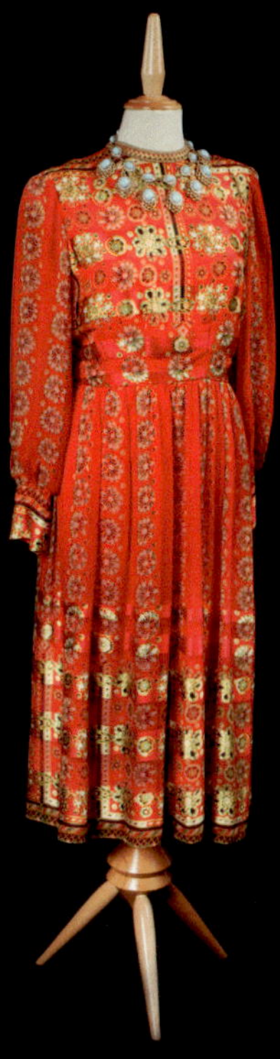

[6]

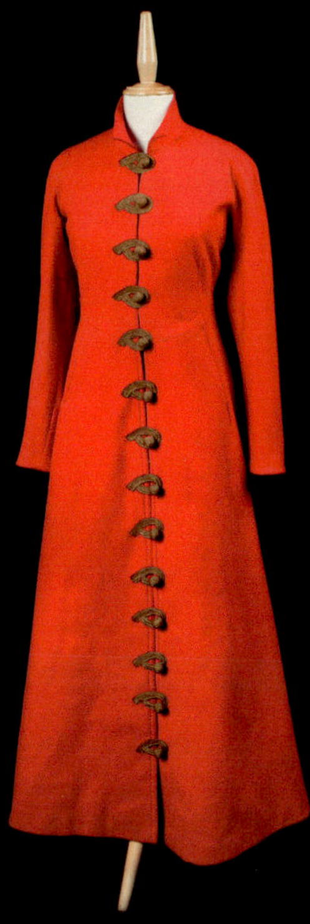

fashion in the interwar years. Based on knitwear, Schiaparelli's designs were strongly influenced by the surrealists. Schiaparelli's designs produced in collaboration with Dalí are among her most well-known: the lobster-dress, the tears-dress, the skeleton-dress and the shoe-hat that Gala wore sometimes. Among her clients featured the heiress Daisy Fellowes and the actresses Marlene Dietrich, Gloria Swanson and Mae West.

Apart from the collaboration of the grand master with Elsa Schiaparelli, Dalí collaborated on designing clothes for other firms. We have a sample of some of these works in the dresses found in the castle of Púbol. For reasons of conservation we only show one of them. It is a two-piece matching set: a long backless dress with full skirt while the jacket is long-sleeved and tight-fitting. The Dalinian pattern is some tiles where pink, fuchsia pink and black predominate. The dress made with patterned rayon and silk taffeta is from the 60s.

We can also see three pieces that are not signed:

The first, a short party dress, in two pieces, is of a simple and geometric line. Made from taffeta and lamé threads in the 60s and bought in the New York shop, Saks Fifth Avenue.

The second, from the boutique of Jeanne Lanvin, is a short dress in geometric line with the waist marked by a belt. It is made with synthetic fibres and lame thread.

Also without an author, a party dress, straight to the feet, with raglan sleeve and no cuff, rounded neck with Egyptian collar style decoration. In white, made with cellulosic fibres, rayon, viscose and plastic and string plaques.

To finalise, the party matching set that takes us to these galas of Gala. It is made up of a long-sleeved blouse with rounded neck matching a long dress of elasticated tulle with black cellulose sequins. It is the piece that Gala wore in the famous photo by Horst that welcomes us into the room.

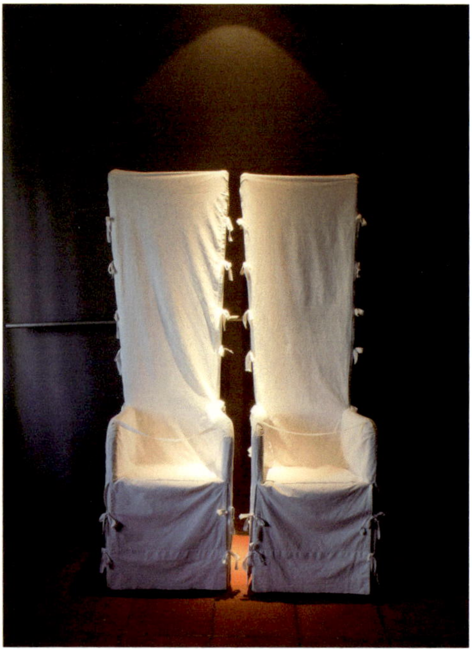

Lined chairs, with the characteristic bow of Dior

Rayon dress with Dalinian pattern

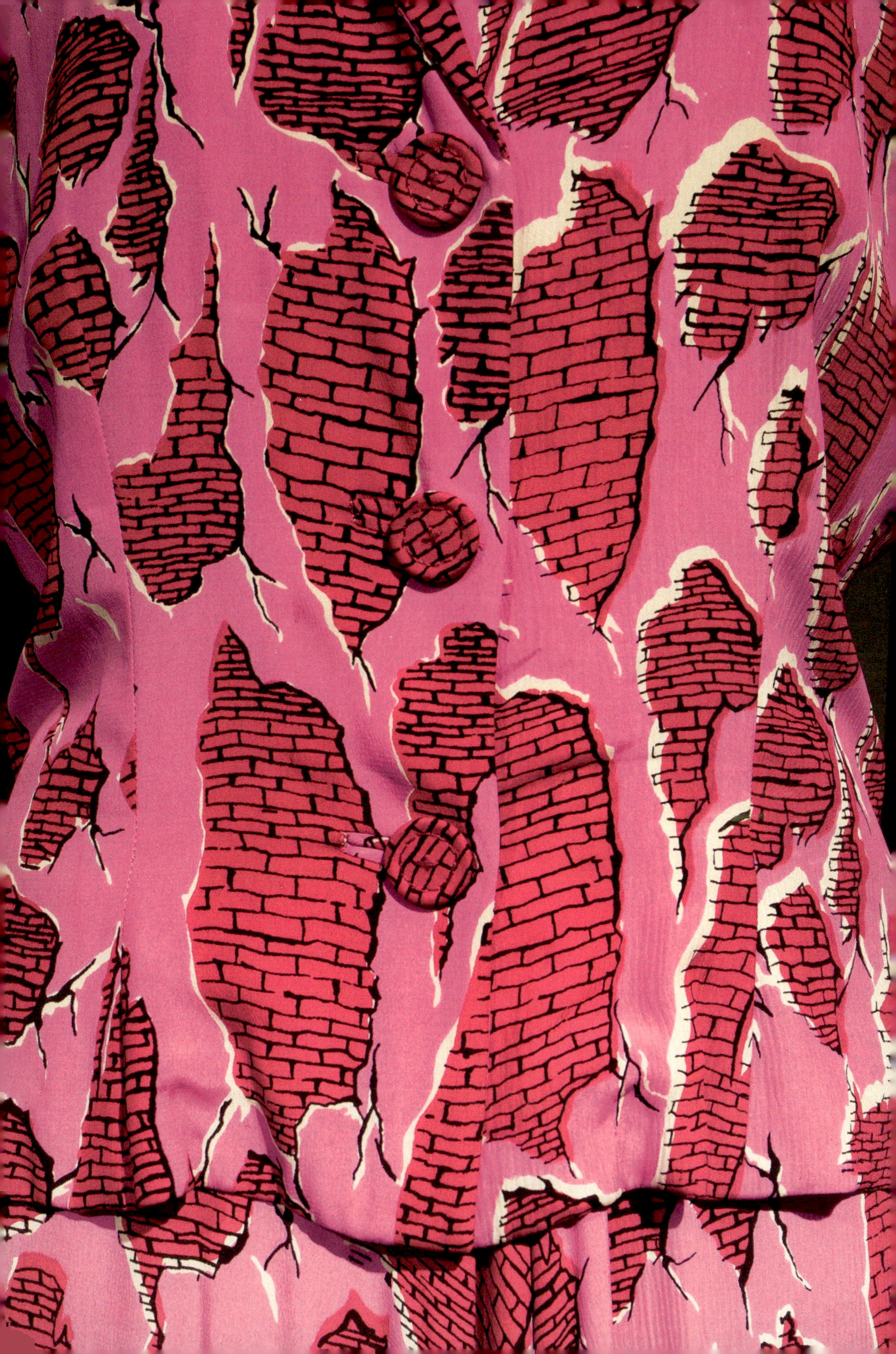

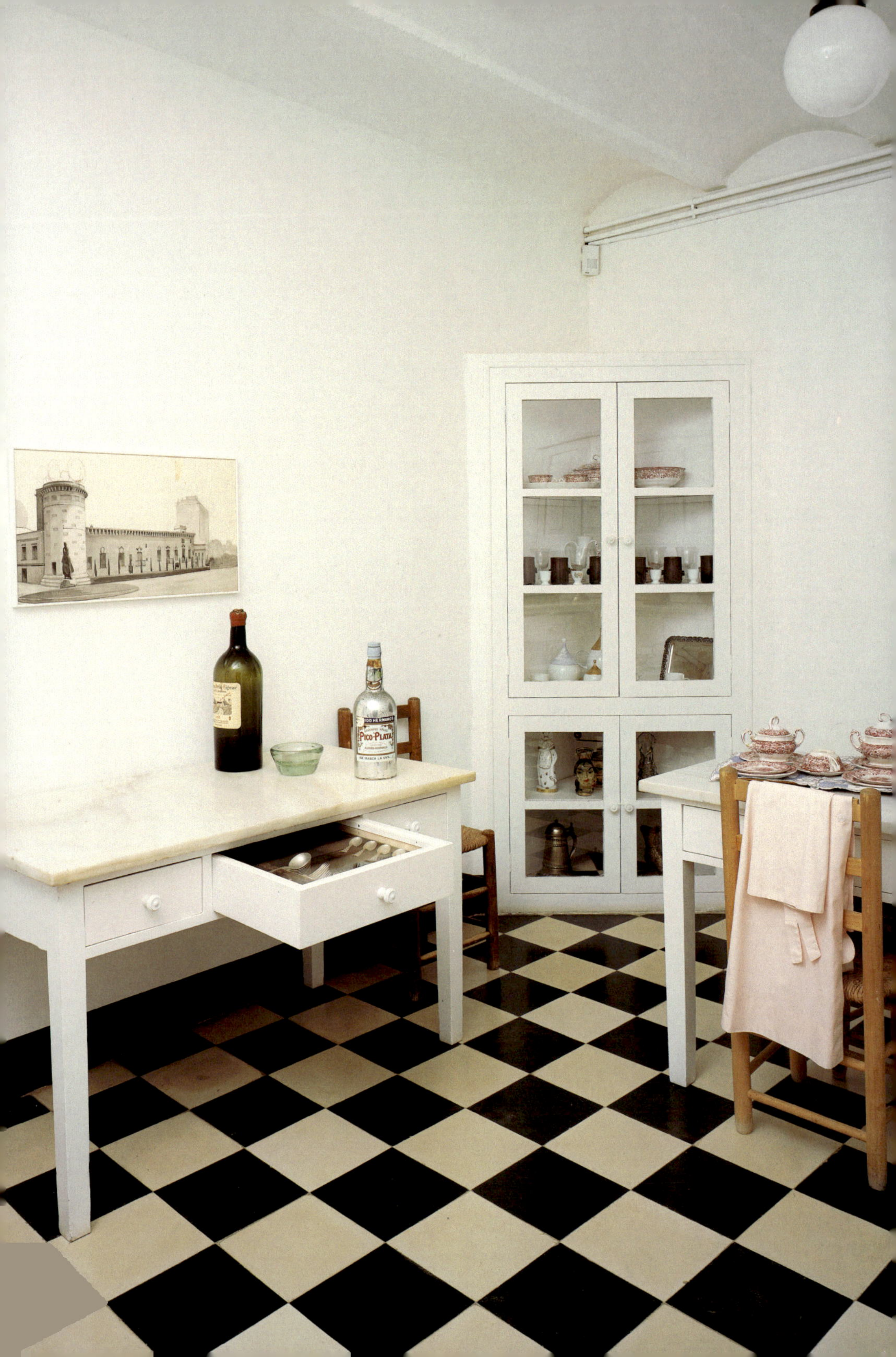
PICO-PLATA

THE OFFICE AREA

Once again on the first floor, we go the temporary exhibitions room, an old part of the kitchen, where the stove was, a part that Salvador Dalí had no involvement in, the reason why it has been able to be used for other purposes. Just beside it is the part corresponding to the office. The checkered floor, just how Dalí liked it, and the window, as in other parts of the castle, with its side benches, give this room, not used much by Gala and Dalí, a friendly and serious air, with practical and sensible furniture.

Some of the objects we find here are of more decorative use than practical and would deserve an outstanding place in the display of the guests' room. In the open drawers of the table is a silver cutlery set from the Tiffany's firm, a gift from Dalí to Gala where each piece of cutlery has Gala's name engraved. The series of bottles deserve a special mention, such as the brandy bottle that forms the head of a gypsy woman from the Nogueras Comas distilleries in Barcelona; the sherry bottle from the Const Terzakis distilleries in Greece in the form of Greek dancer or the white porcelain decorated with the form of a Valencian *falla*, a folkloric figure, that contained double curacao from the El Lorito de Benetuser distilleries in Valencia. It also features a curious bottle of cava of green glass with seven holes, beside two glasses with an optical effect that makes them seem full.

We also find porcelain coffee sets, such as that by Rosenthal, and some porcelain plates, this time from Limoges, with design by Salvador Dalí. In the corner cupboard, between the crockery, is a coffee grinder with a reproduction of *The Angelus* by Millet, which we will come across again in the dining room. The table, laid, shows a breakfast from a normal day of the lady of the castle, and on one of the chairs the apron worn by Dolors, the head of the castle's domestic service.

Before moving on to the dining room, we see one of the sketches for the decoration of the Torre Galatea of Figueres, which Dalí did while he was in Púbol. It is a technical drawing over which the painter sketched, using a felt tip pen, the silhouette of the eggs that crown the façade of the building, headquarters of the Gala-Salvador Dalí Foundation.

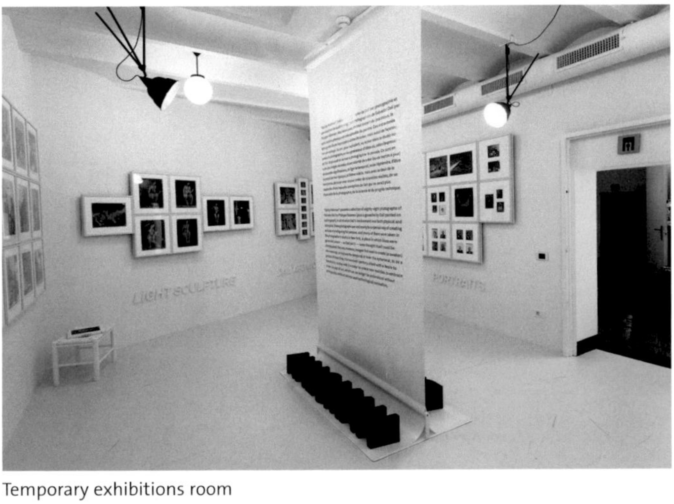

Temporary exhibitions room

The office

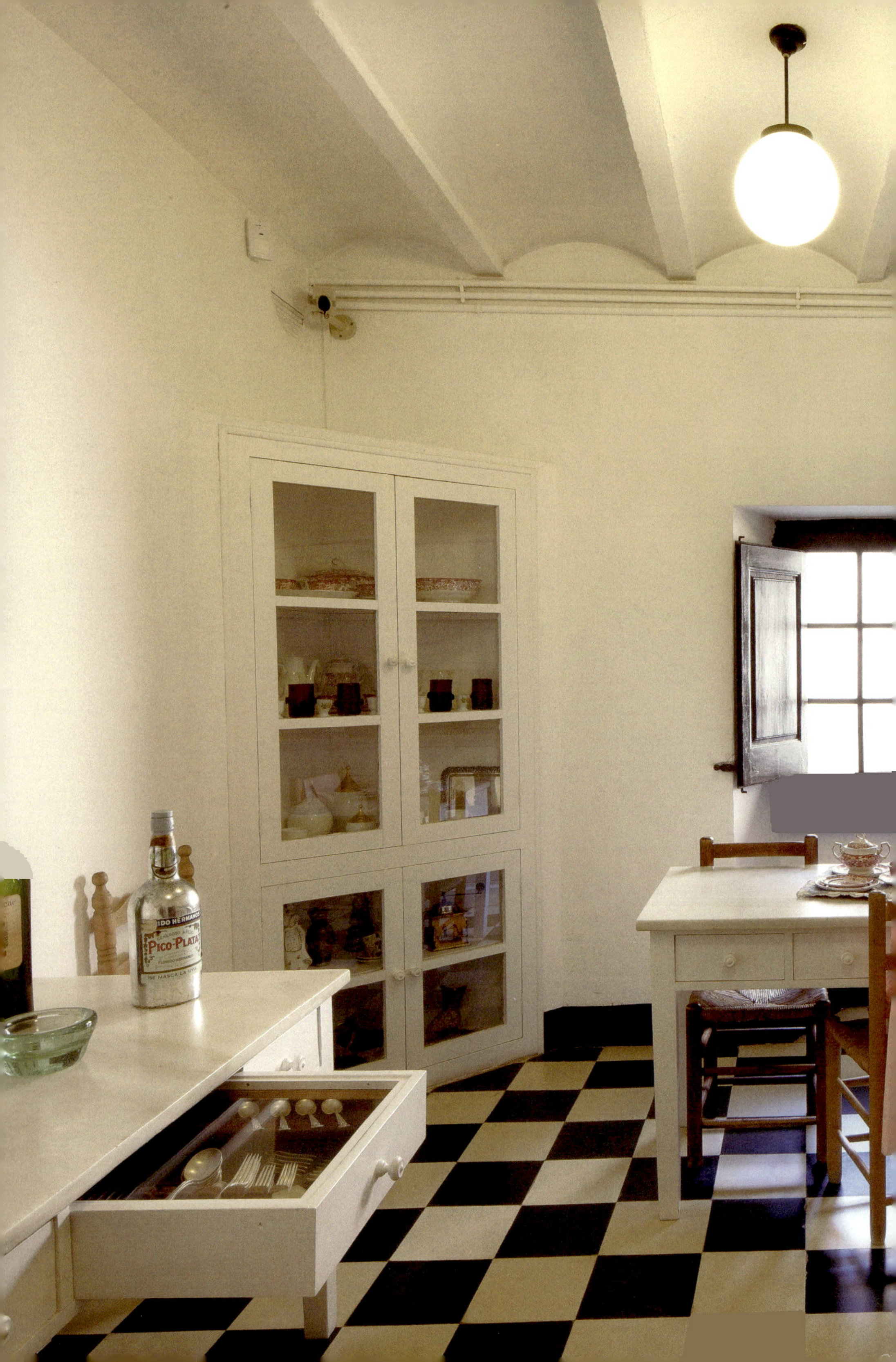
IDO HERMANOS
PICO-PLATA
SE MASCA LA UVA

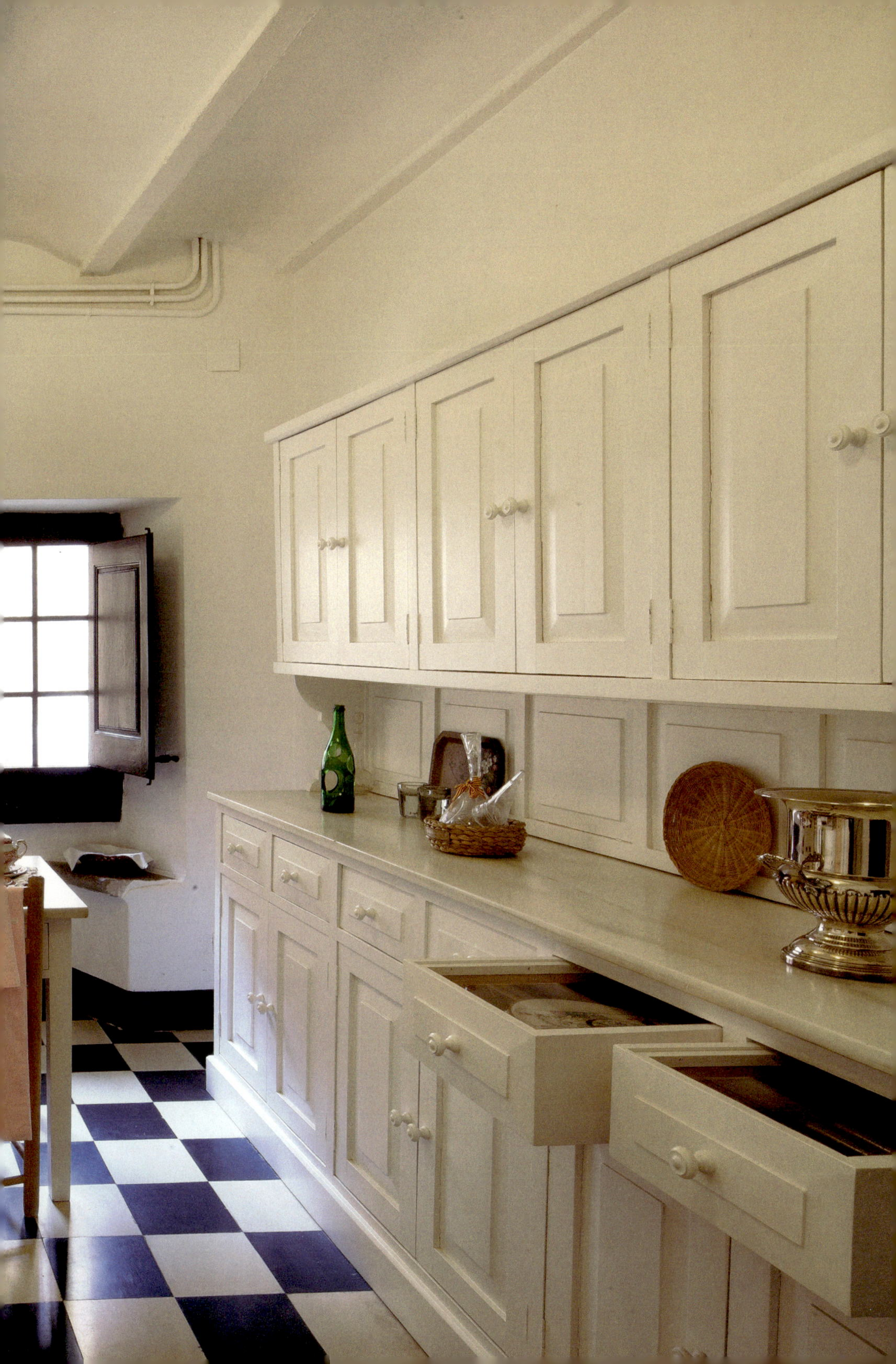

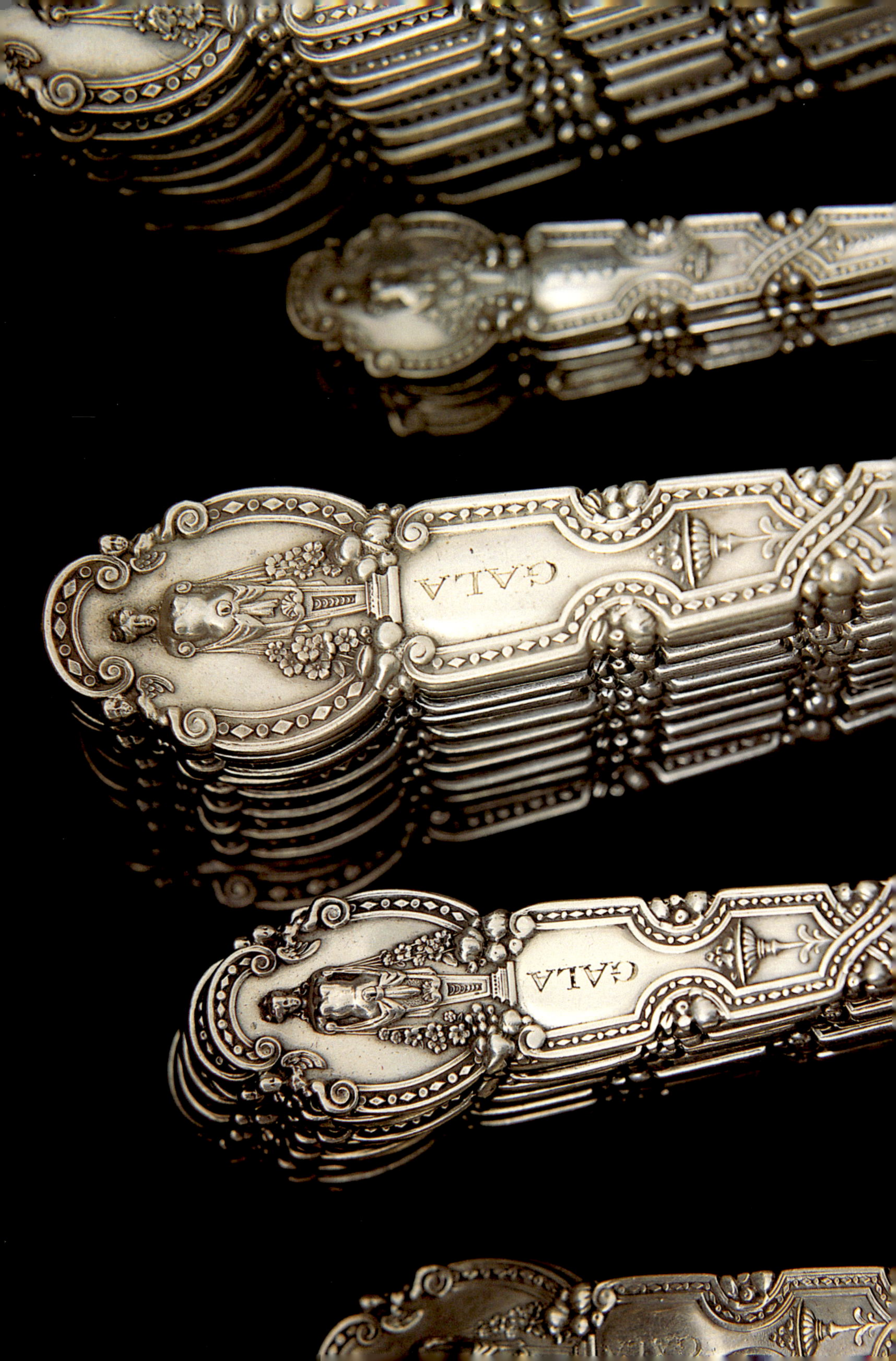
GALA
GALA

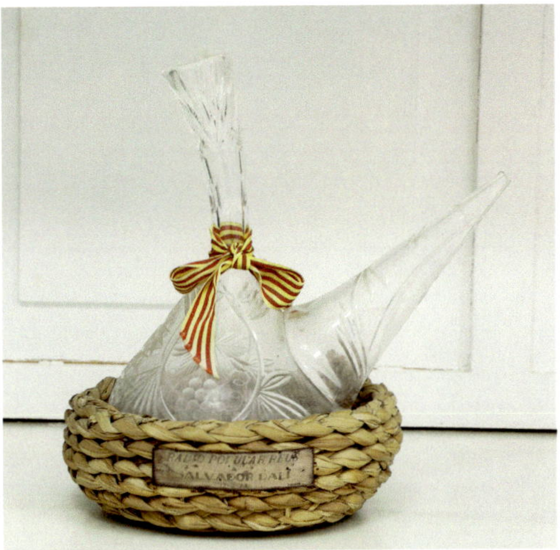

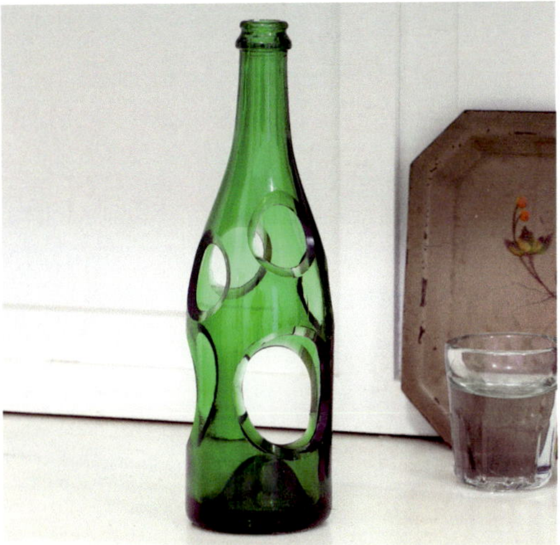

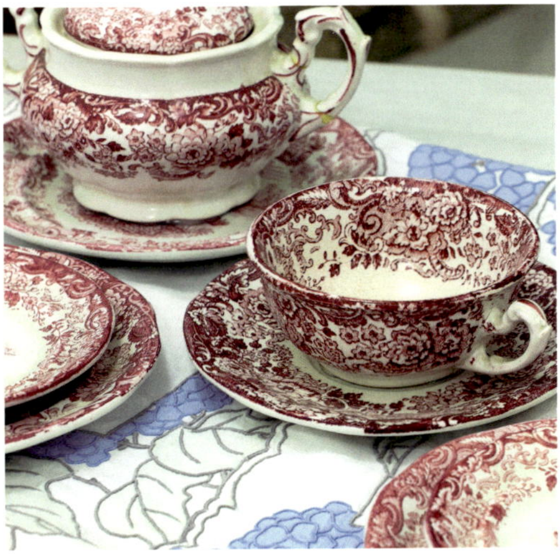

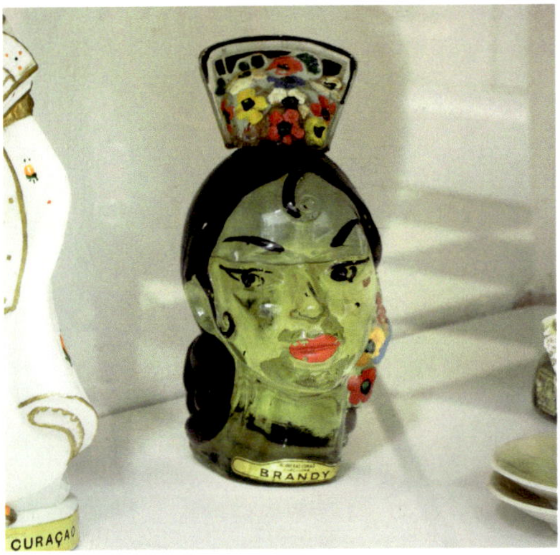

Details of the office

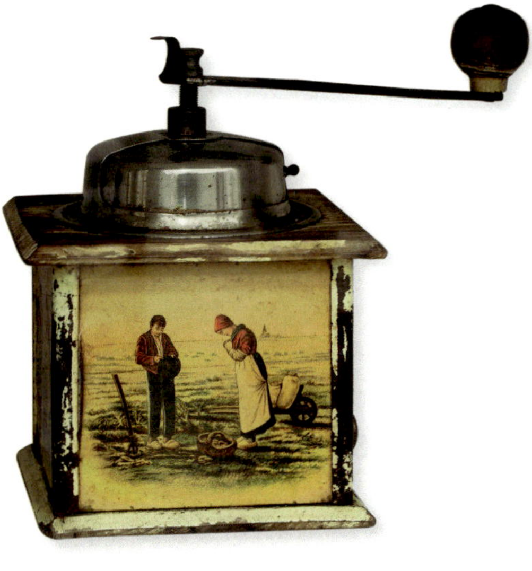

Silver cutlery from Tiffany's

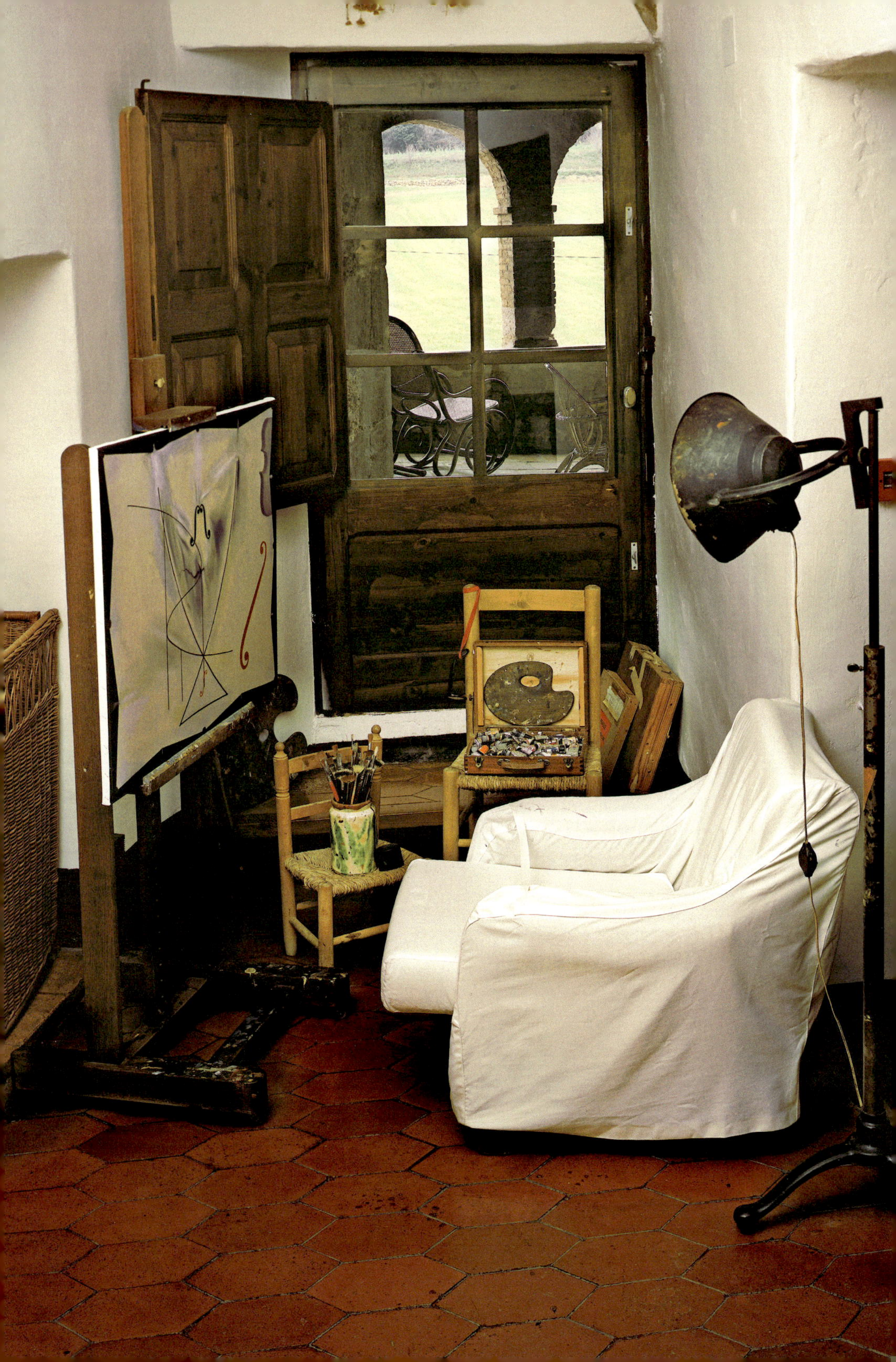

THE DINING ROOM AND LAST STUDIO OF THE ARTIST

We now go to what was the dining room, which, at one end, connects with the coat of arms room. At the end of the room is what was the artist's last studio, where he produced his final works.

The small display cabinet stands out, on the dining room wall, that we could consider as an extension of the display in the guests' room, but mainly dedicated to the best known work by Millet, *The Angelus*. We find an accumulation of porcelain tea sets, ordered by size, from large to small, like a set of Russian dolls. Also, with the image of the work by Millet, we discover some jars for keeping coffee, flour, sugar, pepper and spices.

The references to *The Angelus* by Millet are recurrent in the painter's work, which is why it should not surprise us to find this work represented in many ways, even on decorative objects such as those in this cupboard-display cabinet. As he himself explains in his autobiography, *The Secret Life of Salvador Dalí*, it is an image that pursued him from childhood, when he saw it in one of the corridors of his school, La Salle in Figueres, and which he contemplated in the darkness, precisely after the hour of the Angelus prayer, "This painting produced in me an obscure anguish, so poignant that the memory of those two motionless silhouettes pursued me for several years with the constant uneasiness provoked by their continual and ambiguous presence"[36].

[36] Dalí, *The Secret Life of Salvador Dalí, op. cit.*, p. 64

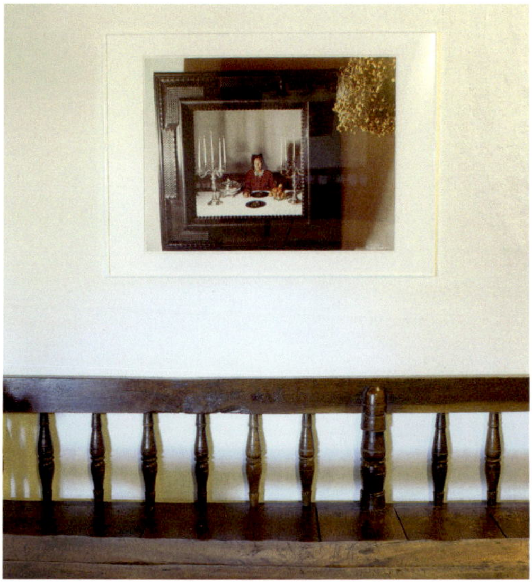

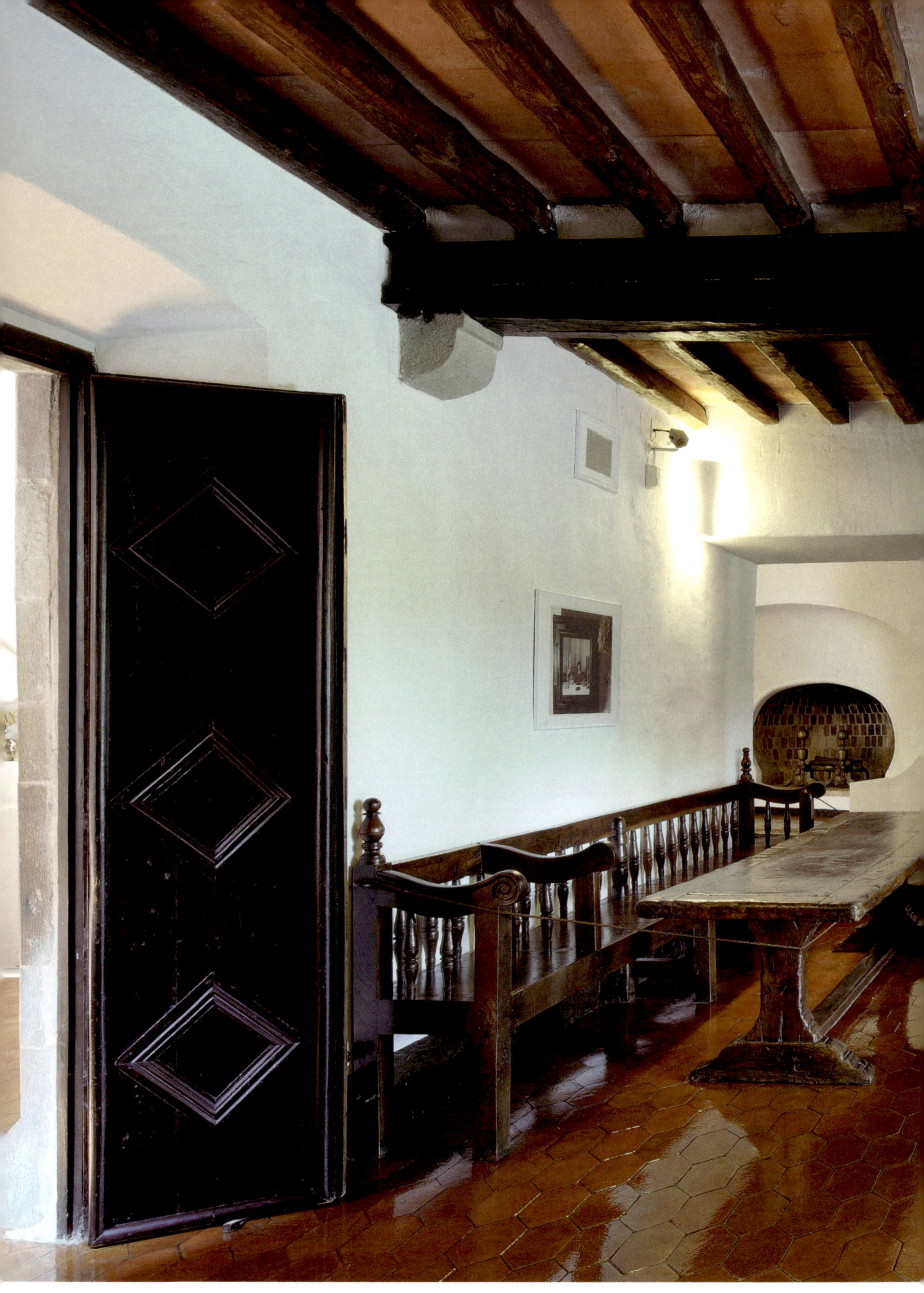

The dining room

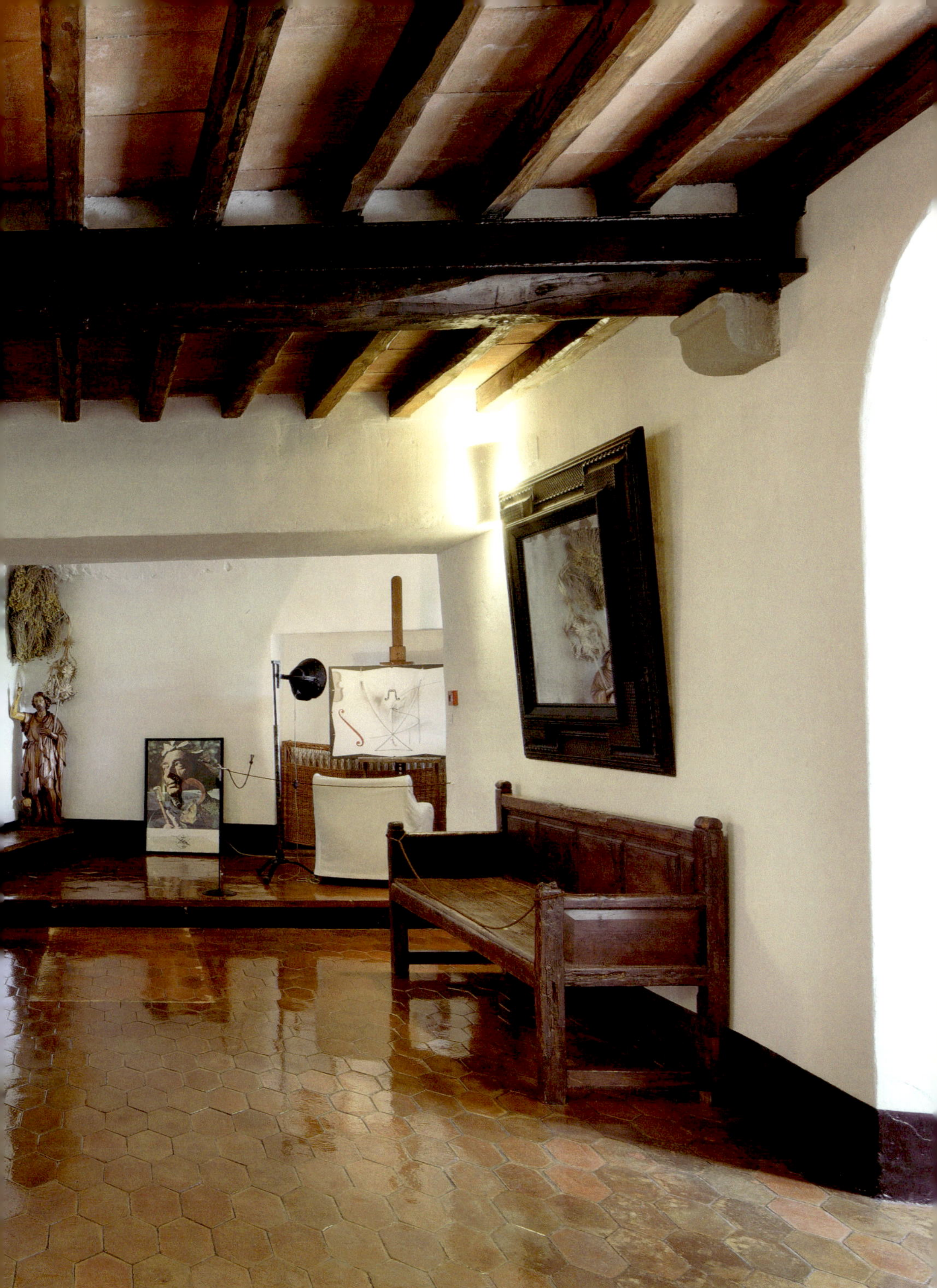

The other objects that accompany them are a small bust of a warrior, a doll with a 'Catalanised' dress, carved stones, more jars and an egg with an arrow passing through it. And, in the middle of all these objects, appear four works in miniature by Dalí that are particularly interesting. The most outstanding is *View of Púbol* from 1971 which represents the castle and church of Púbol in the middle of a landscape of trees, using the suggestive veins of the slate itself. The following dedication is inscribed: "to Gala of Puvol (sic). Dalí" (Oil on slate, 9 × 20.5 cm). Inserted in a shell of a spider crab, we find a polished agate over which Dalí painted the face of Gala in 1970. There is also a sculpture of Christ nailed to the cross in a very twisted position that recalls the *Christ Twisted* in the Dalí Theatre-Museum in Figueres and other figures made with the lost wax technique or from modelling silver paper.

Another piece that attracts our attention is an oval stone, *Christ Naked on the Cross*, rounded by the action of time and the sea, over which Dalí painted in oil the figure of Christ nailed to the cross, of 5 × 4.5 cm. Commenting on this work, Dalí said that "for the love of Gala, I can become a good Venetian painter". The work is from the late-50s, but later Dalí painted over it "For Gala 1974 (sic)". This type of dedication confirms that they were gifts that Dalí gave to Gala every time they met again or when he went to Púbol. Sometimes they were works he had just done, but sometimes they were paintings, or objects that, like this one, he already had in Portlligat, the shared home, and which Dalí wanted to give exclusively to Gala.

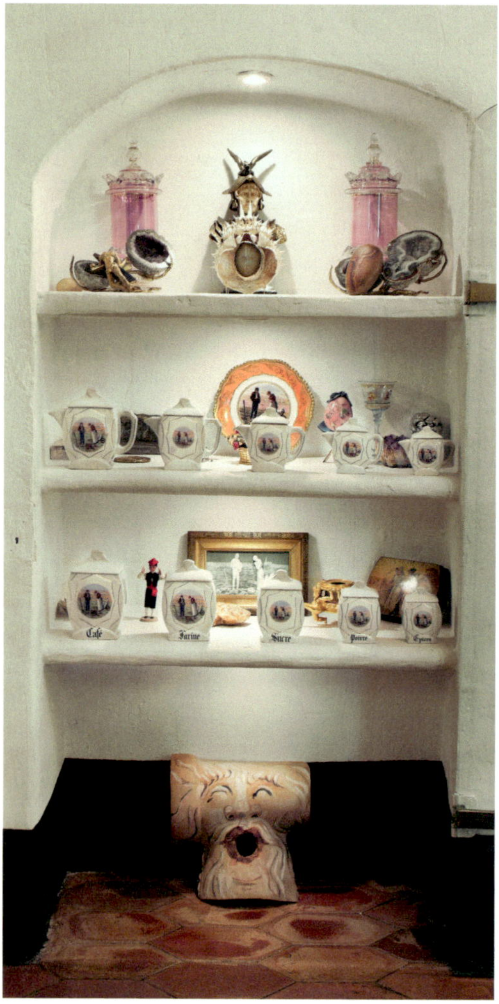

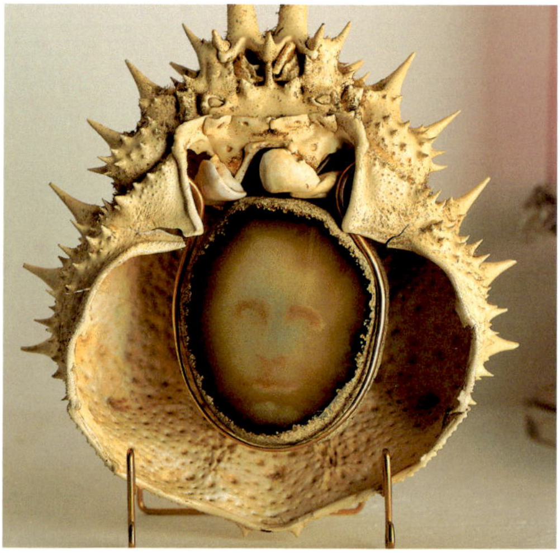

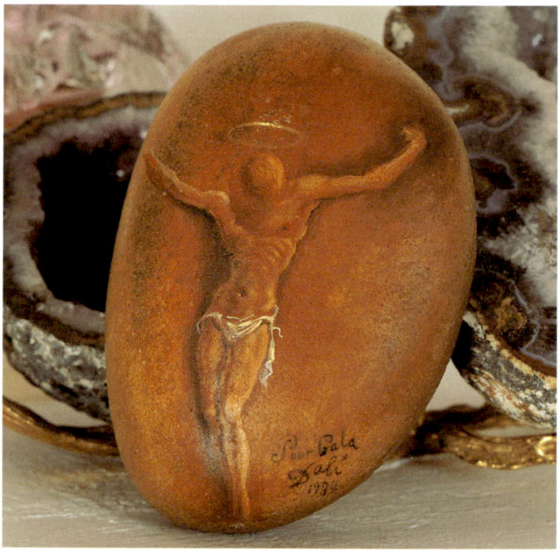

Dining room display cabinet | Polished agate with the face of Gala | *Christ Naked on the Cross*, 1950

At the foot of the cupboard we come to an object, conceived as a test for the base of the eggs that crown the Torre Galatea in Figueres, which for a while was used to cover the loudspeaker over the throne that was replaced by the coat of arms of the marquis. It is a corner piece roof tile, with a face painted on it. On the part that corresponds to the mouth there is a hole. The figure represented could be the *Tramuntana* wind. This object was to be used as the base of the eggs of the Torre Galatea although it was never undertaken.

There is also some reference to the Russian origin of Gala such as two pieces of costume jewellery, which imitate the jewellery of Fabergé and a piece attributed to Salvador Dalí. Another example of the nostalgia she felt for her birthplace is the photo of the last tsarina Alexandra Feodorovna Romanova, wife of the last tsar Nicholas II. She was born Alicia Hesse, a German princess and granddaughter of Queen Victoria of England.

In the dining room we find, as in the rest of the castle, diverse items of furniture from antique shops and auctions in the area. The furniture, like the rest of the house, was the essential minimum: an antique refectory table with two benches; a mirror with an ebony wooden frame decorated with Dutch-style geometric forms, from the 16th century, and much loved by Dalí for its connotations with Vermeer; a wooden chair from the Pyrenees with three columns on the back and a carved flower that dates from the 17th century; a kitchen cupboard from the Pyrenees with the doors divided into caissons decorated with a chestnut wooden x from the 17th century. Above this cupboard adorned with houseleeks is a lion's head that Dalí

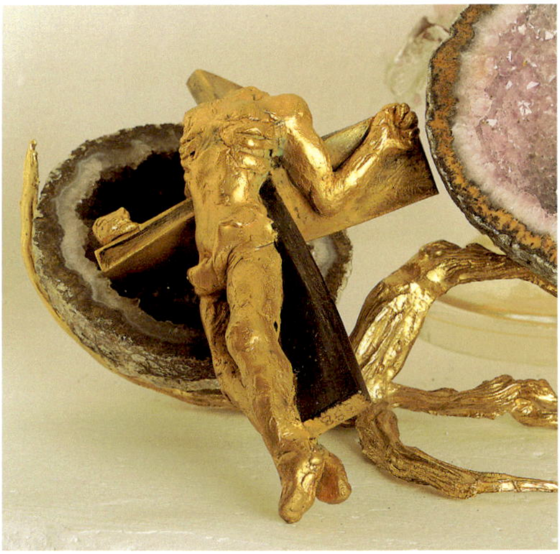

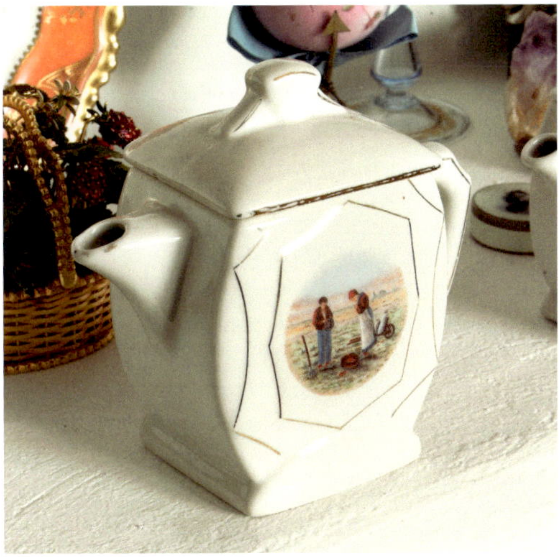

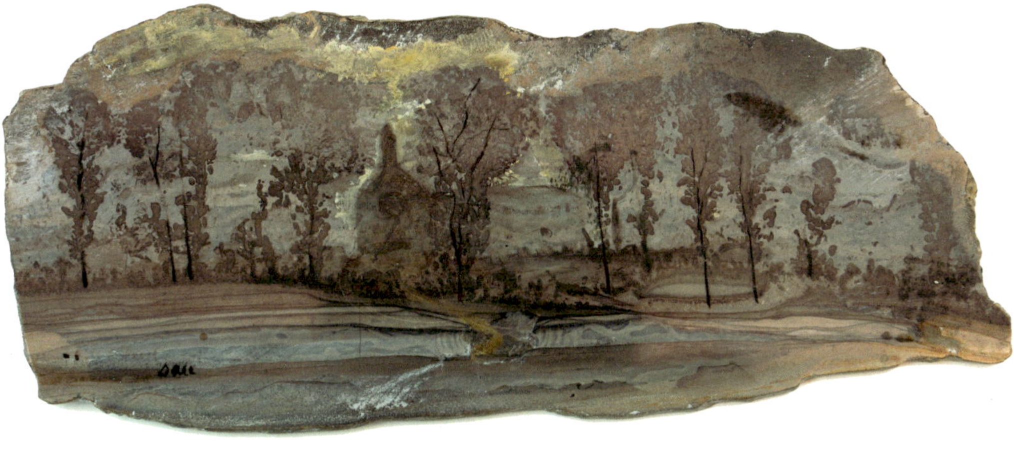

Christ nailed to the cross | Teapot with the *Angelus* by Millet | *View of Púbol*, 1971 (Oil on slate)

sometimes used to frighten Gala, as well as other more or less determinant objects such as a salakot, used by Dalí himself when he went out into the garden to sunbathe in both Portlligat and Púbol.

In this room we find the wooden bench where in 1982 the filmmaker Luis Revenga shot a long interview that later appeared as the final sequences of an unissued film, *Enigma Dalí*, in which Dalí wanted to repeatedly represent different intonations of the old popular Catalan song *La filla del marxant*. Dalí emphatically increased its tone until tiredness made him fall. In the image of the film, a yellow shadow passes before the camera that was Antoni Pitxot, who stops Dalí from hitting the floor. The whole sequence was to take to Mexico the communication from Dalí to Luis Buñuel at the hand of Javier Solana, along with a very precise pilot script where Dalí proposed to Buñuel the idea of making new film. Buñuel answered him from Mexico that his time had already passed by. The short script was set in the small entrance stairway to the metro of an imaginary city with a sole leading player, lame, "the little devil", who repeatedly intoned the song while time and the weather passed by.

At the end, climbing a small step, we enter what was the old oratory of the castle, which Dalí wanted to join with the dining room and turned into an area for the fireplace. The former barons of Púbol had the right to hear mass through a grille, a privilege that the Church conceded to some nobles so they could follow the religious rituals. On buying the castle Dalí thought that they could do without the step. Curiously, the Torre Galatea, the old Casa Gorgot, also had a door that gave the privilege to the lords to go directly to the boxes of the theatre, and is currently what connects the two sections.

This area of the dining room is where the easel is conserved that shows where Dalí did his final works. In fact it shows a copy of what is considered the last oil painting he produced, *Untitled. Swallow's Tail and Cellos (Catastrophe Series)*, 1983. Dalí was used to painting on a seat that had a white cover, in which there still remain inevitable stigmas in the form of stains from the last activities of the painter. You can see his glasses, the last brushes he used, a stick, and the sofa which, as in Portlligat, in his later years, he used to paint while seated and thus dedicate more time to painting. We can also see a poster with the face of Dalí, crowned, and that of Gala, the photo being by Jean Clemmer.

In these later works, there are very personal references such as his concern with catastrophe theories of the French mathematician René Thom and the homages to Velázquez and Michelangelo, grand masters who he had always admired. His thoughts at the time are well explained in his declaration: "What I do now is no longer the imagination at the service of fancy and dreams, or automatism; now I paint meaningful things taken directly from my own experience, of my illness or from my most present memories". For some months his activity was still very prolific and he was sometimes accompanied by Isidor Bea, a former stage designer and very efficient in his work of preparing canvases, the man who from the mid-50s helped him in the studio. In April 1983, shortly after having opened the large anthological exhibition in Madrid, he finally stopped painting.

The chimney and plastered wooden carving, with houseleeks

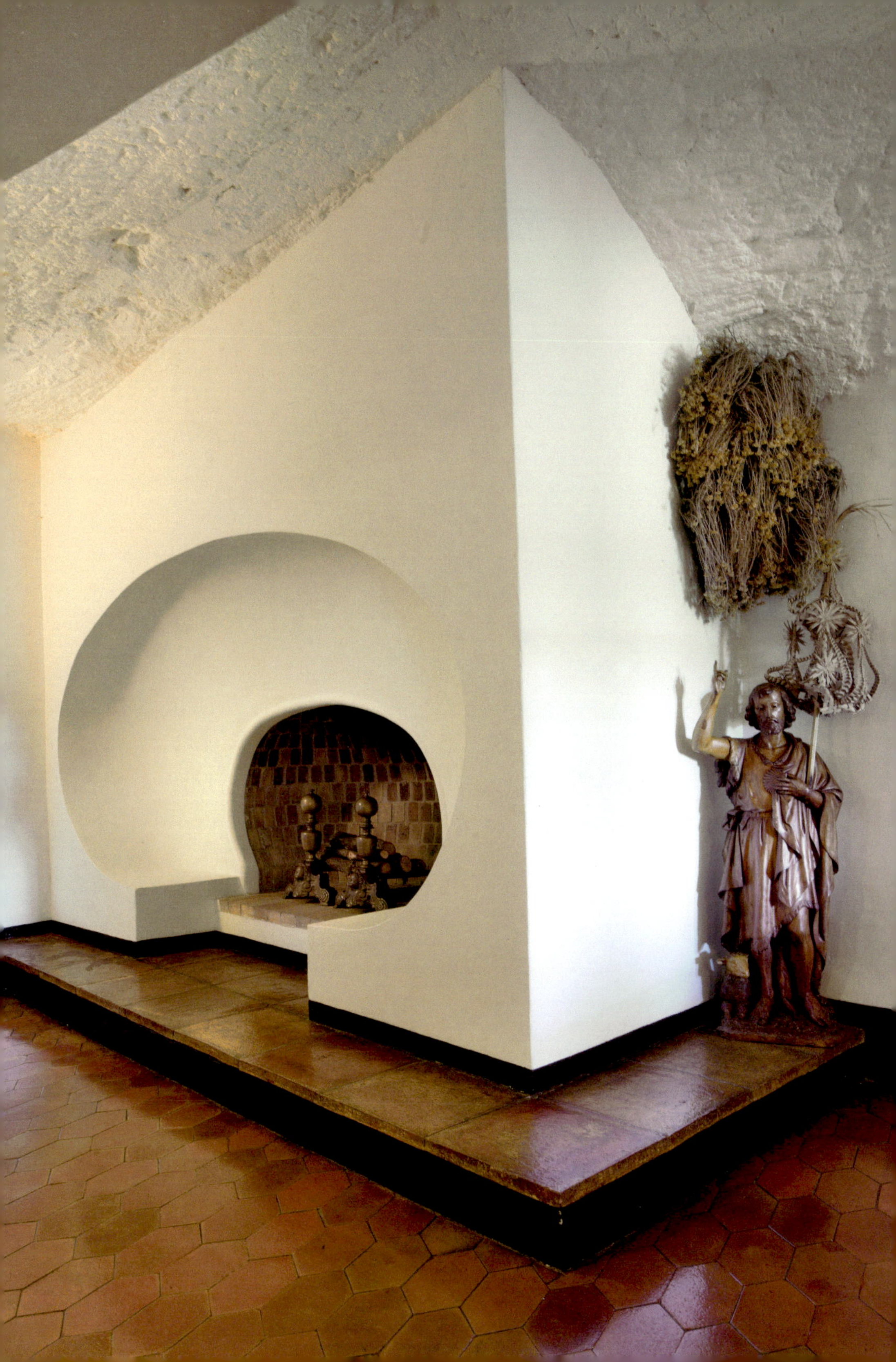

In this period Dalí painted almost without light, because he said it bothered him and this room has little. He had the easel placed between the fireplace and a now-covered door, which previously had led to the church. The setting of this part of the dining room, the wall of which joins the church, has a religious piece, the stuccoed and painted wooden carving of Saint John the Baptist with his finger raised, with his other hand holding a shell that alludes to baptism. At his feet there is a lamb.

The fireplace has a lower opening in the form of a double curve, in accordance with a drawing by Dalí and the outline he made directly on the wall. His idea, repeatedly proclaimed, was that the curve corresponds to what a drop of water has before breaking. "It is the principle of the drop of water that holds together due to a physical law of surface tension but ends up becoming a cosmic act", he repeated breathlessly. Two 18th-century bronze firedogs accompany it decorated with a bas-relief that forms a face.

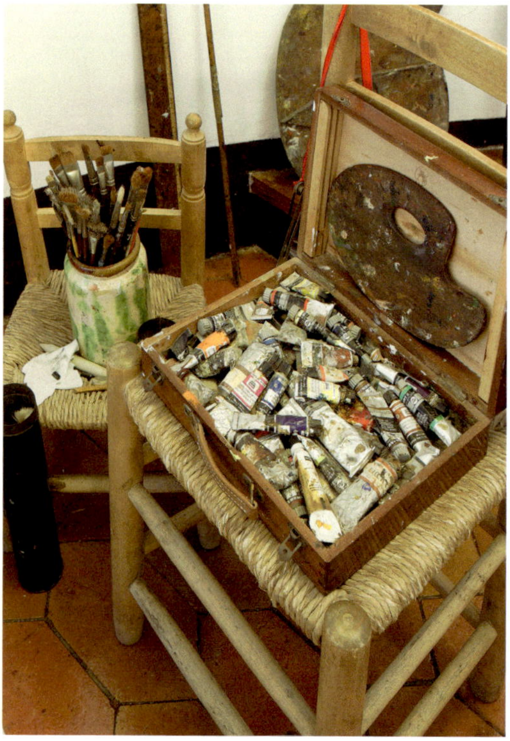

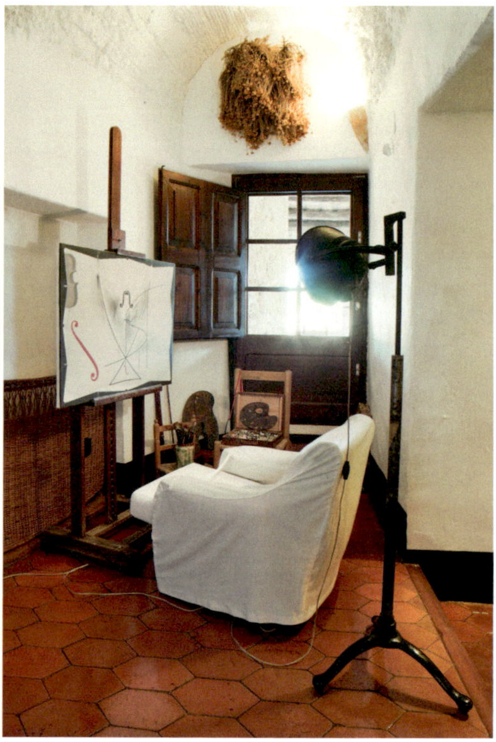

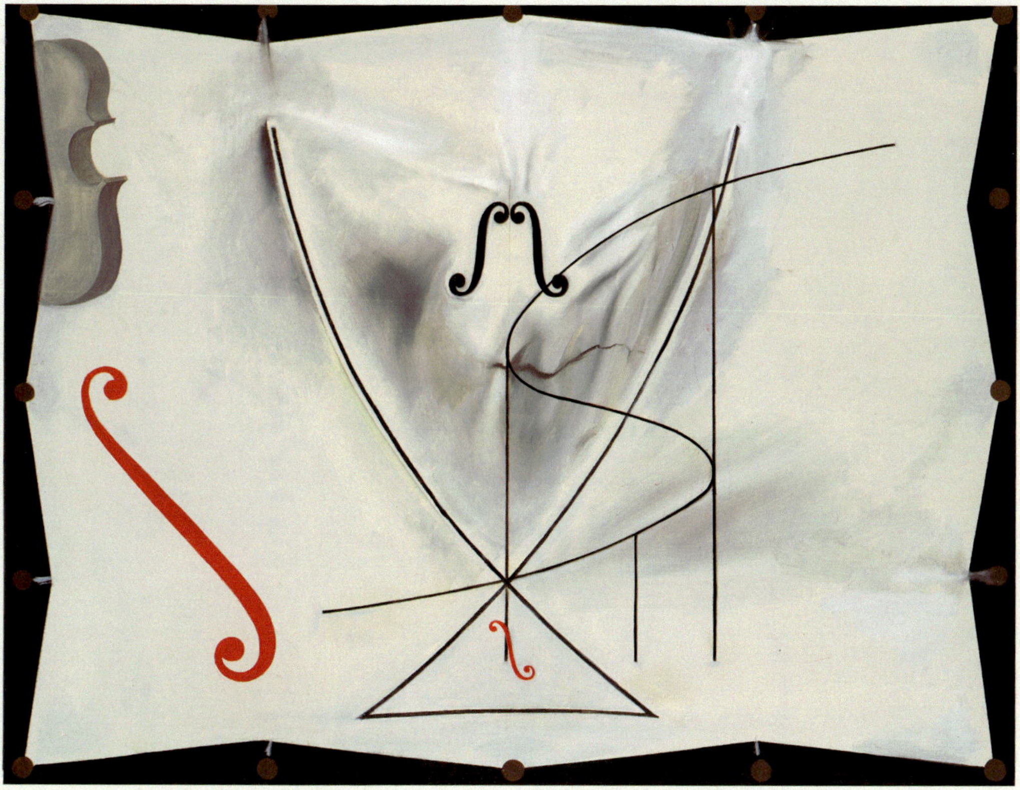

UNTITLED. SWALLOW'S TAIL AND CELLOS
(CATASTROPHES SERIES), 1983. Oil on canvas (73.20 × 92.20 cm)
Dalí Theatre-Museum in Figueres Optical Illusions Room

This is the last oil painting that Dalí painted. He did it in the castle of Púbol and in this applied knowledge expressed by the mathematician René Thom in his book *Paraboles et catastrophes*. Dalí uses the form of the cello, to which he attributes symbolic functions of sentiment rather than any musical presence. In this last Dalinian period, the cello is the main subject matter, always with a painful mission; in other canvases it appears attacked by bedside tables. It is rather like a wounded ego and, in this case, it participates in the representation of a swallow's tail, the most determinant element, due to its poetic content, of all the descriptions and graphic art that he had produced in the catastrophe theory. He therefore brings these two coinciding points together: pain and beauty.

THE GALLERY

From the dining room we can go out onto a large gallery with magnificent views over the garden and the surrounding fields. There are remains of the old fortification that recall bygone times. Gala intended to buy the field on the other side of the street to plan a Venetian-style bridge that would join it to her terrace. In a corner of the terrace, we see the plaster figure of a warrior on a pedestal that reproduces an imaginary coat of arms. One part of this gallery, to the left, which from the outside can be distinguished by some

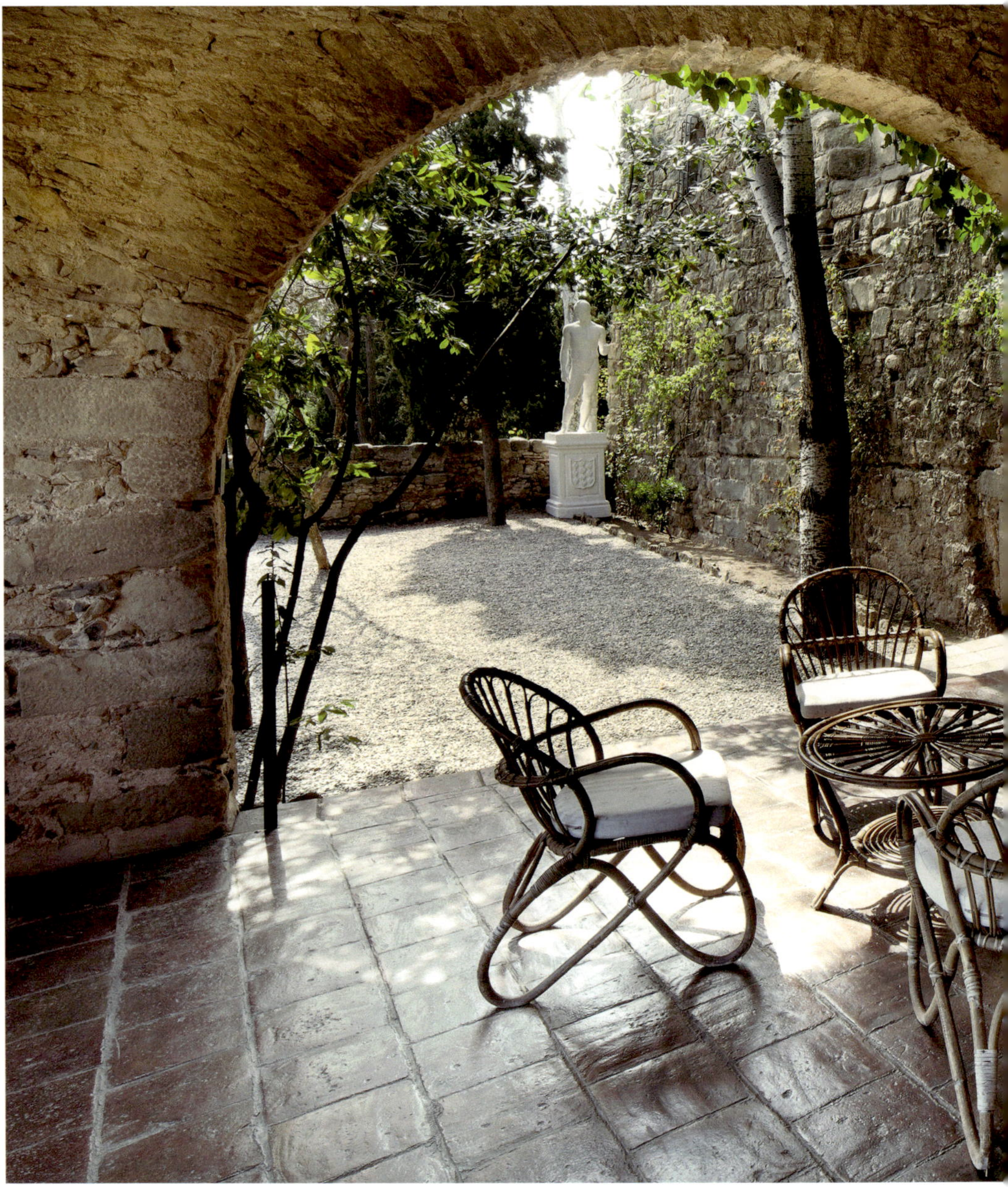

porches, is covered. It was an ideal spot for Gala to rest in summer on some *chaises longues* that can still be seen. There is also a rocking chair and pouf that must have come from Portlligat (like those that there were in the swimming pool area). In the lower part is the sacristy of the church, which shows the overlapping that there had been between the area of the nobility and that of the clerics with the neighbouring temple. A new stairway to enable us to visit it leads us to the exit.

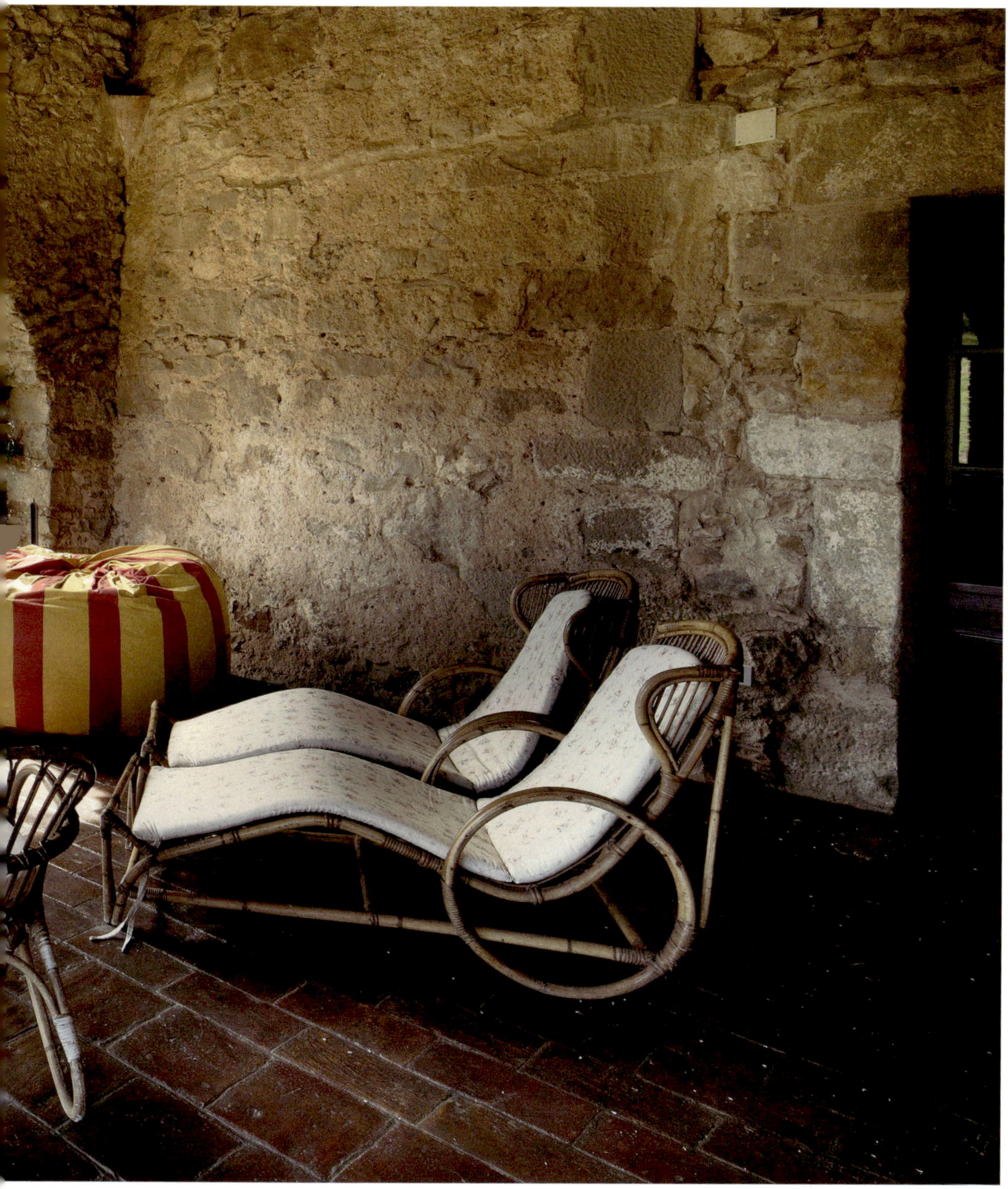

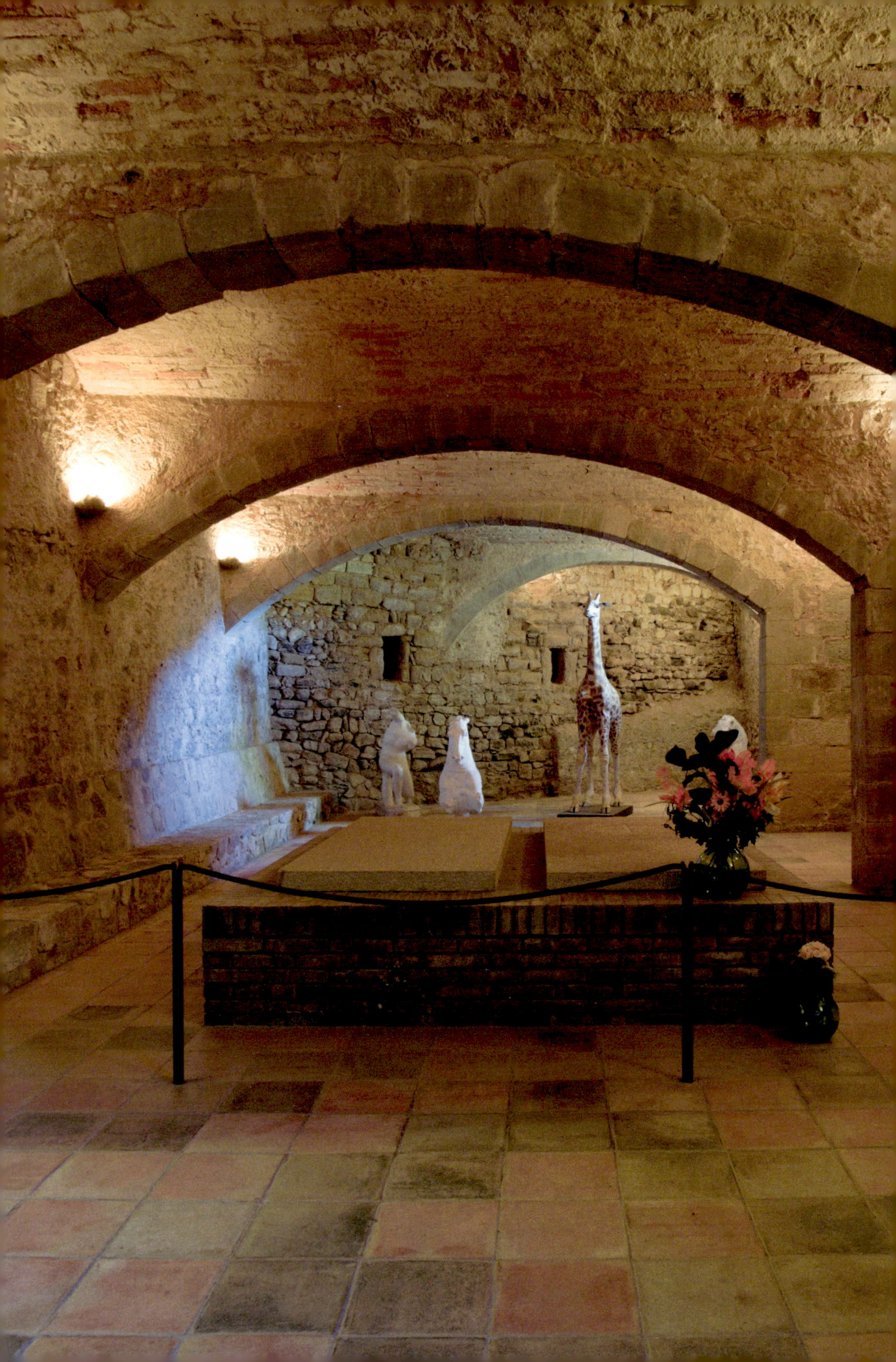

THE CRYPT

On being close to the crypt area, we can speak structurally of two differentiated spaces within the same part: the 15th-century castle and the basement converted into a tomb that becomes yet another room.

Let's go towards the garden going through the porch, the ceiling of which is a starry sky painted by Gala to amuse herself. Beforehand, however, we come to the door that leads to the basement. This basement was known as the 'tithe': this was because of the ten per cent tax or tithe imposed on the produce from the land to ensure the maintenance of the clerics and the religious buildings. Between the 13th and 16th centuries, in Catalonia, some serfs of the glebe paid the feudal lords. In the castle of Púbol, the space reserved for paying taxes was this basement, converted, on Gala's death, into a crypt.

Before reaching this space, however, we have crossed a small hall or antechamber. The first thing that attracts our attention is the three cardboard lions' heads, which watch us from the opposite wall. On the rights hangs a poster that shows the model of a chair created by Charles Rennie Mackintosh in 1902. This poster, which was given to Dalí, on transparent acetate paper, was designed in the early 70s by the architect Pep Bonet for the Boccaccio Diseño company. It is the reproduction in elevation, and life size, of the famous Modernist chair initially designed for a restaurant in Glasgow. It must have served as inspiration to Dalí to create the high-backed chairs, of a much more popular type.

From the drawings that are preserved [37], we can deduce that Dalí had planned this space as a reception room with a stairway that ended with a banister of Modernist ornaments. The projects, however, were not completed since it seems that for Gala, this floor of the castle was not a priority and did not form part of the first restoration stage. It was confined to removing the barrels, widening the stairway and placing some wall benches and some statues. He also wanted the floor to form a type of chessboard, with black and white squares, in homage to Marcel Duchamp. This project was entrusted to the constructor Emili

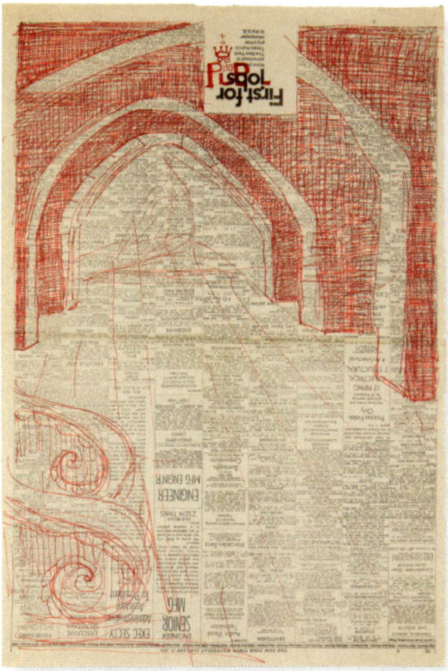

[37] More than 3,000 drawings by the painter are conserved in the Gala-Salvador Dalí Foundation. Among them feature some sketches for different aspects of the castle, both architectural and decorative. Dalí once again shows his interest in the total work. The details end up giving meaning to the whole, a meaning that the visitor will round off.

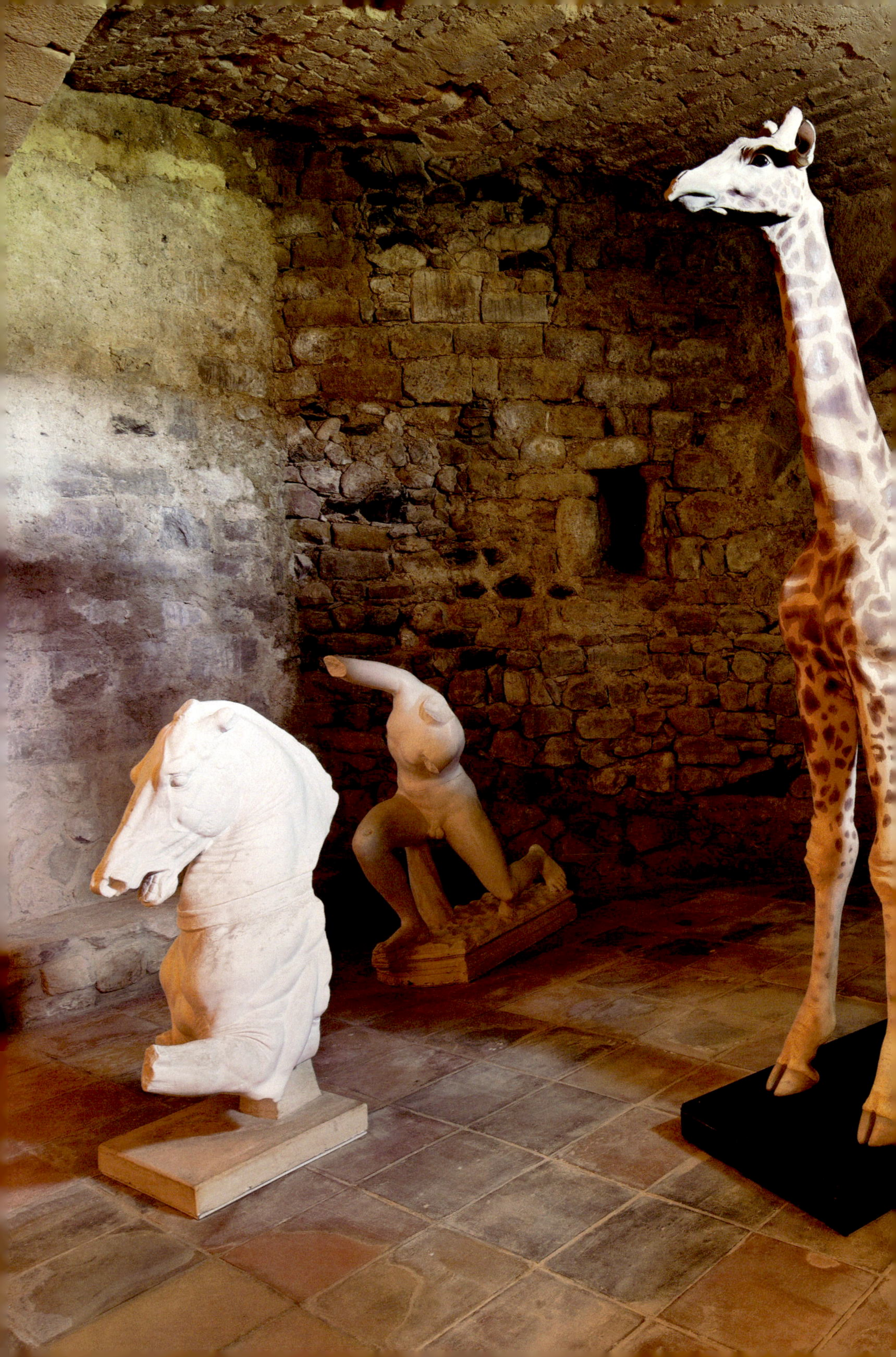

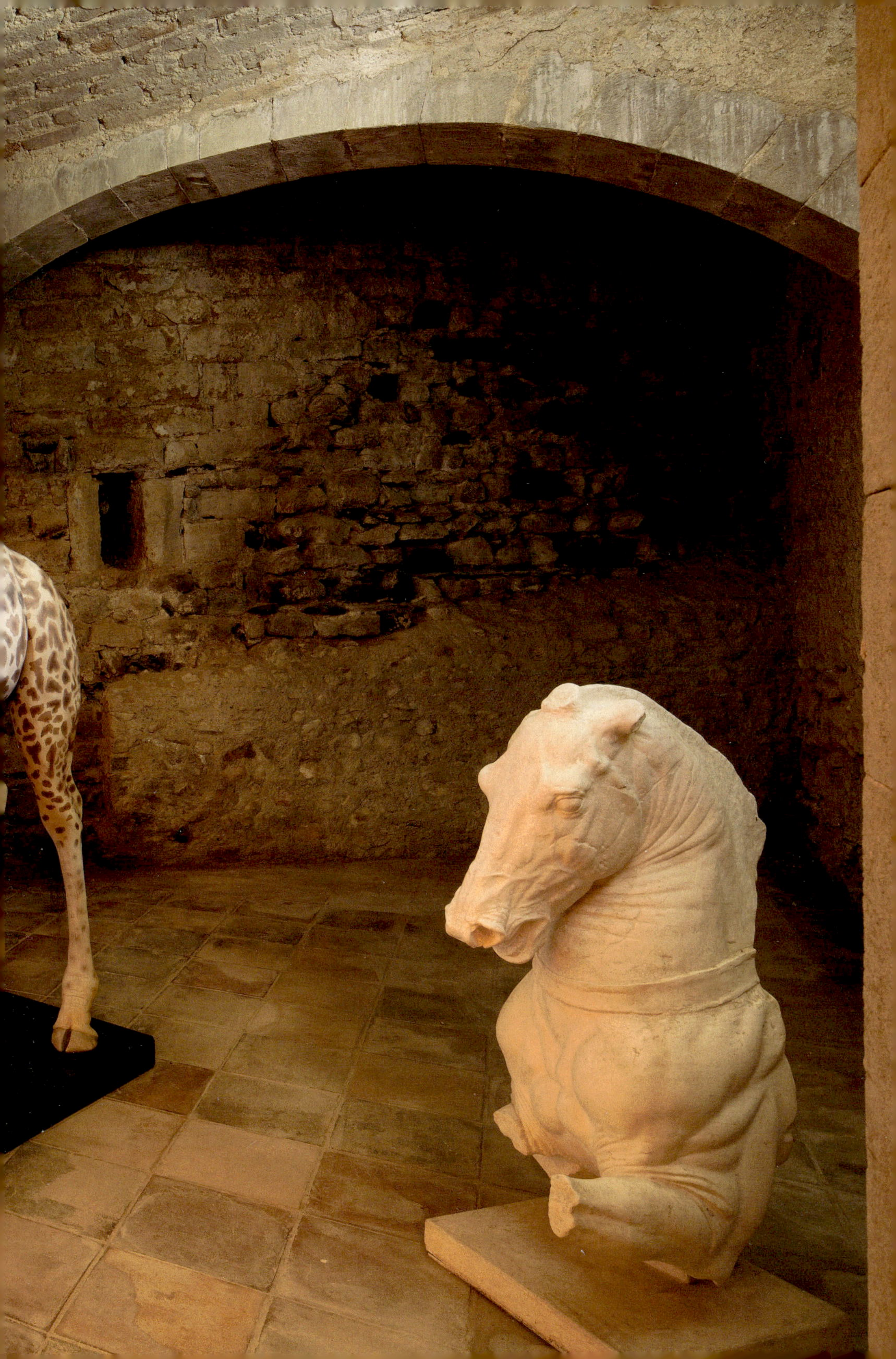

Puignau, who looked for some special tiles; however, when he got them, he realised that the black ones were too discoloured. To solve the problem, he plated some tiles with a natural colour to darken them. Over time they became discoloured again and the chessboard remained as just a project. In any case we should highlight the technical part: the floor was raised to avoid water filtrations, since in Púbol there are many springs.

During the first years of Gala living in the castle, she was asked if she could open the basement to the people of the village to hold the summer festival in case the rain stopped them from holding the ball in the square. She did not only allow it but even made an economic contribution to the festival. On another occasion Gala also donated a batch of thirteen engravings to the La Pera local council, which are on show in the council offices.

Dalí, then, thought of building a funerary monument in this space known as the "tomb of the Carmelites" like the one that exists in the cathedral of Nantes, made at the behest of the Queen of France, Anne of Brittany, to guard the mortal remains of her parents. But when the fire occurred, the project became forgotten.

Towards the end of May 1982, when Gala was already ill in Portlligat, it was decided to build a crypt in the space corresponding to the basement to bury her in. The commission was given directly by Dalí to the mayor of La Pera, Benjamí Artigas, the day he came to the village with the priest, to administer the last rites to Gala. It was the surveyor of La Pera who made some plans for the crypt, with a single interior space, but planned for two people and with two tombstones above. Dalí gave his approval without showing much interest since he was very upset by Gala's condition. The works were undertaken speedily and discretely. Gala died in Portlligat, but was embalmed and buried in Púbol (beneath the tombstone that now remains, seen from the entrance, on the right).

At Gala's funeral, which took place at six in the afternoon on the 11 of June 1982, only a dozen people attended, Dalí's closest collaborators. The painter stayed upstairs accompanied by Antoni Pitxot, and only

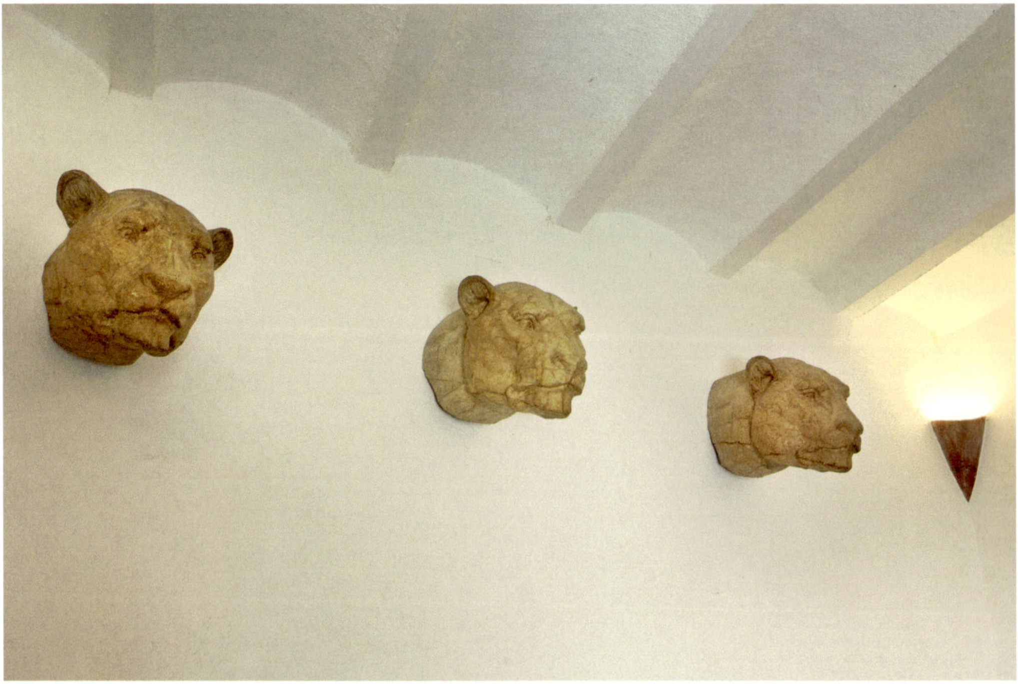

Cardboard lions' heads, in the entrance to the Crypt

when everyone had gone, went down to the crypt with him, and spent a while crying in silence before the tomb of his partner and muse. He never went down there again, except one rainy day, making use of a distraction on part of the nurses. Dalí kneeled for a few moments before the tomb, shivering with cold, in a great state of excitement.

There is an expressly theatrical touch in the space that wants to avoid as much as possible the mortuary elements. Dalí planned the basement as the space where Gala rests, the chamber where a series of characters protect her and keep her company: a giraffe, some classical horses and a kneeling horseman, situated in the last fascia of arcades, where the light of the sunset enters, in a way that a ray of sunlight illuminates the three figures. We should also mention the presence of the vase of B.D. Edicions, inspired by a decorative vase by Lamberto Escaler, always with houseleeks, just as Gala wanted.

Despite the fact that Dalí's condition was worsened due to the lack of enthusiasm he had to move or eat, Dalí did not talk about death. "Geniuses never die", he told a journalist when he was by then settled in the Torre Galatea in Figueres. The search for immortality was an obsession in his life. It is true that in 1985 he still told his closest friends that he wanted to be buried in "with my face covered" and no flowers. But he never spoke of the matter again, until the end of 1988, when he was admitted to the Quirón clinic in Barcelona, and now realising his death was close at hand, he asked to see the mayor of Figueres, Marià Lorca. He informed him that he wanted to be buried in the Theatre-Museum, right beneath the dome.

Many people were surprised by this revelation, which broke with the idea of the two bodies together, buried in Púbol hand in hand beneath the ground and, once again, he broke with conventions. However, the root of this went back to 1968, when Gala and Dalí promised each other the castle and the Theatre-Museum as gifts, and ended with the conversion of the two settings into their pantheons: Gala, in the basement of Púbol, and Dalí, beneath the stage of the old theatre of his birthplace, his last great work, on a vertical line that runs through the centre of the dome and rises heavenwards. Two symbolic constructions, with unity of meaning, at the service of art and its creators[38].

[38] Pitxot, Playà, *Gala Dalí's Castle: The Road to Púbol*, *op. cit.*, p. 52.

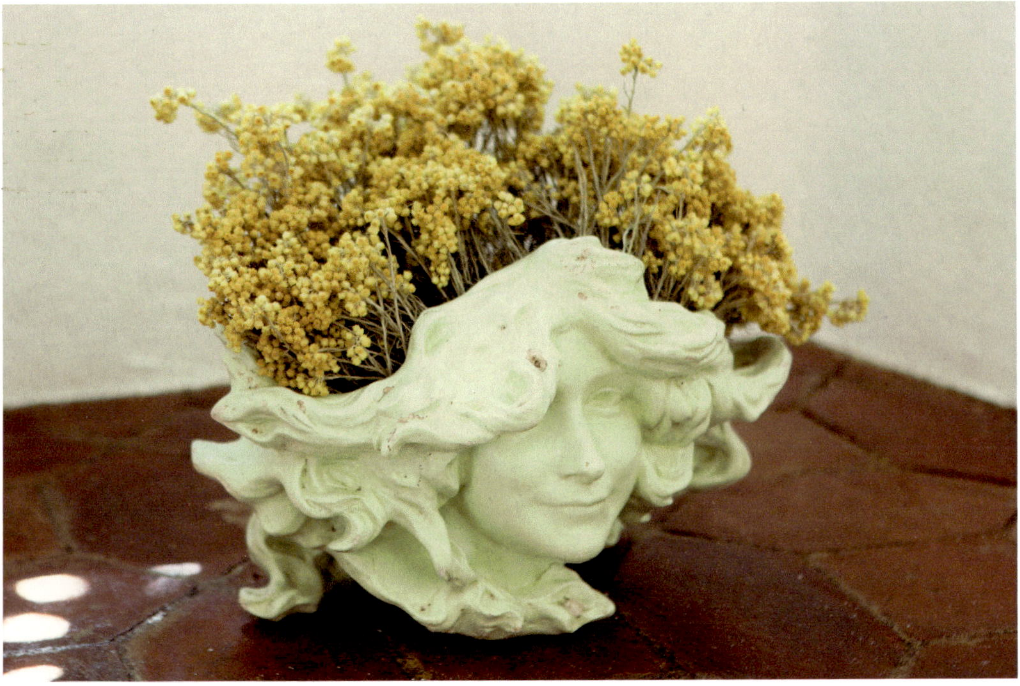

Vase by B.D. Edicions —inspired by Lamberto Escaler— with houseleeks

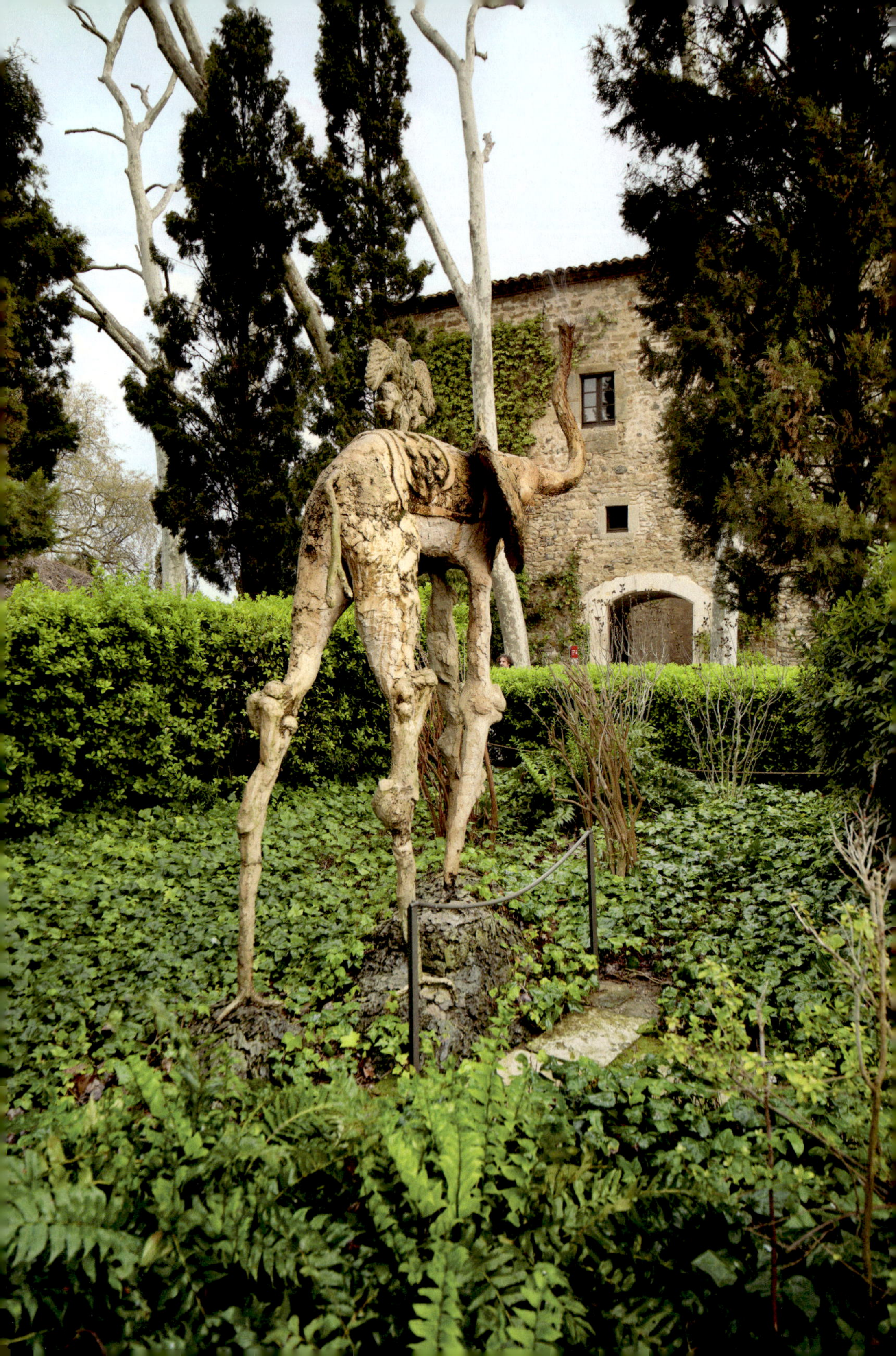

THE GARDEN

We now go through the imposing entrance of the south façade of the building, from 1798, and we come to a small avenue of plane trees that starts on the eastern wall of the garden, by which Gala arrived at the castle with the Cadillac or orange Datsun, which are in the garage.

We should remember that Dalí referred to the garden in his work, even alluding to the widespread idea that the Empordà county is a garden. In his creative work he also referred to water, the fountain, poetry, and the ideals of peace and nature. He very often provided a utopian vision.

The avenue of plane trees is an element that that articulates the fortified country house with the garden, structured from a main central path and two side paths that distribute the space into two sectors, each of them organised from hedges from the old French-style garden, from the time of the Barons of Púbol, with reminiscences of a rural Catalan garden of axial symmetry. An early structure that Dalí, while conserving it, gave it an Italian style in the way it became overwhelmed by the plants that Dalí chose at the time —cypresses, fruit trees, lilacs, rosebay, jasmine and honeysuckle. We should not forget that shortly before discovering the castle Salvador Dalí had been fascinated by the Baroque magic of the gardens of Bomarzo, near Rome. Walking along any of the three paths that the garden outlines we gradually discover the different types of vegetation, and the sculptural and architectural elements, with which Salvador Dalí decorated the different spaces bordered by the hedges. The three paths lead us to the private space of the swimming pool.

The east path, the shadiest, runs between the flower beds and the outside wall which, crowned by prickly pears in 1983 to maintain the painter's privacy increased its height. From the barons' horses' drinking trough and the small rosebay copse, just at the entrance to the path, one can appreciate the false perspective that affects the visitor's sight in the reproduction of a neoclassical structure. Salvador Dalí loved false perspectives, and the one that interested him most was that of the Palazzo Spada in Rome —famous for the false perspective achieved by Borromini, a Baroque architect—, where at a crossing there are three real dimensions and one fictitious one that shows more illusion of depth, once more deceiving the senses to escape from the duality of reality and fiction. In the case of this "corridor" of the

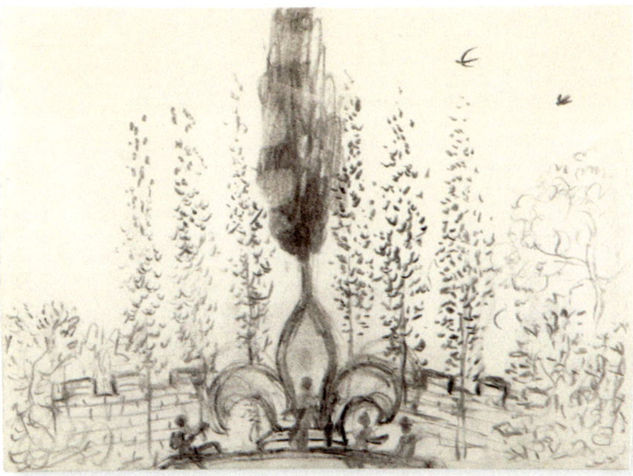

Design by Dalí for the bench with back in the garden

Elephant-waterspout with insect legs

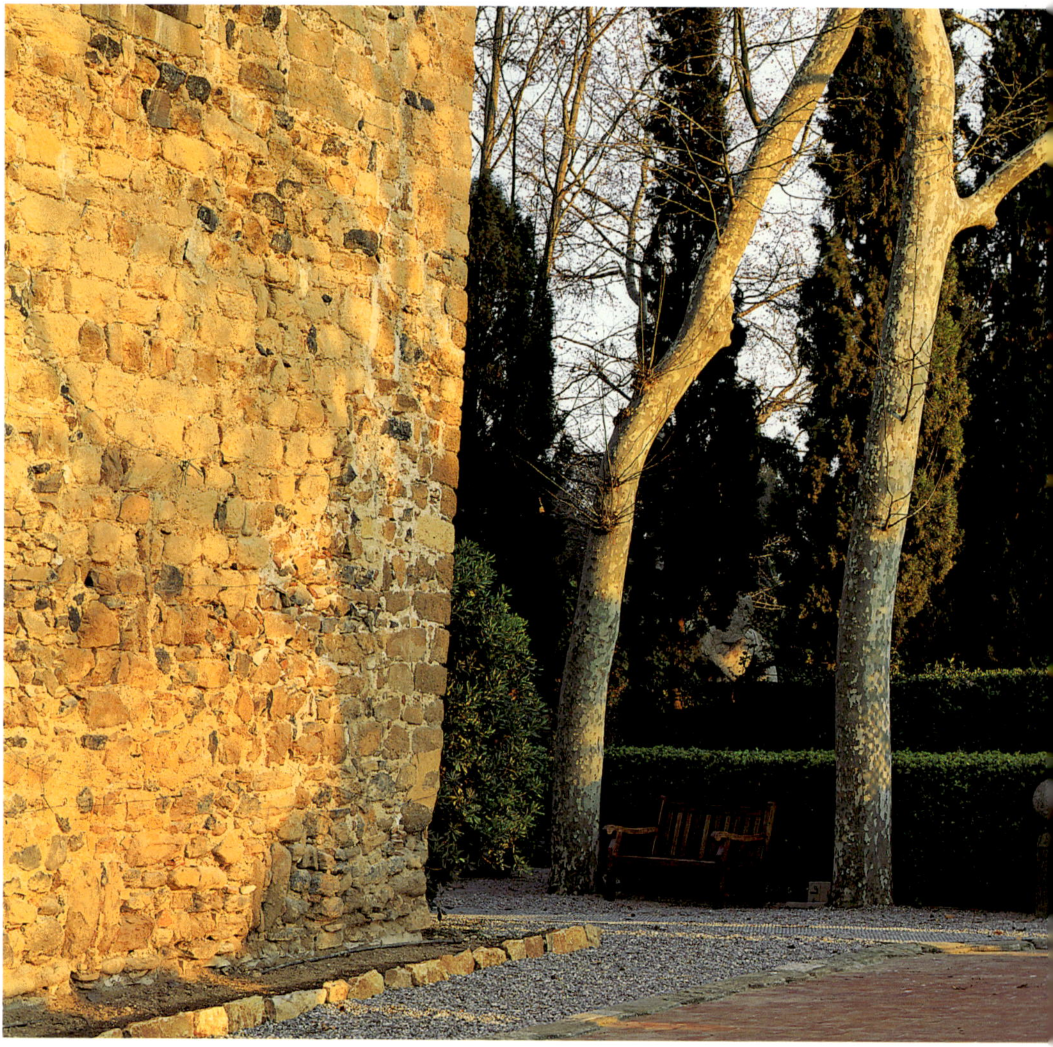

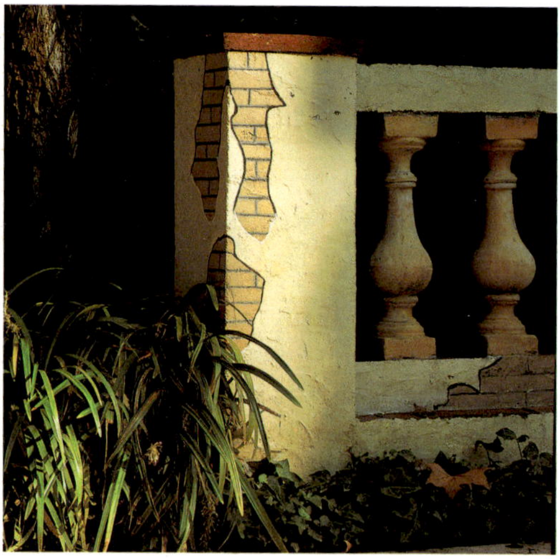

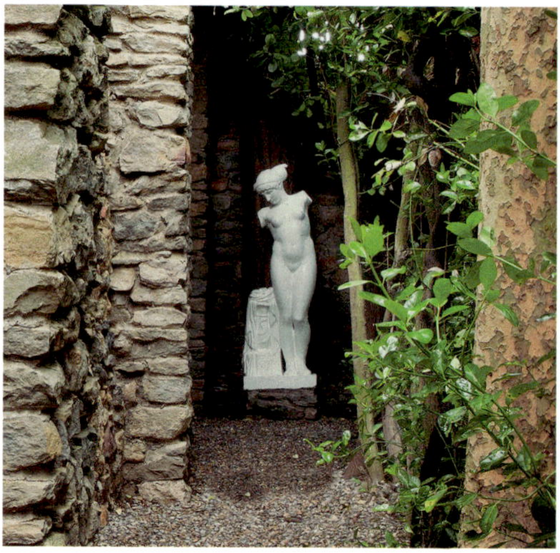

Balustrade with trompe-l'œil | Neoclassical sculpture

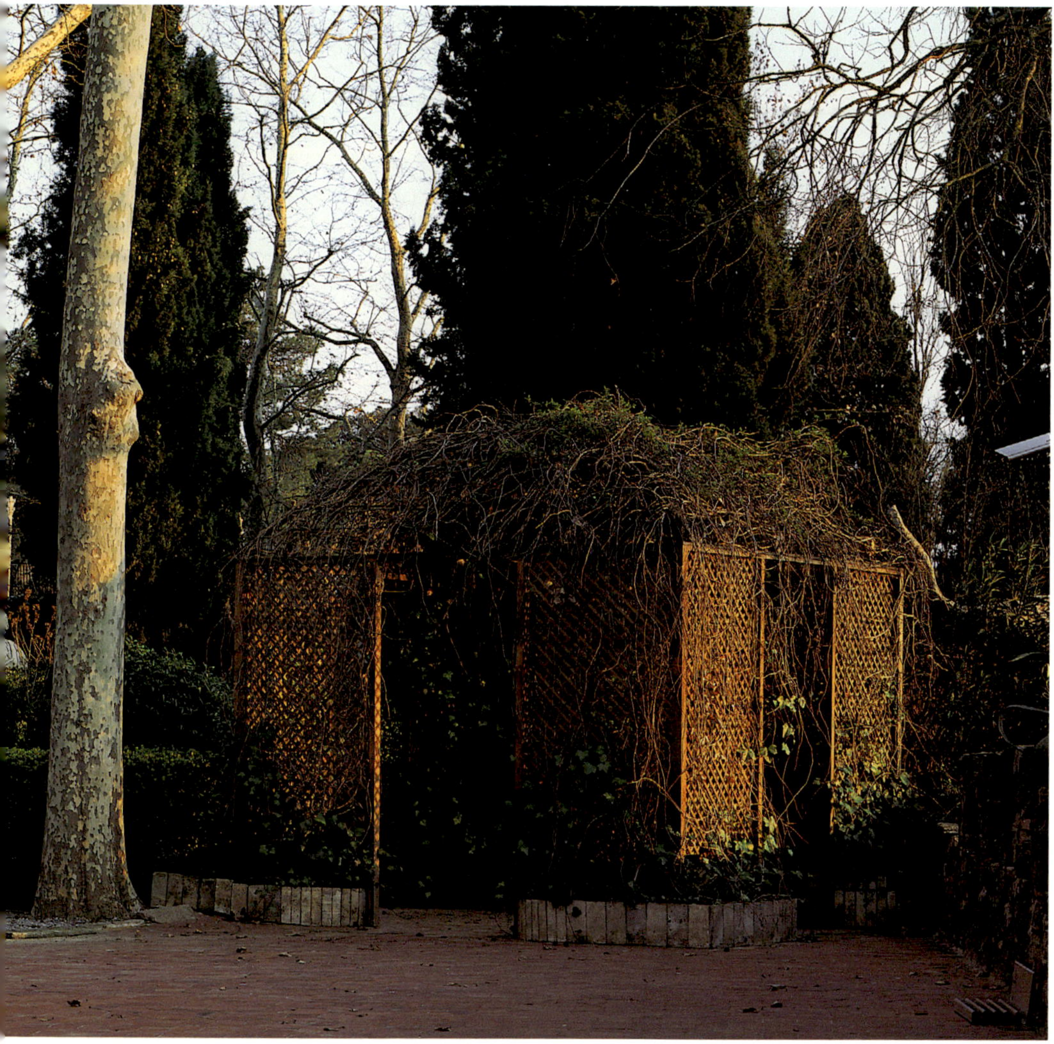

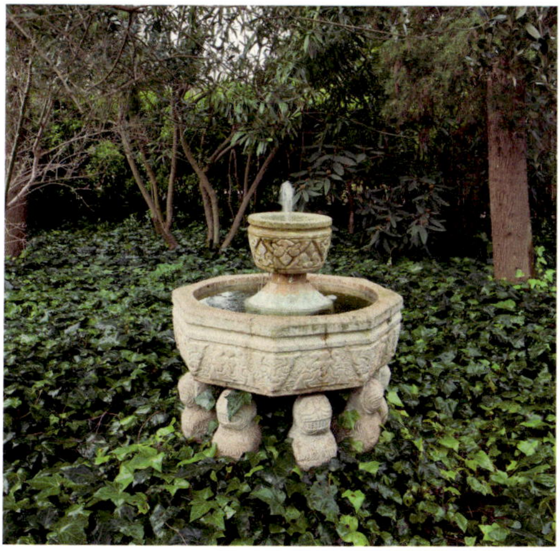

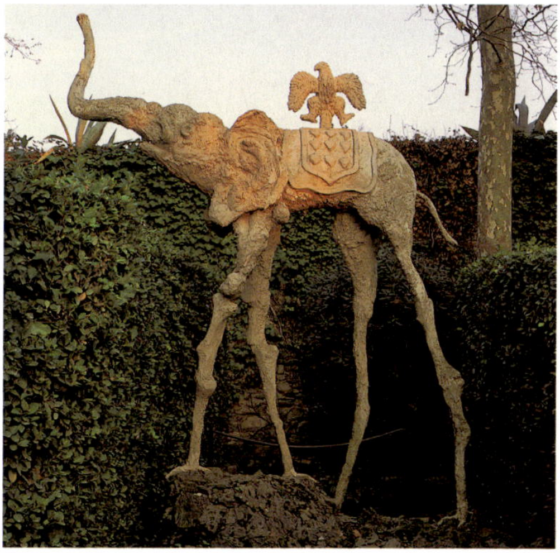

Replica of the Lions' Fountain of the Alhambra of Granada | Elephant-waterspout

castle, the artist played with the straight line of the enclosing wall, which marks our line of sight, while he placed several plants in a way that as they become distant from the spectator, they are closer to the wall; the final result is two lines that converge on the white Venus, becoming the vanishing point. The thick vegetation of the path also works as a hideout for elephants that are gradually revealed as you advance, even from the start, we can only see the trunks that shower water to freshen the atmosphere in summer.

In contrast, the western path opens the garden up to the landscape of the village of Púbol, but from a raised viewpoint that provides a privileged and distant position to the inhabitant of the castle. The path is hidden behind the bower of the terrace, covered by ivies and jasmine, which Dalí defined as "a place to have a sentimental chat". The passage leads us to one of Gala's favourite corners, in the shade of an old fig tree, while we discover, between the hedges and the ivies, a replica of the fountain of lions of the Alhambra that reminds us that during those years Dalí was also working on the decoration of the swimming pool of his house in Portlligat.

The main entrance to the garden, nevertheless, in a clear hierarchical order compared to the rest, is the central path. We enter it going beneath a small iron structure that the jasmine threads itself around and leads to the swimming pool, framing the main sculptural structure. Half way along, in a space overlooked by two mulberry trees, on either side there are two elephants with locust legs and claws of birds of prey —remember that it is an outstanding element of Dalinian iconography— which, according to Dalí, together with two more elephants hidden among the trees, "advance threateningly towards the castle"; an idea easily perceptible in winter from the castle windows and the gallery. Of the four elephants, all made from cement with an iron inner structure and slightly raised on stones from Cap de Creus, three were made in the olive groves of Portlligat and transported to Púbol immediately, and one, which appears unfinished, was made *in situ*. While the elephants from known Dalinian iconography have an obelisk in the group, those from Púbol show a crow with the wings open, a heraldic element of noble family of Corbera, barons of Púbol in the early 15th century, and of the coat of arms of the village. At the end of the path, another metallic support with jasmine leads to the pool.

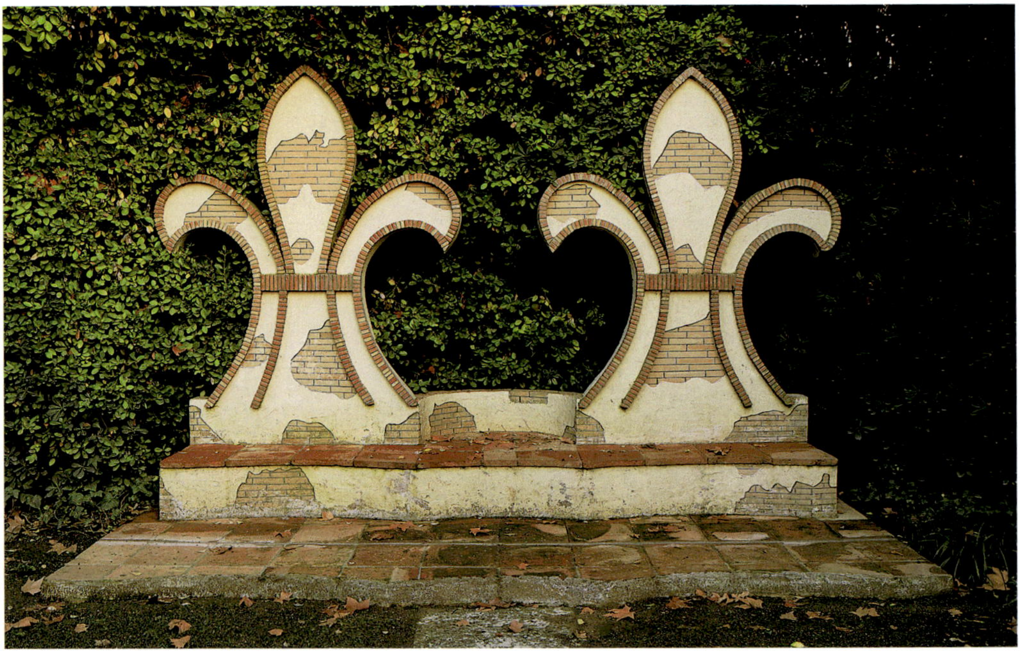

Bench with back in the form of a fleur-de-lis, with trompe-l'œil

THE SWIMMING POOL

The first impression on reaching the space of the pool is significantly different if you reach it by one of the side paths, through the leafy vegetation and in an unexpected way, as if we were coming out of a hideout, or by the central path, where the central architectural elements are a prelude of the space from the first moment we enter the garden.

This area was completed in spring 1974, in the period in which the works on the Theatre-Museum in Figueres were also finished. The back wall features a sculptural series in stone that recalls a classical shrine, with two caryatids that serve as columns and a fountain with the figure of a boy and a dolphin. All this series comes from a private garden in Figueres, the painter's birthplace. Again, the past appears from the present and the very Dalinian use of decontextualized remains of old constructions. Before the shrine there is a fountain that is the head of a monkfish. On either side of the fountain, there are 14 sculptural reproductions in different colours of a bust of the German composer Richard Wagner, who Dalí admired greatly.

Around the pool there are three constructions —in the high part of the shrine, on a hedge that separates the pool from the garden and on a bench with a back— on which Dalí had some trompe-l'œil painted, in the style of Magritte, and also with the idea of recovering the *Camera picta*, with structures of cracked tiles that let us see both the cracks and the bricks that make them up, to recover the illusion or the intention of leaving a mark of the passing of time. The balustrades, on the left, have the structure of a fleur-de-lis, of so many dynastic meanings for history.

This space is therefore conceived as an area of isolation, a sealed world to seek refuge in and devote oneself to contemplation. A space full of personal references that underline the general concept that from the whole restoration that Salvador Dalí undertook on the castle: a marble tower in homage to Gala, with a heavy romantic and symbolic content. The castle transmits a Proust-like air, where Dalí delightfully analysed each of his memories and offers Gala moments of sublimation and intense communication that there had always been between them. Moreover, here Dalí wants to go beyond two-dimensional representation, maintaining the magic of that reality, and always leaving room to chance. We, the visitors, are guests in a unique space, the space of the Dalinian Triangle where we are shown the most about Gala.

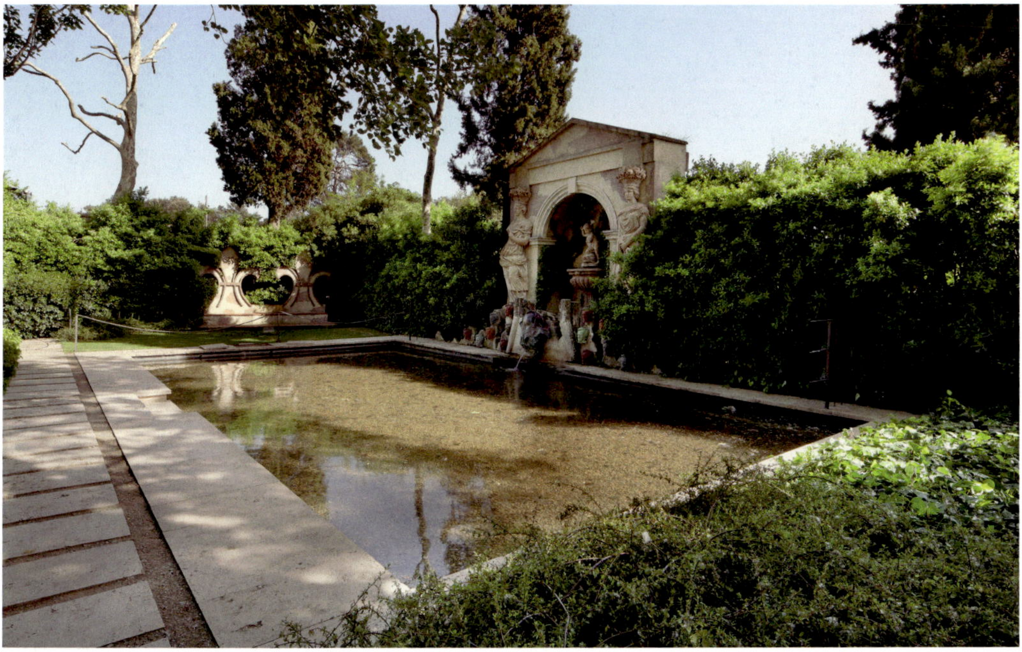

The swimming pool

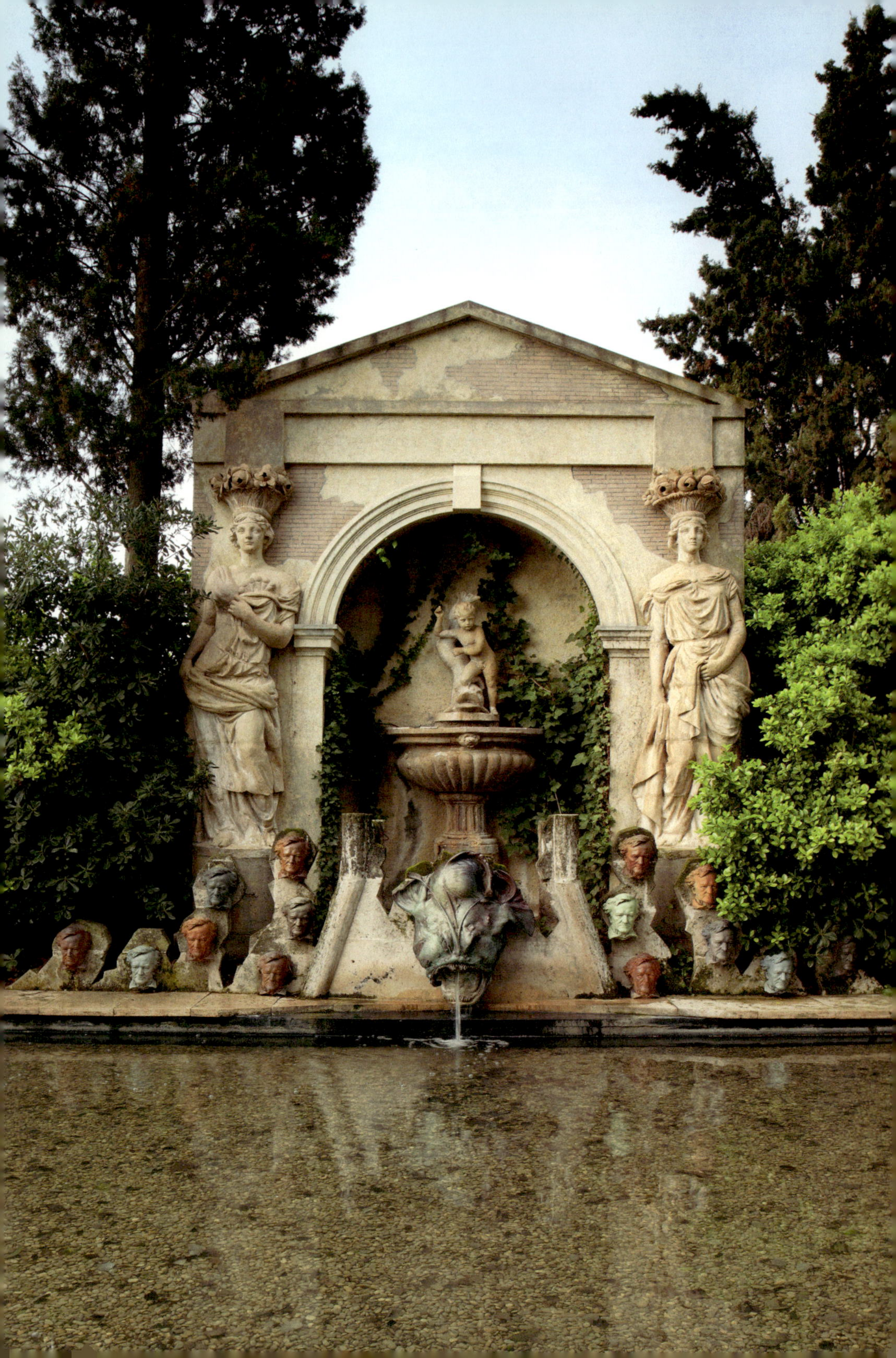

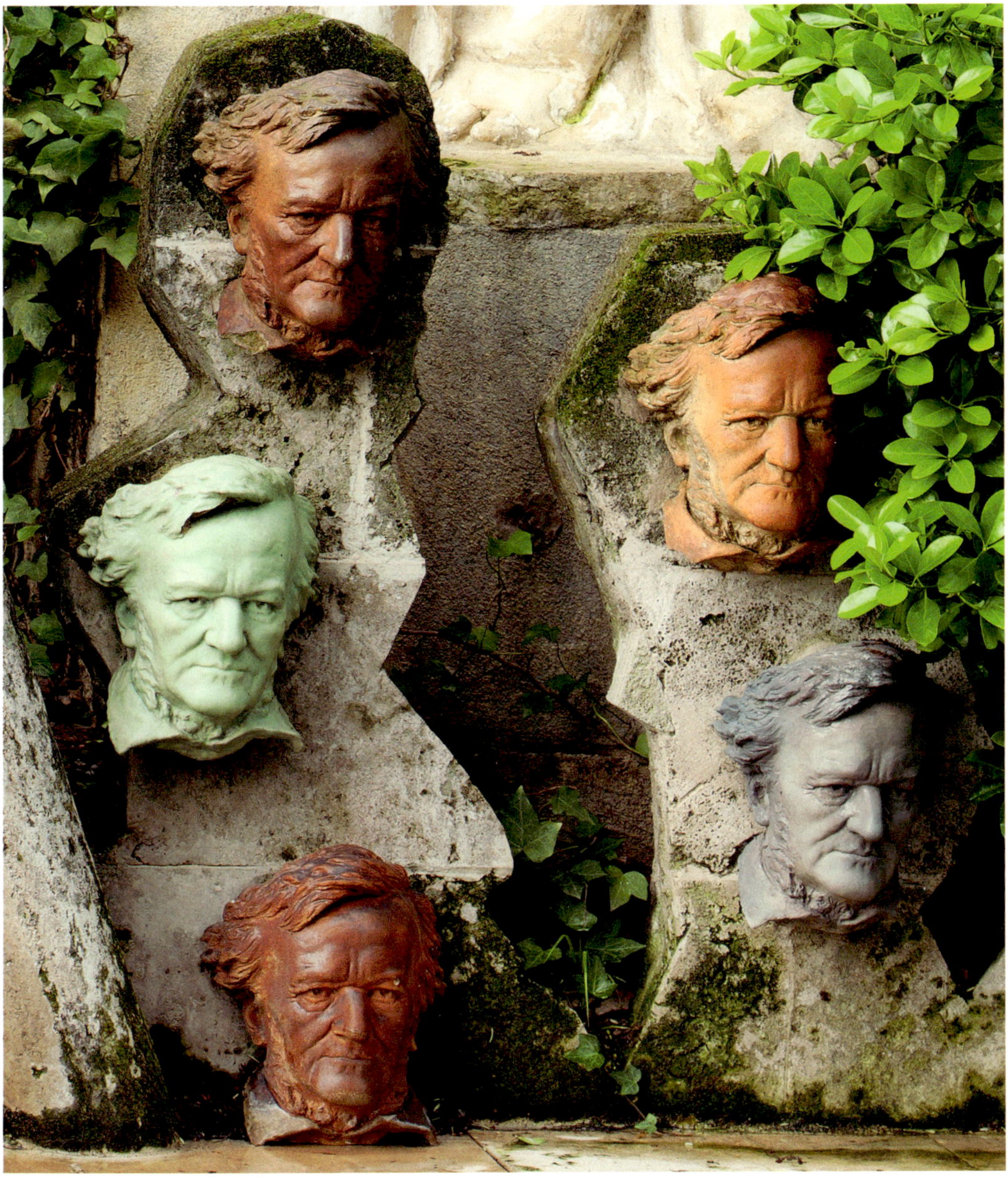

Busts of Richard Wagner

HOUSE-MUSEUM
GALA DALÍ CASTLE

GROUND FLOOR AND GARDEN

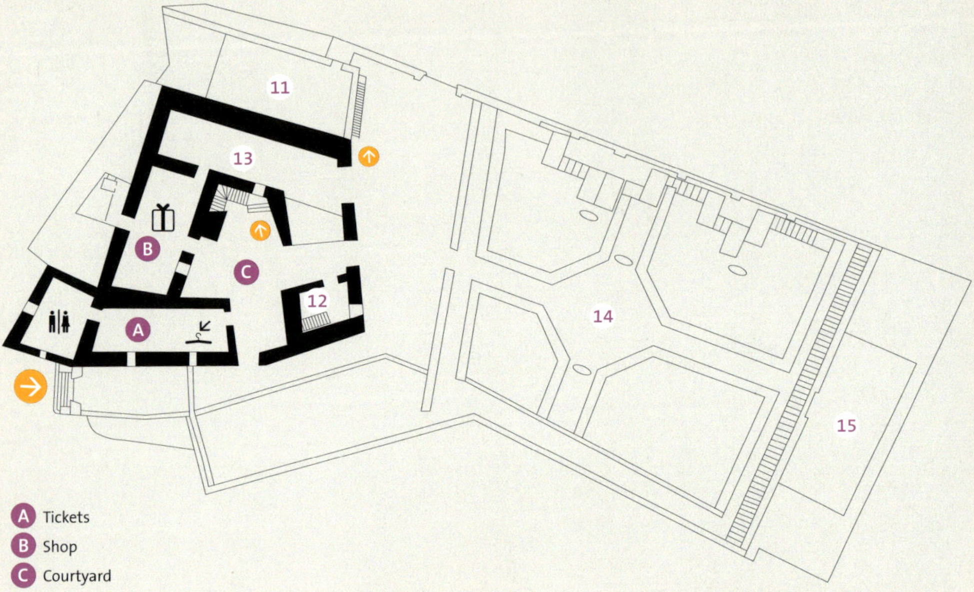

A Tickets
B Shop
C Courtyard

FIRST FLOOR

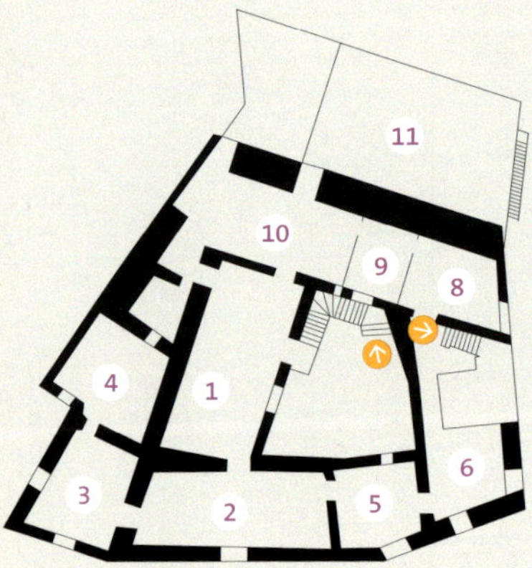

SECOND FLOOR

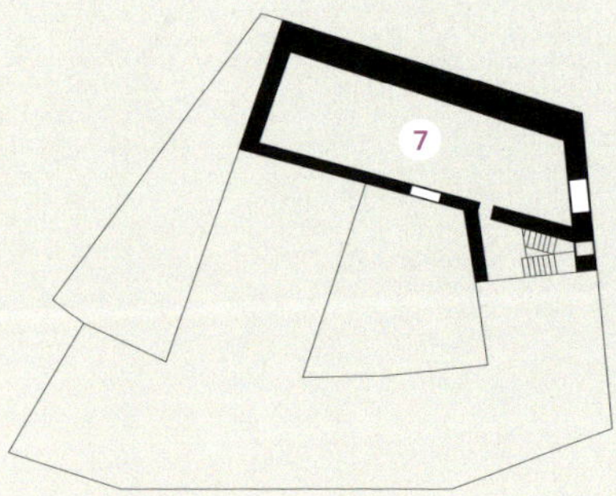

1 Coat of arms room
2 Piano room
3 Gala's bedroom
4 Badroom and dressing room
5 Library
6 Red room
7 "Gala dresses" of Gala
8 Temporary exhibitions
9 Office area
10 Dining room
11 Gallery
12 Crypt
13 Garage
14 Garden
15 Swimming pool

DALÍ TRIANGLE

The House-Museum Gala Dalí Castle in Púbol is included, along with the Dalí Theatre-Museum in Figueres and the Salvador Dalí House-Museum in Portlligat, in the museum complex run by the Gala-Salvador Dalí Foundation.

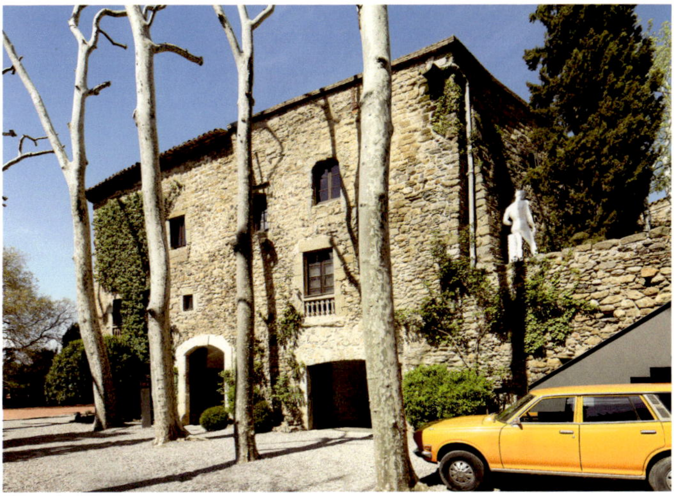

House-Museum Gala Dalí Castle in Púbol

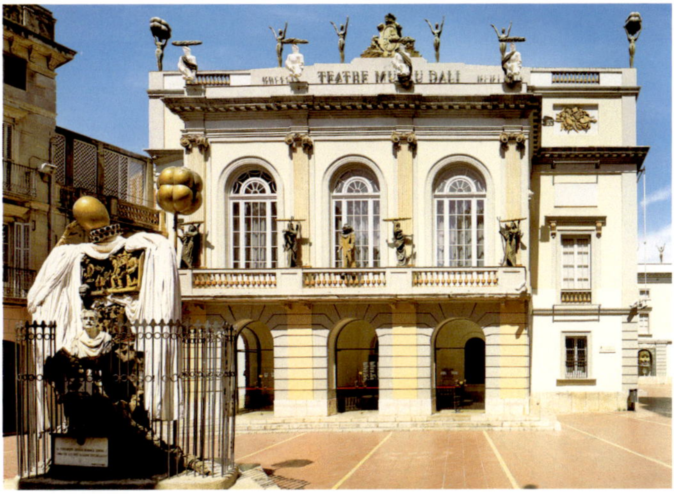

Dalí Theatre-Museum in Figueres

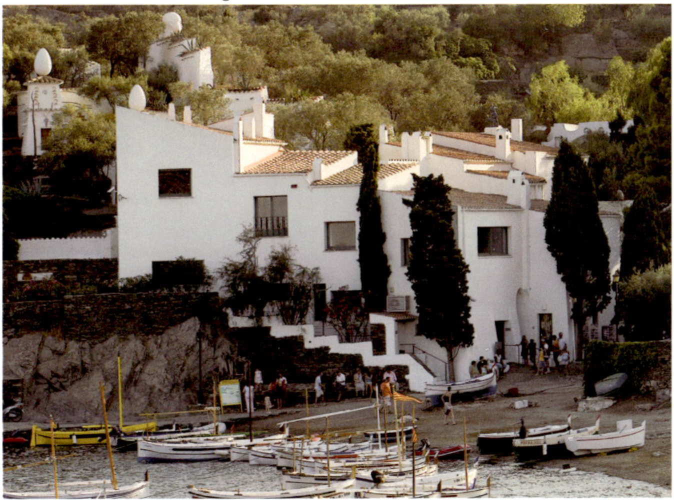

Salvador Dalí House-Museum in Portlligat, Cadaqués

FUNDACIÓ
GALA-SALVADOR DALÍ

TRIANGLE ▼ POSTALS

Published by
FUNDACIÓ GALA-SALVADOR DALÍ
TRIANGLE POSTALS, SL

Direction
Jordi Puig

Art direction
Ricard Pla

Editorial coordination
Joan Manuel Sevillano Campalans,
FUNDACIÓ GALA-SALVADOR DALÍ
Imma Planas,
TRIANGLE POSTALS, SL

Text
© Antoni Pitxot,
Montse Aguer Teixidor, 2011

Photography
© Jordi Puig, 2011

Page 17, © Studio 46, Roma
Page 25, © Melitó Casals
"Meli" /Fundació Gala-Salvador
Dalí, Figueres, 2011

Rights of image of Salvador Dalí
reserved. Fundació Gala-Salvador
Dalí, Figueres, 2011

Works by Salvador Dalí
© Salvador Dalí, Fundació Gala-Salvador Dalí, Figueres, 2011

Archive photos
Centre d'Estudis Dalinians,
Fundació Gala-Salvador Dalí

Graphic design
Joan Colomer

Layout
Vador Minobis

Translation
Steve Cedar

Supervision of contents
Centre d'Estudis Dalinians,
Fundació Gala-Salvador Dalí

Printed by
Sanvergrafic

Printed in Barcelona

© of edition:
FUNDACIÓ GALA-SALVADOR DALÍ
TRIANGLE POSTALS, SL

Registration number
B-17.879-2011

ISBN
978-84-8478-522-4

This is the second version of the guide to the castle of Púbol. The first, important edition has been its base and support:
Pitxot, Antoni; Playá, Josep, *Gala Dalí's Castle: The Road to Púbol*, Fundació Gala-Salvador Dalí, Escudo de Oro, Figueres, Barcelona, 1997.

We would also like to highlight the important collaboration of Jordi Artigas, head of the Dalí house-museums, and Carme Ruiz, coordinator of the Centre d'Estudis Dalinians.

TRIANGLE POSTALS, SL
Sant Lluís, Menorca
Tel. +34 971 15 04 51
Fax +34 971 15 18 36
www.triangle.cat